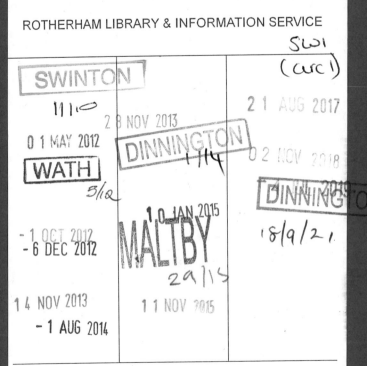

Memories of
Milligan

Memories of
Milligan

NORMA FARNES

FOURTH ESTATE · *London* and *New York*

First published in Great Britain in 2010 by
Fourth Estate
a division of HarperCollins*Publishers*
77–85 Fulham Palace Road
Hammersmith
London W6 8JB

www.4thestate.co.uk
Love this book? www.bookarmy.com

A catalogue record for this book is available from the British Library

ISBN 978-0-00-735638-6

Typeset in Minion by Birdy Book Design

Printed in Great Britain by Clays Ltd, St Ives plc

Mixed Sources
Product group from well-managed
forests and other controlled sources
www.fsc.org Cert no. SW-COC-001806
© 1996 Forest Stewardship Council
FSC

FSC is a non-profit international organisation established to promote the
responsible management of the world's forests. Products carrying the FSC
label are independently certified to assure consumers that they come
from forests that are managed to meet the social, economic and
ecological needs of present and future generations.

Find out more about HarperCollins and the environment at
www.harpercollins.co.uk/green

For Jack
My Champagne Charlie

CONTENTS

ACKNOWLEDGEMENTS

I wish to thank all those who contributed to this book, for their kindness and willingness to talk to me and giving freely of their time in very busy schedules. It was a pleasure to meet some old friends again. Eric Sykes, a good friend, for his guidance and support about this book. Louise Haines, my editor, who drives me mad because she's always right. Janet Spearman, for her devotion and putting some order into my life. A special thank you to John Fisher for allowing me to quote from his *Heroes of Comedy – The Goons*. Pamela Lester for all her encouragement – 'Just get on with it.' The lovely Bill Kenwright, who has taken over from Spike by spoiling me. Lastly, Lawrence Drizen, my mentor, for his advice, his unending patience with me, and most of all, for his friendship.

INTRODUCTION

The concept of this book, as far as I was concerned, was a coffee table book, and that is how it started. After a few months, I was quite happily going along when Louise Haines, my editor, dropped a bombshell. She didn't 'want a book of articles. I would like a more chronological memoir.'

Let me tell you about Louise. What Louise wants, Louise always gets. She has a certain way of saying N-O-R-M-A, long-drawn out, very quiet. You know then she's about to get you to do something you don't want to do; in this case ten times more work than I had anticipated. However, she's terrific and knows exactly what is needed, so I forgive her. And you know what – she was right again.

Throughout Spike's illustrious career – thank God he's not around to read that. I can hear him say, 'What career? They'll say Spike Milligan wrote *The Goon Show* and died,' or 'It's all for fear of the bank manager,' or 'It's just that Van Gogh couldn't stop painting and I can't stop writing.' All these remarks were repeated to me many times over the years. Well, I think he had an illustrious career and throughout that career he made some friends, a lot of acquaintances and a few enemies.

In this book I've tried to capture the varied recollections of some of the people who did know Spike; so many professed to know him, but they didn't know him at all. He was loyal, and his friendships, the true ones, lasted all his life. I can think of two, alas, no longer with us: Alan Clare, brilliant pianist and composer, and Jack Hobbs, his editor – friendships that lasted over forty years. There were ups and downs with Jack, but Spike never had a cross word with Alan. When he was down and feeling alone, he used to go to Alan's flat in Holland Park and sit and talk to him for hours, or just go and sit in silence after asking Alan to play for him. When Alan died, Spike missed him terribly and said to me, in such a haunting tone, 'Oh, Norm. We are all beginning to die.' One week later, I was the one who had to tell him that Jack Hobbs had died.

The relationship with his brother, Desmond, was a love/hate one. It was either 'I have a God-sent brother,' or 'That stupid brother of mine.' His book *Rommel? Gunner Who?* was dedicated to Desmond:

> To my dear brother Desmond
> Who made my boyhood happy and with whom
> I have never had a cross word
> Mind you he drives his wife mad

Obviously written in a 'God-sent brother' period. The one thing that never changed was the wonderful memories Spike had of their idyllic childhood growing up in India and Burma, and Desmond's memories of this time reflect the stories Spike had told me.

Eric Sykes was an established writer when he met Spike. He was writing the very successful Peter Brough and Archie Andrews radio shows, *Educating Archie*. Eric was lying in bed in the Homeopathic Hospital in Great Ormond Street awaiting an operation, the first of many for an infected mastoid. He was listening to the radio and a new comedy show which he thought was fast, furious and very, very funny. It was *Crazy People* written by Spike Milligan and Larry Stephens. Eric wrote them a letter saying what he thought about the show. It was such an accolade for them, an established writer sending them such a letter of praise. The next day Spike and Larry paid a visit to Eric and that small incident of fate began an enduring friendship between Spike and Eric which culminated in sharing an office for over fifty years.

In about 1953, Ray Galton and Alan Simpson, like Spike and Eric, had only just started their writing careers. They met Spike at a rehearsal of a *Goon Show* and they were introduced after the recording. Together they formed a company, Associated London Scripts (ALS), and stayed together until April 1968 when they went their separate ways, Eric and Spike staying together at Orme Court, their offices in Bayswater. Ray and Alan have wonderful memories of 'the early days' when they thought the world was full of laughter.

Friendships, laughter and writing scripts wove them together. It was new and exciting, breaking new ground, and that's when Spike met Liz Cowley, a journalist and broadcaster. Another relationship that lasted fifty years, though relationship is the wrong word, it belies the love and affection they had for one another until his death. What was always amazing to me, apart from their love for each other, was their deep friendship, and he cared so much for her and her wellbeing. She is such a natural to share her memories with the reader.

Denis Norden is one of the great scriptwriters of the Fifties, Sixties and Seventies. With his writing partner, Frank Muir, he was responsible for the highly successful radio series *Take it From Here* which ran for twelve years. He also wrote and presented *It'll Be Alright on the Night* for twenty-nine years. He is a great raconteur and has an immense fund of showbusiness stories and anecdotes of stars of the last sixty years.

Spike had great affection for Marcel Stellman. He was an A & R man and producer at Decca records. In the late Sixties Marcel approached Spike, having heard the *Goon Shows*, to ask him if he had any comedy songs as he was interested in recording him. The first song Spike gave Marcel was 'I'm Walking Backwards for Christmas' and he even had a B-side for him, 'Bloodnok's Rock 'n' Roll Call'. Then came the famous 'The Ying Tong Song', still popular today, so much so it's the ring tone on my mobile.

Another lasting friendship for over fifty years was with Sir George Martin. George was best man at Spike's second marriage, to Paddy, and Spike was godfather to George's son Giles, not that you would know. He was a very bad godfather and when I reminded him of this he'd say, 'I know, Norm, but Gentle George [Spike's favourite name for George] will forgive me. I just forget and I'm getting to be an old man.' He wasn't an old man until the last two years of his life when his body started to fail him. He was just an old fake. And Gentle George always forgave him. For Spike, Gentle George could do no wrong. In the late Sixties I'd just taken over as Spike's manager and Spike was going to a recording session with him. I hadn't then met George. In my green years and trying to be efficient, I told Spike that I hadn't seen a contract for the recording session. Very indignantly, Spike replied, 'I don't need a contract with George. He's my friend,' and for the rest of their working lives together it remained so.

The early Sixties had established Spike as a writer with *The Goon Show* and his first poetry book, *Silly Verse for Kids*, with the inevitable plethora of fans turning up at the studios and, of course, fan letters. One from Alan (Groucho) Matthews led to another fifty-year friendship. He and Spike corresponded until about two years before Spike's death. And to this day I still see him.

Also in the late Fifties Spike had flown to Australia to see his mother and father and while he was there he went to the theatre to see Barry Humphries in his one-man show. He never forgot that wonderful performance. Long before Dame Edna was even thought about. My memory of Barry was when he came to Orme Court to see Spike in 1966/1967. He was so flamboyantly dressed – that picture of him waiting in the hall to go upstairs to see Spike still remains with me – tall, large black coat, which might have been a cloak, and wearing a fedora. After his visit I asked Spike, 'What was that?' Spike's reply: 'That was talent. You watch and wait, he'll really hit the big time.' How prophetic.

It was in 1959 that Spike had the most fun with Peter Sellers and the director Richard Lester. Richard made the first film in which Spike and Peter appeared together – *The Running, Jumping & Standing Still Film*. Spike thought this young American director had the right idea about comedy. How many times did he relate to me, 'Dick and Pete and I went into a field with a camera. Dick shot it and it was one of the best times of my life, free and easy, no worries. Just Pete and me.' I heard the same story from Pete. No doubt they drove Dick Lester mad, but their memories were pure gold.

In 1961 *Private Eye* was founded by Richard Ingrams and after the magazine's initial success Peter Cook became involved. They were two men Spike admired. It was inevitable that he would support them with spoof advertisements, jokes and cartoons. It was such a loss to Spike when Peter Cook died. 'Of all of us,' Spike said, 'Peter was the most talented.' In the early days Peter would come to the office and they would sit upstairs in Spike's office chatting and laughing for hours though I remember quite clearly one day Spike saying to me, 'Peter needs to watch it. He wanted to go out and have a drink. I told him not to start drinking at this time.' It was four o'clock in the afternoon. What a tragedy he didn't heed Milligan's advice, all that wonderful talent wasted because of alcohol.

Richard, on the other hand, was so down to earth. I always found him to be such a gentleman. Quietly spoken, always looking something like a dishevelled retired Classics master from a public school. He looks forgetful but don't be fooled: his mind is as incisive as a well-honed, old-fashioned razor.

How did Jimmy Verner survive? He spent seven years as an entrepreneur, taking Spike on tour with his one-man show. There were heartaches and people at the box office demanding their money back when Spike had done a 'no show', with Jimmy trying to keep the money and offering tickets for other performances. Then there were the tantrums when a false nose was missing from the prop basket. And yet, Jimmy recalls, 'Underneath it all he was a good human being.'

Now, I have to explain at the outset that Peter Medak can do no wrong as far as I'm concerned. In this business you meet hundreds of people but there are very few 'you would walk through fire for'. Peter said this of Spike, and I'm saying it of Peter. He directed Spike in *Ghost in the Noonday Sun* in 1973, and although the twelve-week filming in Kyrenia was a nightmare, with Peter Sellers behaving abominably, my memories are of the laughter between Spike and Peter Medak. Their friendship grew out of what can only be described as hell on location. Their respect and admiration for each other remained until the day Spike died. When it comes to Peter, I'm just biased.

The Sixties and Seventies saw a broadening of Spike's remarkable and diverse talent. His first novel, *Puckoon*, published in 1963, sold over a million copies and was followed by his play *The Bed-Sitting Room*, later made into a film directed by Richard Lester. Then in 1964 came his memorable theatre performance in *Son of Oblomov* at the Comedy Theatre. This had been a failure as *Oblomov* at the Lyric, Hammersmith, but Spike rewrote it as *Son of Oblomov*. It ran for eighteen months and he ad libbed throughout each performance, and broke all box office records. A torrent of talent!

In 1971 at the age of fifty-three he wrote the first volume of his war memoirs *Adolf Hitler: My Part in His Downfall*, followed by a further six volumes. Then came his first serious poetry book, numerous records and the first of the Q series for television. Also a milestone, on 30 April 1972, *The Last Goon Show Of All* was recorded at the Camden Theatre, at Spike's insistence, because that is where most of the *Goon Shows* had been recorded.

This burgeoning period brought him many new admirers and some became friends. At times he drove the jovially philosophical Terry Wogan almost to despair, but I think nothing or nobody could do that, Terry has such a personality that his warmth and mischievous character will always have shone through anything that Milligan could have thrown at him. Spike also joined forces with Joanna Lumley and together they set about saving the animal world. He greatly admired Joanna and it is my regret that he didn't live to see her successful fight for the Gurkhas. He would have been so proud of her and rightly so.

Spike's talents have been applauded by some remarkable people. Alan J.W. Bell, producer and director of some of the most prestigious BBC television shows, directed him in *There's a Lot of It About*, and one of the Q series. He remembers how hard Spike worked, as well as the laughter they shared. According to Alan, there were no tantrums, just laughter. I find that hard to believe – a TV series with no tantrums? Who is Alan talking about?

Dick Douglas-Boyd was the marketing director of Michael Joseph who published many of Spike's books, including the seven volumes of his war memoirs. I think at first Dick was very apprehensive with Spike and didn't know how to handle him. Mind you, who did? But as the working relationship progressed they found common ground, because they had both been through the war, and a friendship was built on mutual respect.

The fiercely intellectual Jonathan Miller, who takes no prisoners, directed Spike in *Alice in Wonderland*. Although he didn't like Spike as a person I found his comment very illuminating. 'His work is as important as *The Pickwick Papers*.'

Michael Palin was hooked on the *Goon Shows* as a schoolboy. He and Spike became friends and Michael has some wonderful memories of Spike. I recall a memory that Spike had of Michael. He was on holiday in Tunisia, nothing to do with the fact that the Monty Python team were filming *Life of Brian* there. Naturally, they met up and on his return to the office we exchanged the normal pleasantries: 'Good hotel, food OK, wine lousy,' he said. Then, 'I met Michael Palin out there. You'd like him. He's very funny, a warm person, and something unusual about him, he's a good human being.' It wasn't until months later I discovered the whole team had been in Tunisia and that Spike had appeared in the film. This was so typical of Spike. Filming meant nothing to him – it was something to be dismissed but the fact that he had taken a liking to Michael Palin was the one thing he thought worth mentioning.

For Stephen Fry it was not just Spike's originality that he so admired, it was 'the fact that he was afraid of nobody. And the fact that he didn't toady to anyone.'

I wanted to include Eddie Izzard in this book although he didn't really know Spike, was neither a friend nor an acquaintance. But I wanted to know from Eddie, as a more recent newcomer, what he thought Spike's legacy would be. I knew he had memories of Spike, but more importantly Spike had asked me whether I had seen Eddie perform. At that stage I hadn't and told him so and Spike said, 'Go and see him. Out of this new breed he's going to be the one that will last. He's original and going to be around a long time. Most of the others are flash in the pan compared to him.'

So, *Memories of Milligan*, some good, some not so good, but that's what he was like – the little girl with the curl. When he was good he was very, very good but when he was bad he was horrid. But aside from all this was his unbridled talent – an original, a free spirit. He genuinely didn't care what people thought of him and if he didn't like someone he would dismiss them. He just didn't want to know anything about them.

Within an hour he could be mean, cruel, hateful and despicable, then generous, compassionate and understanding – a most complex man. In business he could betray me without a second thought and I would remind him, 'I'm not your enemy.' A typical Milligan reply would be, 'Well, don't act like one.' And yet in my personal life he was a true friend. He was always there when I needed him and he never let me down.

Life is not so much fun without him in my world. I miss the old sod.

Norma Farnes, 2010

DESMOND MILLIGAN

Desmond Patrick Milligan, born 3 December 1925 in Rangoon, younger brother of Terence Alan Milligan, born 16 April 1918 in Ahmednagar, Poona. Simple, straightforward names, but this is the Milligan family where nothing is simple or straightforward.

Their father, Captain Leo Alphonso Milligan, was a charming, eccentric Irishman. Their mother, Florence Mary Winifred Kettleband, was a resolute Englishwoman, strong and determined. She ruled her family with military precision. Both were from military backgrounds. For years I had assumed they had married in England, Leo had been posted to India, and they had gone there as bride and groom. The reality was rather different. Florence was taken to India where her father had been posted. It was 1901 and she was eight years old. Leo was posted to India in 1912, arriving in Kirkee, where the Kettlebands lived and where their romance was about to begin.

When he was in England Leo had developed a love for the theatre. So much so, he changed his name to Leo Gann and had reasonable success appearing in the Imperial Palace in Canning Town, doing a soft-shoe shuffle dance, and a song and dance act. It was inevitable when he arrived in India he would form a repertory company and he performed at regimental balls and concert parties. It was in St Ignatius church he heard Florence playing the organ and singing in the church choir. She had a trained contralto voice and Leo was hooked – 'I fell in love with her voice.' Together they formed a double act 'entertaining the troops' performing at the Poona Gymkhana Club. They were both accomplished horse riders, and Leo became riding master and gave instruction on equestrian drill. One can only imagine what a wonderful life they had together.

Leo was a wonderful storyteller, always insisting the stories were truthful, until one day, as a boy of about seven years old, Spike caught his father telling lies about a tiger he had shot. He said to Spike, 'Now listen, son, would you rather have the boring truth or an exciting lie?' For me, this sums up Leo more than any of his stories. No wonder Spike spent the rest of his life embellishing the truth.

In her later years I grew very fond of 'Grandma', as I always called Florence. On her yearly visit to England (from Australia, where the family, apart from Spike, relocated) she would stay with me for a week. It was always a joy. We would go out to dinner in the evenings and she would relate stories of her time in India with 'her boys'. The wine would be consumed, sometimes a little too much, and I do recall one evening in the Trattoo restaurant the resident pianist was Alan Clare, a very accomplished pianist and composer. In the middle of one of her stories she suddenly stopped talking and shouted over to Alan, 'Alan, you played a bum note there.' Then went back to telling her story. That memory will stay with me forever.

A devout Roman Catholic, when she was staying with me I had to drive her to confession on a Saturday evening. I once asked, 'Grandma, why do you still go to confession, what do you have to confess at your age?' (She was about 83 or 84 years old at the time.) She replied in that strong voice, 'Norma, please don't you get like Terry.' She was very artistic, she made beautiful clowns, hand sewn in bright coloured velvets, large pointed hats and stars for their eyes. The one I have sitting on a chair in my office is 3 feet high. She named him 'Nong', from Spike's poem *On the Ning Nang Nong*. On one of her visits she knitted a beautiful white rabbit and gave it to me on the last night of her visit, attaching this little gift card (*above right*).

And Grandma, I miss you very much.

In one of our early conversations Spike told me he had a brother, Desmond, who lived in Australia. He extolled Desmond's virtues, explaining that he was a great artist and his portraits were worthy of being hung in the National Portrait Gallery. How was I to know that the rest of the family called Desmond Patrick, or that, while Desmond called his brother Spike, the rest of the family called Spike Terry?

I only discovered this idiosyncrasy when Spike was going to Australia and I received a phone call from Grandma Milligan. 'Will you please tell Terry that Patrick will pick him up at the airport. He needs to know the flight number and time of arrival.' Who was she talking about? Confused? Well, it gets better.

Desmond was married to Nadia Joanna Klune who was born on 21 May 1932 in Alexandria, Egypt. Their son Michael Sean was born on 10 December 1965 in Sydney, Australia. According to Spike, apart from his own mother's 'curries', Nadia's mother's cooking – Mama Klune's – had to be tasted to be believed. He went on about it for years, and finally on my first trip to Australia with him we were invited to Mama Klune's for dinner – a 'welcome home, Spike' dinner. I asked why 'welcome home' when he had never lived there and I was told, 'Well, everyone thinks he lives here.' And that was that; total acceptance. But I wouldn't let it go. 'Spike, you have never lived here. How can it be a "welcome home" dinner?' His reply has stayed with me for nearly forty years. 'Norm, your home is always where your mother is.' Some twenty years later I was going to Yorkshire for the weekend, and although I hadn't lived there for over thirty years, I said to Spike, 'I'm going home for the weekend.' He had remembered. 'There, I told you so. Your home is always where your mother is.'

So, welcome home dinner or what, Spike couldn't wait to taste Mama Klune's food again. No one had prepared me for the torrent of languages, a baffling clamour of conversation in three or four tongues, and the realisation that everyone seemed to understand except me. As we sat around the table, Mama Klune spoke to Nadia in Greek and Nadia answered in Greek. Michael answered in English, while Papa Klune spoke to Nadia in Italian and she answered in Italian. Nadia spoke to Michael in Greek, but again he answered in English. In all, Nadia spoke five languages fluently: Greek, Italian, French, Arabic and English. I asked Michael if he spoke these languages as he seemed to understand what was being said. 'Oh yes, but I was born in Australia so I speak Australian.' It was a wonderful evening, Nadia acting as interpreter for me. There was a lot of laughter. Spike was right, the food was excellent, and so I was catapulted into the Milligan family.

DESMOND: Terry is almost eight years older than me, but the story I heard as a boy, over and over again, was the calamity of his birth. Of course, it had to be in the middle of a storm and the nearest transport to get my mother to the military hospital in Ahmednagar was a bullock wagon taxi called a dhumni. The hospital was several miles away and the roads were rough dirt tracks. She had started in labour, she was in great pain. When they arrived at the hospital the duty nurse had to unlock the door, that's how small the hospital was. By this time my mother was in the advanced stage of labour and when the battery doctor arrived – Dr Anderson – she screamed at him, 'Get out of here! I never want to see another man in my life again.' Dr Anderson replied, 'Don't blame me, Florrie. I didn't do it.' So, at 3.30 p.m. on 16 April 1918, screaming his lungs out, Terence Alan Milligan was born, all 8½ lbs of him. From now on I'll give him his nickname,

Spike. He had been given this name when he was in the army because he was so thin.

Apart from hearing the story of his birth a thousand times, we had a wonderful happy childhood. My father had been transferred to the Third Field Brigade Port Defence in Rangoon, Burma. I was born there in December 1925. We had a big house within the military grounds, and we had servants, including a gardener. My earliest memory of Spike was in 1930 when Rangoon was struck by a huge earthquake, the epicentre being in the north. It was evening and after the earthquake my mother and father had been expecting a major riot and looting. I remember, as we sat down to dinner, Dad had on his pistols. Mum had her .44 Winchester rifle alongside her, and Spike, being Spike, was upstairs having a cold bath. He too had a pair of pistols on the chair alongside the bath. As the first shocks arrived Father Milligan reached over and grabbed me. 'Everybody outside,' he shouted and rushed into the garden.

Everything was shaking. The noise was terrifying, added to by all the birds being shaken out of the trees. Up in the bathroom the double doors shook violently. Spike thought that rioters were breaking in and shouted, '*Koowan Hai? Koowan Hai*?' (Who's there?) Of course, no reply, so he picked up his pistols and fired through the doors. He soon realised it was an earthquake, threw a towel around himself and ran to join us in the garden.

The shocks subsided but the town to our north, by the epicentre, was totally destroyed. I was looking over my father's shoulder directly at the Golden Shwe Dagon Pagoda. It was all illuminated and as I looked the umbrella crown at the top broke off and crashed to the ground. It contained a casket of jewels placed there by the last king of Burma in 1930. It's extraordinary, but it was not put back until 1960, and I wondered if the jewels got put back up. Lucky for us this did not happen during the monsoon season. In the East, when the rainy season moves in, boy, does it rain. It's like a solid wall of water hitting the ground, and it goes on and on. All social activity comes to a halt. The Burmese priests, called pungees, walk through it with giant umbrellas, in their saffron-coloured costumes. Then when the rain stopped, everything grew like crazy. All the little creatures came out of hiding: snakes, lizards, little furry things and insects by the million. Gorgeous butterflies and more . . . but back to the earthquake. There were many aftershocks over the following days, but it is surprising how quickly life returns to normality. Mum and Spike were soon playing on our tennis court or going on outings with his school, as if nothing had happened.

NORMA: In spite of the age difference, did you still play together as children?

DESMOND: Oh yes, life for us kids was heaven. Spike went to St Paul's High School, run by the Brothers de La Salle, and I went to a tiny school run by Catholic nuns in the convent grounds. Father, as a military man, taught us to play soldiers and drill with our toy guns. We would have battles in the bits of jungle and three lakes that surrounded us. We made a flag and we called ourselves 'The Lamanian Army'. Spike wrote an anthem, 'Fun in the Sun'. We recruited three soldiers, Sergeant Taylor's son, Haveldar's son and our servant's son – wait for it – Hari Krishna. It was here that the fun started, the lampooning of people and places where Spike's stretching of reality began. He decided we needed a proper trench. We dug a big one right in the middle of Mum and Dad's garden. My God, were we reprimanded.

Even the word Goon goes back to when we were reading Popeye cartoon strips in the English papers that we received. There were some blob-like characters in the strip that were called Goons, and that is where the word came from. When we were fooling around, we would impersonate these characters as we saw them. We would literally become them. I suppose one could say it was the beginning of *The Goon Show*. The world of the Raj gave us so much material for fun. For example, there was an Indian businessman who had dealings with Dad's battery. His name was Percy Lalkakaa. He bought himself a bright red motorcar. There were very few privately owned motorcars in this little town at the time. But a bright red one! Wow! So Spike (we stilled called him Terry) wrote a song about him and his car. It went something like this:

Oh Percy Lalkakaa in his red motorcar,
Oh Percy Lalkakaa we see him from afar.
Oh Percy Lalkakaa he comes to see Papa,
He comes to see Papa in his red motorcar . . .

We loved the lakes that surrounded us. In the heat of summer they dried up and grass grew across them. The villagers grazed their cattle on them, but when the thundering monsoons arrived the lakes filled to the top. Then Spike came into his own. He would persuade his school friends to play truant and swim in the Chorcien lakes which weren't exactly healthy, and Spike would develop severe tropical fevers. But he still kept on doing it.

Nothing daunted Spike. He decided to build a machan – a tree platform for shooting big game – but this one was to be in our garden. A homemade ladder gave access to the platform. I would dress up as a tiger and Hari Krishna as a deer. Spike would always have the toy gun and he would fire at us. We spent many happy hours playing this game and with all the kites we made. Spike always drew funny faces on his, and then we would vie with each other who could draw the funniest face.

Spike was about twelve when he joined the 14th Machine Gun Company as a cadet and drove Mum mad. He would dismantle a Vickers .303 machine gun and reassemble it about a hundred times. Possibly to stop this continuous practice Dad bought him a banjo and undoubtedly this started him off on his musical career, and from then on music was the order of the day.

Entertainment came right to our front door – snake charmers, dancers, the shoe repair man (the Mooche Wallah), the barber (the Nappie Wallah). There was no television or radio so as a family we entertained ourselves. Dad formed a concert party that toured the army camps performing everything from comedy sketches to Shakespeare. The Milligan boys were drawn into productions so this was a very good grounding for Spike.

But time was running out. The Great Depression had struck, the size of the army was cut down and the Milligan family came to London, in winter 1933, when Spike was 15 years old. I remember we were returning to England from Bombay on the SS *Kaiser-I-Hind*. A makeshift canvas swimming pool had been erected on the deck. I was about six or seven years old and was just learning to swim, or drown as Spike put it. I jumped into the pool and panicked, I was saved only by the squeaky high-pitched voice of a stick-thin four-year-old girl, saying to my father, 'He's fallen in the water!' That memory never left Spike and it would later become one of the most famous catchphrases in *The Goon Show*.

NORMA: I never believed Spike when he told me that story. You have to remember, he would make up a story, swear it was the truth, then say, 'Well, it made you laugh, didn't it, so what the hell?' The child is father to the man. [And although Desmond has confirmed that it was true, don't forget that he is from the same stock.]

DESMOND: Returning to England in winter – cold, drizzling and wind-swept, a shock for us colonial-borns. Spike could never get used to the grey skies and drizzle. He missed all the magnificent colours of India. No more big houses with servants. Suddenly, Mum had to do everything. Cooking, cleaning, shopping etc. and we were stuck in one of those long lines of two-storey houses. And in London there were line after line of them going on for miles.

Spike wrote a poem, 'Catford 1933':

> The light creaks
>   and escalates to rusty dawn
> The iron stove ignites the freezing room.
> Last night's dinner cast off
>   popples in the embers.
> My mother lives in a steaming sink.
> Boiled haddock condenses on my plate
>   Its body cries for the sea.
> My father is shouldering his braces like a rifle,
>   and brushes the crumbling surface of his suit.
> The Daily Herald lies jaundiced on the table.
> 'Jimmy Maxton speaks in Hyde Park',

My father places his unemployment cards
    in his wallet – there's plenty of room for them.
In greaseproof paper, my mother wraps my
    banana sandwiches.
It's 5.40. Ten minutes to catch that
    last workman train.
Who's the last workman? Is it me? I might be famous.
My father and I walk out and are eaten by
    yellow freezing fog.
Somewhere, the Prince of Wales
    and Mrs Simpson are having morning tea in bed.
God Save the King.
But God help the rest of us.

We were no longer the Burragh Sahibs. We were just one of the crowd. It was a let-down for us kids, but we quickly adjusted to the working-class district we were living in. Dad was out of work for six months. Finally, an old army buddy got him a job with the American Associated Press in the news division. He became photo news editor in a very short time. Spike had odd jobs of no consequence, but was soon making his way with the local band groups, joining 'Tommy Brettell's New Ritz Revels' playing at St Cyprian's Hall, Brockley. By this time Spike had mastered four instruments: the banjo, guitar, double bass and finally the trumpet. So he was well in with the young band scene. But we spent lots of time together during the long cold winter nights, drawing everything you could imagine. I suppose this got me on the road to being an artist.

NORMA: [I told Desmond the remark Spike had made regarding the standard of his paintings, that they should be hung in the National Portrait Gallery. Desmond told me he had painted an extremely good portrait of Spike, parcelled it up and posted it to him from Australia. Spike opened it and returned it just as it had arrived; no acknowledgement, no comment, nothing. Desmond was quite clearly hurt by this appalling behaviour, but all he said was, 'My brother at his worst.']

DESMOND: As we became adults we tended to go our own ways. Spike was finishing High School and mixing with his mates, and then things changed dramatically. Mum, Dad and I emigrated to Australia and Spike stayed in England. He was just getting established, had written the first *Goon Show*, but was planning to follow – the rest is history. Of course, he visited us once, sometimes twice a year, and when he was with Mum, up at Woy Woy, he was always so happy. He did the odd television and radio show. That's why so many people think he was an Australian. We wrote to each other very frequently. We worked together and I illustrated a couple of his books. We had our ups and downs as brothers.

NORMA: I'm sure you know that your brother, like your father, made up wonderful stories and he would swear they were the truth just to make you laugh. This is a wonderful opportunity for me to find out if the story about your father is true. Spike told me his name was to be Percy Alexander but he was baptised Leo Alphonso. The story goes that, on reaching the cathedral, the priest officiating at the baptism suggested he should be named after popes or saints, hence Leo Alphonso.

DESMOND: It does feel like something my brother could have written, but it's absolutely true.

NORMA: When did you become aware that Spike was famous?

DESMOND: I remember going to local music gigs to listen to Spike playing his trumpet and realising he was mixing with a different set of people: artists and musicians. But I think my first visit to a recording of a *Goon Show* – to hear the laughter and applause – and thinking 'my brother wrote that'. I knew then.

ERIC SYKES

'A piece of gold in showbusiness' – Spike's description of Eric Sykes, and to know him is to know the meaning of the word courage.

Early in the Seventies, Spike told me how Eric had tackled a burglar in his house and pinned him against the wall until the police arrived. 'You know, Norm, Eric has the courage of a lion.'

As Eric's manager for nearly thirty years I know him to have a different kind of courage. As most people are aware, Eric has been deaf for over forty years, but for the last fifteen he has been partially sighted until now he is almost blind. To a lesser mortal this would herald the end of six decades of a truly great laughter maker – director, writer and comedy genius – but not Eric. When Sir Peter Hall asked him to appear in his production of Molière's *The School for Wives* in 1997, Eric was hesitant, until Peter mentioned the word vaudevillian. 'Molière was a great lover of vaudeville and you are the last of the vaudevillians.'

Eric was hooked. He loved working with Peter and enjoyed the experience immensely. Then some years later Peter was back. He wanted Eric to play Adam in Shakespeare's *As You Like It*. 'That's a bridge too far for me,' Eric said, but I knew the persuasive charm of Peter, who invited us to lunch. My money was on Peter.

'Do you know, Eric, Shakespeare appeared in only one of his plays and he chose the role of Adam. Don't tell me you can't do it, because I know you can.'

I encouraged Eric. 'You have to do it. Shakespeare, for the first time, at eighty. After all these years we will be legitimate!' Then came a gesture that will stay with me for the rest of my life. Sir Peter, the greatest authority on Shakespeare in the world today, recorded the part of Adam on to a cassette to enable Eric to learn the correct inflections. In Bath, on opening night in 2003, only one thing marred the evening for me – Spike was not sitting beside me to watch 'his old mate' perform Shakespeare. He would have been so proud. But I have no doubt he would be up there telling God, or anybody who would listen to him, 'That's my old mate. He has the courage of a lion.'

ERIC: I was in bed in hospital awaiting a major operation on my ear, and while I was enjoying the comfort of a proper bed and listening to the radio I heard a comedy half-hour. It had me laughing and I was so taken by it I promptly wrote a letter of appreciation, a whole two pages telling the writers what was admirable about it. It was a new type of comedy, and it was breaking new ground. Hearing it for the first time was like walking through clear air after being stranded in a fog, infinitely laughable and funny.

Next day I had the operation. It was a long job – about four hours. I was sitting up in bed with my head swathed in bandages like the Maharajah of Shepherd's Bush. The door of my room opened and the nurses were coming in and out in a constant stream and I was coming in and out of semi-consciousness, and I saw two figures, little white faces peering at me, making 'Psst Psst' noises. I thought, 'What the hell's that?' Then the matron came in and hauled them out. I learned later their reason for being there was to thank me for the letter I had written. It was Spike Milligan and Larry Stephens. I had briefly met Spike at the Grafton Arms and he had impressed me as a man with comic ideas, exploding from his mind like an inexhaustible Roman candle.

We met later and that meeting proved to be the seed which turned out, over the years, to become Hyde Park. I came to know Spike fairly well and a few weeks after that we rented an office, five floors above a greengrocer's shop in Shepherd's Bush. It's difficult to believe we turned up every day in suits and collars and ties. We were almost a registered company and trying to behave like one. Spike and I, with Frankie Howerd, named the company Associated London Scripts [ALS]. The aim was to corner the market in scriptwriters. That office over the greengrocer's shop saw probably some of the happiest days of my life. I was newly married and lived in Holland Villas Road which was just round the corner. It suited me down to the ground, and the office became the centre of attraction for many jewels of our profession – Gilbert Harding, Irene Handl and her two pet dogs, Gretzel and Pretzel. They were little things, one under each of her arms, and we could hear her stopping on every landing to catch her breath, or possibly it was the dogs that were tired.

NORMA: It was such a pleasure to see Eric's enjoyment, recalling the obviously happy times he shared with Spike. They lunched together every day at Bertorelli's which was just across the road. Shepherd's Bush was a busy metropolis and crossing the road was hazardous so they took it in turns to limp, and the other one to help the limper across the road. The traffic always stopped and as soon as they got to the other side they marched to their lunch like members of the Household Cavalry. Next door to Bertorelli's was a funeral director's where, in a now legendary scene, Spike knocked on the door and then lay on the pavement and shouted 'Shop!'

Eric at that time was writing *Educating Archie* and Spike, who had now progressed from *Crazy People* to *The Goon Show*, was busy with his new creation, but they were still in the same office, sitting back to back. Spike had a typewriter and Eric was usually on the telephone. They had a 'hilarious time', but you can't spend all your life laughing. Spike was writing a *Goon Show* a week and the pressure was taking its toll. By this time, Eric noticed the change in Spike. He was very drawn and tired and he asked Eric if he would write some of the *Goon Shows* with him.

ERIC: I looked at him and I thought, 'Yes, because otherwise Spike's going to end up as the youngest death in the graveyard.' So we wrote and it was amicable and I saw the colour come back into his cheeks.

But when you get two highly combustible people working together there's invariably an explosion, and it came one day when Spike and I disagreed over one word. It was either 'the' or 'and'. I said it was important to put 'the' in and Spike said it wasn't, and I said it was. This got so heated that Spike picked up a paperweight and threw it at me. Now, had I been prepared I would have ducked, in which case I would be in the graveyard, but I didn't. I stood there, frozen, and it missed me by about a foot and went through the window – remember we were on the fifth floor – to smash itself onto the pavement. When I collected myself I walked straight downstairs, picked up the pieces, came straight back and put them on the desk in front of him and I said something very banal, which was, 'Remember what day this was.' It was like a B-movie. It was silly, it's like a sentence that would go down in history and he was a bit sheepish at the same time. Also he was wearing an open-neck shirt and I saw these red spots on his chest and neck that I hadn't seen before and I realised that his manic depression was something physical. And so I said, 'I'll tell you what, Spike. You write one week and I'll write another.'

So for a few *Goon Shows* that's how we wrote, until one Sunday I went to the recording of one of my scripts and they were standing round looking gloomy, the three of them. Peter Eton was the producer and I said, 'What's happened?' And Peter said, 'It's not funny,' and the three of them were mute – Spike, Harry and Peter. Suddenly, I lost my rag and I said, 'Listen! Whatever happens, it's too late now to do anything about it so you'll have to go on and do it tonight. And I'll tell you something. I'll never set foot in a *Goon Show* studio again.' And with that I made my exit, better than made by Laurence Olivier.

Every Sunday night after the show we used to eat at the Czech restaurant in Edgware Road. I went and had dinner alone and when I came out a taxi pulled up and Peter Sellers got out. He came over and he was actually crying and he said, 'That's the funniest show we've ever done,' and he flung his arms round me. Me being a Lancashire lad, thick and stubborn, said, 'But remember what I said. I'll never set foot in a *Goon Show* studio again.' And I never did and I've never forgiven myself for that.

Spike and Peter, the three of us, remained friends after that. It was a friendship and I was relieved not to have the responsibility of writing the *Goon Shows*. After all, I was only copying Spike's style and I didn't want to paint the shoes of a choirboy on a Michelangelo painting. But when I think back to those days when we rented that office in Shepherd's Bush, I think it was so natural. Spike and I were drawn together as if we'd been brothers. We just went together like bacon and eggs.

NORMA: Eric and Spike shared an office for fifty years. For Eric the *Goon Shows* are 'golden nuggets that will last for eternity'. And thanks to Mary Kalemkerian at BBC Radio 7, Eric's favourite radio station, they are still played frequently. Surprisingly, Eric admitted that he had not been the butt of Spike's outbursts. He explained that from the moment they had first met it was understood tacitly that he was the governor. There was no way Spike would lose his stripes by behaving badly in front of him and he never expected it of him.

ERIC: That side of Spike had to be borne on your poor young shoulders, but for all those readers who are starting to grieve, you survived and so have I.

In a way I was a bit strait-laced and Spike was free of his corsets. I remember we went from Shepherd's Bush, moved up into Cumberland House in Kensington. This was before the hotel was built opposite and I remember the Aldermaston marchers were marching past. Spike and I were both going through somebody else's scripts and Spike looked up, saw them through the window and he dashed out and joined Father Huddleston and Michael Foot at the head of the procession and he walked with them to Trafalgar Square. I thought, 'What a cheeky sod. Those poor devils have walked for miles and I bet when he gets to Trafalgar Square he'll be breathing heavily as if he's done the trip.'

Then from Kensington we moved to Orme Court. We spent the rest of our days as writers. And Spike was very fortunate – he met you. You and Spike came together when you were a green shoot and Spike was on the bottom rung of the ladder, and you moulded each other into a whole. You became his manager, his mentor and, if the occasion demanded it, his mother.

Spike led the life of a slightly retarded gypsy. He would sometimes lock himself away in his room with a notice on his door not to come in, but that's polite. It was F.O. When you saw that on the door you knew that to enter you were taking your life, and even the building, in your hands. As far as writing was concerned I had gone my way and he'd gone his, but we used to get up to some real pranks. I remember one day Spike's secretary came in with an envelope addressed to me. Our offices were only across the landing, five paces. I slit open the letter and it said, 'Dear Eric, where do you fancy going for lunch?' And I got my secretary to type 'Dear Spike, I think Bertorelli's would be very nice. But it'll have to be about 2 p.m. Sincerely, Eric.' And that was delivered and his secretary came back again with another letter. 'Eric, why 2 p.m.? Sincerely, Spike.' And I wrote 'Because I'm in the middle of something and I don't want to break the thread. Sincerely, Eric.' Then the door opened and Spike came in and said, 'We've got to go now.' And I said, 'Why?' and he said, 'Because I'm running out of paper.' And so we both went to lunch.

On another occasion he came into my room and he was stark naked. He was carrying a script and he put the script in front of me and said, 'What do you think of that?' and I read it. 'Well, that line can come out there,' and I made certain criticisms. 'The end is fine like that.' Then Spike said, 'You bastard! Here I am bollock-naked and you haven't mentioned it.' 'Yes, but you asked me to read the script, not examine you.'

NORMA: Eric explained that Spike was 'driven by his whims' and could be unreliable. He remembered once Spike was in the car when his first wife (he thinks it was his first wife, not the one he eventually ended up with) was driving and they were having quite a row. They were driving in the Bayswater Road and Spike had had enough, opened the door and got out. They were doing forty miles an hour. That could hardly be called the action of a responsible person. Eric also remembered one time when Spike was due to appear on stage.

ERIC: I think with Peter Sellers and Harry Secombe. Something upset him and he locked himself into his dressing room. They couldn't get him out and he wouldn't go back on stage. This again doesn't stoke up a CV of reliability. Peter and Harry had to go on to fill in. It's very difficult to tell an audience that Spike will not be appearing as he's locked himself in his dressing room, because that would take away some of the steam.

Although he was unreliable, he was trustworthy. And I say this, because if you left a thousand pounds on your desk and he came in, it would still be there when he left. And also you could leave your children with him knowing he would enthral them and entertain them with his stories and poems. Which reminds me of a hilarious Christmas Eve. His wife had left him and rather than spend a lonely festive season we invited him to spend Christmas with us in Weybridge, which he accepted because he had no intention of cooking the turkey. The four children, two of ours, Kathy and Susan, and his two, Laura and Sean, got on like a house on fire. They were all the same age, five or six years old.

Spike was the sole organiser. It was pitch black and my wife Edith had given him empty jam jars that he filled with candles. He dotted them all around the lawn, those flickering little lights. He told the children they were fairies, then speaking through a tube from the Hoover, through a little gap in the window behind the curtains, he said, 'Ho! Ho! Ho! This is Father Christmas speaking. Now where exactly are you staying tonight?' and they were all whispering they'd heard Father Christmas himself and he was coming to see them. Spike's energy was boundless. He was creating things for the children and I realised he'd hit the bullseye. I envied him this because I was less attentive to my brood, I knew Edith would bring them up properly. The children loved it. It was a very happy Christmas Eve.

We saw the children into bed and filled their stockings. As usual on the Christmas morning Edith and I, and the four children, were up early and we were all unwrapping our presents. I had lit the fire so it was cosy, with a big cardboard box to put the wrapping in, but where was Spike? What had happened? Had he left? We went up and searched all the rooms. He wasn't anywhere. Perhaps he'd been kidnapped, although I didn't think he was worth a lot in those days. About 11.30 in the morning a rejuvenated Spike came into the room.

He had locked himself in the attic and spent the night there so he wouldn't be disturbed. I thought he had missed the best time of a child's life, when they are opening their presents. It was rather typical of the man.

NORMA: One of the qualities Eric admired in Spike was his extraordinary generosity.

ERIC: He would give you his last halfpenny. If he saw what he thought was a cause he would probably mortgage his house in order to swell the charity coffers. He was a very generous man. If he saw a man limping in the street I would know he'd buy him a pair of shoes. He was impulsive – he lived on impulse half his life. Money didn't mean anything to him. It ran through his fingers like lukewarm water.

NORMA: Eric spoke of Spike's love of jazz and the wonderful times he spent at Ronnie Scott's jazz club. It was a real home from home and he used to go there three or four nights a week. For both Spike and Eric, Ronnie was a hero.

ERIC: Spike was such a friend to Ronnie, and then came startling news in 1983 that Spike was getting married again and was about to move to the wilds of the country, temporarily at first in Ticehurst, then in Rye, East Sussex. Now, it is my belief that the Thames separates one part of London from the other and never the twain shall meet, and on this occasion Spike was in a foreign country miles out, so that his new-found wife had cut him off from all that was familiar and all that he loved, including his beloved Ronnie's. And sadly I regret I never went to see him for the simple reason I didn't have satnav or enough petrol to get there, but that's where he ended his days. For me it was like I'd lost a brother.

NORMA: Spike once said to me, many years ago, 'Eric had a sister in Hattie and I've got a brother in Eric.' As Eric prepared to leave (to film an episode of *Poirot* with David Suchet, one of his favourite actors, he was so looking forward to working with him), I asked him if he had heard this quote. Such a look of sadness came over his face.

ERIC: Do you remember the story I told you at the beginning about Spike knocking on the funeral director's door, shouting 'Shop!'? I was lucky. It took fifty years for them to answer. I used to think, 'When our time comes I hope we go together. I would hate to live in a world where he wasn't.'

On 26 February 2002, one of the jewels fell from the comedy crown. It was the day Spike Milligan, with whom I'd shared an office for over fifty years, passed away. I use the phrase 'passed away' for that is exactly what he did. Spike will never die in the hearts of millions of us who were uplifted by his works. For me and you, Norma, he still prowls the building in unguarded moments. He will always be welcome. As Hattie was my sister, so he was my brother. Rest in peace, Spike, and say hello to Peter and Harry.

RAY GALTON AND ALAN SIMPSON

On my way to meet Ray and Alan, I reflected on the early days at Orme Court. The building pulsated with talent: Spike, Eric Sykes, Johnny Speight, Terry Nation, Frankie Howerd, Tony Hancock and his two scriptwriters – Ray and Alan – who played such an important part in making him the nation's favourite comedian. At six foot four, Alan topped Ray by an inch. Not much else separated them.

The year was 1966, only a few months into my induction, and Milligan was having what I later termed a mini-tantrum. I hadn't quite got used to 'the wild Milligan', in his own words. He had been working all day on a television script. After several re-writes and accompanying outbursts, heard by everyone in the building, the day's work was thrown into the wastepaper basket. I heard him shout, 'I'm gone. I've binned it. I didn't realise I could be that unfunny.' Over the years to come I must have heard that a thousand times.

The door banged as he charged out of No. 9. I retrieved his 'unfunny' efforts, as I would do many times, and tried to make sense of what he had written. It was late and I thought I was alone in the building when the door opened. Alan, who had obviously heard the outbursts, poked his head round the door. 'Why don't you go and work in a bank?' After the tension of the day I burst out laughing. It was pure Hancock from *The Blood Donor* – that famous line, 'I'll do something else. I'll be a traffic warden.'

A few days after Spike's outburst he had another one. This time I was better prepared. There was the usual shouting and ranting. 'Right,' I told him. 'I'm going home. I'll deal with it all tomorrow.' Unknown to me, Ray was in the hall and had heard what I said. He looked at me. 'I think you'll stay. You have that Scarlett O'Hara attitude.'

All the writers in Orme Court at that time had different methods of working. Ray and Alan were very disciplined. They would arrive every day about ten, have tea or coffee and start writing. Eric didn't come to the office every day, mainly because he was appearing in theatre or filming. Johnny mostly wrote at home. He didn't have an office in Orme Court but would visit Eric once or twice a week.

Spike wrote when he felt like writing. He was in the office every day. From the late Sixties right up until the early Eighties he had a bedroom in Orme Court and he would sleep there Monday to Friday. So if he felt like writing late into the afternoon this is what he would do, and work into the early hours of the morning.

I knew that meeting Ray and Alan again would be a pleasure. They're both oenophiles and lovers of fine food, and I was so looking forward to seeing them. Then an embarrassing memory flashed through my mind. After Spike introduced me to Ray I said to him, 'Isn't he gorgeous? So beautifully dressed and so sophisticated.' (Back in the Sixties I'd never heard of anyone having their shirts handmade by Turnbull & Asser.)

Spike wasn't interested and I thought he hadn't taken any notice of what I had said until later that evening, in a crowded hall when everyone was going home, he shouted, 'Ray! She's got hot pants for you!' I could have killed him. I was young and naïve and I thought I would die of embarrassment.

I met Ray and Alan together at Ray's beautiful Queen Anne house where he has collected one of the most extensive private libraries in the country. Peter Eton, a producer of *The Goon Show*, told me many years ago, 'It's one thing having a fine library, but unlike most people Ray has read every book in it.' As the car turned into the drive Ray appeared in the doorway, a slight stoop now, but as charming as ever, and Alan with that wide, kind but knowing smile that always makes me feel he knows exactly what's going on in my mind before I realise it myself. He has filled out over the years. Ray is as slim and gangly as ever – still beautifully dressed.

Equally well read, Alan is enormously knowledgeable on almost every subject. He is philosophical about most things, having suffered tuberculosis that after the war put him in a sanatorium, where he met another patient, Ray. Their sense of humour sparked a relationship that has survived the years and brought laughter to a nation, first with their memorable scripts for Tony Hancock and later with *Steptoe and Son*. It was after their enormous success that Alan decided he would retire – and did. Ray was disappointed, but this decision never impaired their friendship which, to me, seemed to strengthen after they both tragically became widowers.

Ray showed me into the drawing room. There was a beautiful Christmas tree fully decorated. It was late February! 'Why,' I asked, 'is the Christmas tree still here?' Ray's reply: 'It's so lovely, I didn't want to take it down.' Alan didn't seem to think there was anything extraordinary about this. Enter the world of Galton and Simpson. And believe me you have to be sharp to live in it. Alan has a phenomenal memory and was in no doubt when they had first met Spike.

———————

ALAN: We hadn't been in the business very long when we went to a *Goon Show* recording, about 1953. We would be in our early twenties and like almost everyone else in that age group we were great fans. Someone introduced us to him and we were really thrilled. We thought no more about it. At the time we were working from my mother's house in Mitcham. Months later, probably in 1954, the phone rang.

'Spike Milligan here.' Christ! Spike Milligan! What's he want with us? What he wanted was to find out whether we had an agent. No, we hadn't. 'Well then,' said Spike, 'Eric Sykes and I haven't got one either and we are being picked on by an agency called Kavanagh's.' That was the big showbusiness scriptwriting agency.

Spike said he and Eric were looking around to find writers who were still free from agents so they could team up and form a group as a bulwark against being picked off. We were obviously flattered that they had even considered us. We went to meet them at this really dreadful office above a greengrocer's shop in Shepherd's Bush. We were the new boys on the block so we listened and then said, 'Yeah. We'll come in with you.'

Finally, after a couple more meetings we had a main meeting to decide on the set-up. It was agreed we needed a secretary, someone to organise the office. We said we knew a girl who was doing our typing – very efficient. Beryl Vertue. It was agreed we should approach her. Well, she said, she had a good job in advertising and to leave she'd need twelve pounds a week. 'Gawd Almighty!' said Spike. 'Twelve pounds a week!' Wait a minute, we pointed out, that's only three pounds a week each. 'That's true,' they agreed. So Beryl came on board.

[Beryl Vertue later formed her own company producing successful films and television series, including *Men Behaving Badly*.]

What were we going to call ourselves? I suggested Associated British Scripts. Fine! But the Board of Trade said we couldn't have that name. What about Associated London Scripts? Yeah. We could have that. And that's how it all started. I think our first client was a man called Lew Schwartz, sent by Dennis Main Wilson or somebody like that from the BBC. Frankie Howerd got a script from someone called Johnny Speight and suggested he should go and meet the lads above the greengrocer's shop. He was the next one in. Then there were lots of others – Terry Nation who invented the Daleks, and his mate from Wales, Dick Barry. It gradually filled up from there. Ray can add to that I'm sure.

RAY: Well, I don't know about adding to it. I agree with most of it, but I don't think we were as unknown as you have said. I don't think Spike would have bothered with us if we had been that unknown. But that wasn't the first time we met Spike. I think it was at his house. He called us and we went to meet him. That lovely man Larry Stephens was there [he wrote some of the *Goon Shows* with Spike]. They were obviously sending us up like mad because they both pretended to be drug addicts. Do you remember this, Alan?

ALAN: No, I don't.

RAY: I think the real reason Spike invited us over was to see whether we would contribute or write one of the *Arthur's Inn* scripts [a successful radio series].

ALAN: You're going to get this all the time, Norma. In fact Gail Frederick [BBC] commissioned us to do two things. One was to write *Arthur's Inn* and the other was to write a pilot for Wilfred Pickles. We found out afterwards that there was never going to be a pilot for a Wilfred Pickles sitcom. Gail was just giving us a chance to earn some money.
   [They wrote an episode for *Arthur's Inn* and had Graham Stark playing Sir Humphrey Planner, a Shakespearean actor.]

RAY: But Spike must have been writing it.

ALAN: Maybe. I don't know. I know Sid Colin, a radio scriptwriter, was involved with it. [Colin co-wrote some of the *Educating Archie* scripts with Eric Sykes. He was also a brilliant jazz guitarist and composer.] That was long before we had the meeting above the greengrocer's shop. We started in the business at the end of 1951, so it must have been just before *Hancock's Half Hour* started. And we wrote at my mother's place, but after the meeting we travelled to the greengrocer's shop in Shepherd's Bush every day. We had a room on the fourth floor. Spike and Eric worked on the floor above us and Beryl had a room to herself. We stayed there until 1957. We needed to move to more salubrious offices and I think it was Stanley Dale who found a block on the ground floor of Cumberland House in Kensington High Street.

RAY: They were really prestigious. And we occupied a large part of the ground floor. Two property dealers, Jack Rose and his brother, bought the property then discovered that we were on the ground floor and paying only eight quid a week rent. Jack didn't like that. He was living with his wife and children in a beautiful flat on the fourth floor. He used to bash into our office unannounced and say, 'You'd better get used to the idea. I'm going to get all of you out of here.' We became quite friendly with the guy. I used to go up to his flat – really beautiful – and have a drink with him. He never mentioned getting us out of the building then. He wanted to talk about laughter, but his wife only wanted to talk about somebody's barmitzvah she was arranging and whether she should put so and so next to Charlie Clore or whoever, or perhaps on second thoughts it would be better to keep them apart, so on and so on. He ignored her and kept on talking to me about humour. He and his brother wrote a book about how to be property dealers.

Then one day he came into our office and said, 'Right! Come along! Put your coats on. I'm going to show you something.' We asked, 'What's all this about?' 'Never mind,' he said. 'I'm going to show you something.' We followed him up Millionaires' Row, across the Bayswater Road and into Orme Court. 'Look!' he said. 'Number 9. It's the only one that's got planning permission for business use. During the Blitz everybody got bombed out of London and the City so this house is the only one along here that has got planning permission.'

He already had the key and took us all over the building. We could see it was a wonderful place. But how much? £26,000, he said. God Almighty! Where were we going to get £26,000? Don't worry, he told us. He would get us a mortgage. And he did. So he had his wish – getting us out of Cumberland House – and the four of us owned No. 9. It was a great office. Still is.

NORMA: About early 1968 there was a problem when you, Johnny Speight and some others agreed to a deal, negotiated by Beryl, to join the Stigwood organisation. [Robert Stigwood was an enormously successful international impresario.]

RAY: We thought about buying Spike and Eric out, but what was the point? It would just be a drag so we sold out to Spike and Eric.

ALAN: They made an offer to us and we made a bigger counter-offer to them. But we realised it would be too much hassle, and they were staying in the building so we sold out to them. We'd bought it in 1961 for £26,000, between the four of us, and we sold our half for £52,000 in 1968.

RAY: I believe Eric owns the whole bloody lot now.

NORMA: He does. Spike decided to sell because he thought the place was filthy. He was having one of his bad times and had spent the weekend scouring the basement floor with Brillo pads . . .

RAY: . . . and on the Monday he told me he wanted to sell his half of the building. He said to me, 'I'm nothing more than a fucking janitor.'

NORMA: Spike's accountant and solicitor told him not to be a bloody fool, but he wouldn't listen. He insisted on selling his half. I asked him plaintively, 'But where will you go?' He replied, 'Go? What do you mean where will I go?' I told him, 'You're selling the building. Where are you going to go?' To which he replied, 'Fucking marvellous! I bring you in and now you want to get rid of me!' I told him, 'Well, I wasn't exactly in the gutter.' [Ray and Alan laughed.] Spike asked, 'Why would I want to move from here? As from today I'll pay rent.' He scowled at me and then said in exasperation, 'Well, fuck off, all of you!' So he stayed, and paid rent.

RAY: I'd like to explain about going to Stigwood. Beryl had overtures from him and most of us saw the sense of going with him. He wanted half the company, that's all, but in return we would get very good offices at his place and benefit from all his connections. All the writers, with the exception of Eric and Spike, could see the sense in it. We took a poll and every one of them decided to go with Beryl to join Stigwood. We put it to Eric and Spike, but they said they weren't interested. We knew that what Beryl was doing was the right thing because Stigwood had the money and the contacts to get our work sold to America.

[Beryl successfully negotiated the sale of Johnny Speight's scripts of *Till Death Us Do Part*, and Galton and Simpson's scripts of *Steptoe and Son*, to an American television network. *Till Death* became *All in the Family* and *Steptoe* became *Sanford and Son*.]

ALAN: I don't think Spike was interested in the business side.

RAY: And he didn't want to move out of the building. I remember a meeting of the writers' co-operative. One day I said, 'We haven't had any meetings.' So we looked at Spike and said, 'We'd better have a workers' meeting,' and all the chairs were put out and all the writers came into our office. Spike was there but I don't know if Eric was. The first question came from John Antrobus who was provoked by Johnny Speight. He wanted to know why we two, and Eric and Spike, didn't pay rent while the other writers did. Spike walked out, slammed the door, went to his room and started to play his trumpet. That was really the end of the workers' co-operative.

ALAN: First and only meeting.

NORMA: Why did he walk out?

ALAN: He was outraged at the effrontery and attitude. It's the same attitude he adopted to you when you asked, 'Where are you going to go?' The cheek of it. Basically, his motives or morals were being questioned by a lot of idiots. We never had a row with Spike but I think we were very unsympathetic about his mental problems. We ignored them. When he threw a tantrum we'd tell him to fuck off. I suppose they were bipolar problems.

RAY: We didn't really understand. My missus had clinical depression and I don't think we had any sympathy for that sort of thing until then. Alan and I had spent three years in a bloody sanatorium with tuberculosis [that's where they met Beryl]. People with colds and things – it was a case of 'Piss off.' We weren't au fait with mental problems in those days.

ALAN: Spike used to lock himself away in his office and we let him get on with it.

RAY: Tantrums.

ALAN: We took the view that when he was ready he would come out. And, of course, that's what happened. After two or three days he would come out as if nothing had happened. Others in the office would run round him like blue-arsed flies, kowtowing to him. Ray hit the nail on the head. After three years in a sanatorium we didn't have much sympathy for that sort of thing.

RAY: Having said that, we used to watch his eyes. You'd be talking to him and somebody would bring him a piece of bad news – well, bad news to him. The wife had left the tap on and he had to call the plumber.

ALAN: His eyes would go – dah! That was it.

RAY: He'd lock himself in his office and that would be it. He'd stay there for days sometimes. People would walk around on tiptoe so as not to upset him. We used to think that was showbusiness taking over. I don't think we understood. We just got on with the job.

ALAN: Having said all that, we both had great admiration for him because of his talent. And when he was in a good mood we got on extremely well. He was great company.

RAY: While we were unsympathetic, we admired his work. Wonderful! We used to go to the recordings of the *Goon Shows*. Lots of laughs. And we would have lunch with him at Bertorelli's in Queensway. More laughs! I don't know how we managed to get away from lunch to get back to work. We should have been on the floor pissed out of our heads. Here was a guy who wrote on his own – used to come into our office and ask, 'What do you think of this?' We never asked anybody what they thought of our work.

NORMA: As a person, do you think he was reliable?

ALAN: Well, we didn't have to rely on him. We all did our own work and Beryl and others looked after the business side. The thing that kept us together was that we were a mutual admiration society. Spike was very generous about our work, more so than Eric. She was a great fan of Tony [Hancock] and I think he appreciated what we were doing for him.

NORMA: He called it 'a perfect marriage'.

ALAN: That's the right word for it . . .

There was a junk shop nearby run by an old man, decrepit, wore terrible clothes, and Spike and I would look in to see what we could pick up. Sometimes the shop seemed empty and then we would hear a rumbling and out of a cupboard would pop the proprietor. We loved to drop in there.

RAY: I remember when Spike was restoring the Elfin Oak. He was carving cherubs and elves and things. You don't often come across blokes carving things like that, but Spike was different from anybody in showbusiness. [The Elfin Oak, an 800-year-old tree stump, had originally grown in Richmond Park. It was uprooted and moved to Kensington Gardens in 1928 where the illustrator Ivor Innes carved fairies, elves and animals on the trunk. Innes maintained the tree until he died in the Fifties. It was neglected until Spike led a campaign to restore it. With his team of helpers the beautiful fairies and goblins became as new, and in 1997 the oak was granted Grade II listed status.]

He was always getting involved in something or other. Mind you, his public persona was rather different from his private one. There was that kid he shot with an air rifle because he had ventured into his garden. He was taken to court. And then we would hear he wasn't speaking to his wife. If he was going upstairs and she was coming down he would turn his back on her and look at the wall until she had passed. Mad!

ALAN: I have memories of Spike's laughter. He was a great audience when he was in a good mood. He'd fall about laughing. Very much like Hancock. We only worked with him once, a four-week series called *Milligan's Wake*, fifteen-minute shows for ITV. Spike never attempted to re-write anything. He just did it as an actor and performer and did it beautifully. When something tickled him he was a wonderful audience. It was a shame we did only four shows with him. We did bits and pieces for *A Show Called Fred*. I remember we did a sketch where he was reading the football results, but with a different inflection. When an announcer reads the results you know from how he says 'Arsenal 2', in a certain way, that it's going to be 'Chelsea 2'. But when Spike read them he got all the inflections wrong. It was hysterical. There was another, again when he was reading the football results, when he realised the results were as he forecast them in his own coupon. He got more and more excited until he got to the last, which was correct and he realised he was a rich man.

RAY: Subsequently, that's been used by other people.

ALAN: Like the bingo sketch we wrote.

RAY: I remember that raspberry routine. I think it started over lunch. It was all about blowing raspberries. It got very silly. When we got back to the office the telephone rang and out came a really ripe raspberry. We had to go one better than this.

ALAN: We sent a telegram, didn't we? 'Dennis Main Wilson from the BBC says Hello, and then a raspberry!' It got absolutely mad. To cap it all Spike and Co. were in an office a floor above us and Harry Secombe was there. They lowered Harry out of the bloody window, hanging on to him by the ankles. He had a vacuum hose and they lowered him down to our window, which was open. He poked the hose through and blew a really fruity raspberry. If they'd let go of him it would have been the end of Harry. I mean, it was the top floor! We gave up after that. You couldn't top that.

And I'll always remember Spike for what I thought was the funniest gag I'd heard in years. It was in his live act. He brought out his trumpet and said, 'Ladies and gentlemen. I was going to play Chopin's Etude in B minor. Then I thought, why should I? He never plays anything of mine.' I thought it was hysterical. I'll always remember him for that.

RAY: I remember another side of Spike. I was very moved because when my wife died in 1995 Spike came to see me. It was a tiring trip for him to come from his house in Rye because he was quite frail by then. He was very comforting and friendly, absolutely wonderful. I knew he liked Alsace wine so I went to my cellar and brought up a bottle of a very good vintage. He never touched it. That was the last time I saw him.

ALAN: Yet he loved his wine. We used to go together to wine auctions at Beaver House in the City. Spike became very interested. We'd buy these very old wines, a case, and split them up, four each. I'd been introduced to these auctions by a publican in Sunbury. Spike was a great wine drinker.

RAY: Fantastic stuff!

ALAN: 1874 Chateau Lafite – things like that. Dirt cheap in those days.

RAY: We got some amazing bargains, including three bottles of genuine 1812 cognac. Absolutely gorgeous! Someone nicked a bottle from my cellar and the third one leaked through the cork.

ALAN: It was like caramelised treacle.

RAY: Good days. I remember when we were all having lunch at Bertorelli's on the particular morning Spike had received an income tax demand. He suddenly got up from the table and sat on the pavement outside with his cap turned upside down, asking the public for donations to help him pay his tax.

ALAN: He fancied himself as a trumpet player. I don't think he was very good, but Larry Stephens was a brilliant modern jazz pianist. Up in Spike's office there was a piano and Larry would strum away with beautiful little riffs and then break into 'Once in a While' . . .

RAY: We'd be enthralled . . .

ALAN: . . . then Spike would join in on his trumpet. Compared with Larry he was an amateur. The only thing that used to drive me up the wall was that he never finished anything. It was very sad that Larry died when he was in his thirties. He was very talented. He wrote Hancock's stage act. One thing I always feel is that Spike was unkind in his treatment of Larry Stephens because he used to call him 'the highest paid typist in the business'. Very unfair, because I think Larry contributed quite a lot. He certainly contributed a lot to Hancock's stage act and I think he contributed a lot to the *Goon Shows*. But the thing that used to amuse me was that Spike fancied himself as a trumpet player but he wasn't very good, whereas Larry was a brilliant modern jazz pianist.

RAY: I remember when Spike and Eric appeared with Tony on stage. It was at the time when the Russian Army Choir used to tour the world. So Tony was the conductor of the British Army Choir and Spike and Eric were in it. Well, you can imagine what chaos they caused, singing terrible songs badly – the pathetic British Army Choir as opposed to the wonderful, very professional Russian Army Choir.

ALAN: We had a lot of laughs in Orme Court. There would be a knock on the door and on answering it you would expect to come face to face with someone. But, no. There was this dwarflike figure with his head on the floor. 'Telegram from Lilliput.' That's one of my memories of Spike. [He chuckled.]

   We had one similarity. We both typed the same way – thumpers, with two or three fingers and a thumb for the space bar. But the similarity ended there. We could hear him thumping away on his portable. He was very noisy. We never got into electric type-writers.

RAY: We were quite concerned about the waste of paper. His bin would overflow and the floor was a sea of discarded, screwed up bits of paper. When he didn't like what he had written, instead of crossing it out, he simply pulled the paper out of the typewriter and chucked it.

ALAN: Absolutely right. Ray and I were meticulous and took time over everything. Spike rattled away and when he couldn't think of a line he'd just put 'Eccles: fuck!' Then later he'd go back and re-do the 'fuck'. Sometimes he would do seven or eight drafts before he would be satisfied with a script. Eric used to write by hand, enormous great writing, and he'd finish up with a huge pile. When it was typed out it would be no more than two or three pages. He'd say, 'I'll sort it out when I get to the studio.' We all had our different ways of working.

When I think about it, all my memories of Spike are good. And there's one other – he was fiendishly good-looking.

RAY: Very handsome.

ALAN: And talented.

RAY: Definitely.

LIZ COWLEY

If to plumb the soul of a man it is necessary to share his bed then Liz Cowley, once the producer of what is still regarded as the finest of daily current affairs programmes, BBC's *Tonight*, fronted by the seemingly affable Cliff Michelmore, can claim to be the ultimate authority on Spike Milligan. I watched them closely for almost forty years, both of them taking other lovers but then without rancour, resuming their relationship over intimate dinners, absorbing conversations, anointed by sharing his bed in Room 5 at 9 Orme Court. Others came and went, but Liz remained the constant in his life. There was something special between them.

Liz, small, very attractive and rippling with an innate sexuality that would be the envy of the boob tube generation, still continues to bed her lovers, but it is obvious that the one dearest to her was Spike. In my opinion she was the perfect partner for him – bright, witty, funny, warm and a great conversationalist, one of the few people who, when he was depressed, actually phoned me to find out how he was. She didn't want anything from him, she just cared about his well-being. All she would say was, 'When he's better, tell him I phoned.' A caring person. Very rare.

We have remained friends. She calls us 'The Ladies Who Lunch' and I always look forward to our lunches because I know it will be a couple of hours of nostalgia and laughter.

———————

LIZ: I first met Spike when I was working for an old army newspaper, *Reveille*, which is now defunct, and the editor said, 'This *Goon Show* thing. What's it all about? I don't understand it. Go along and interview them.' So I did and there was this dreadful man, named Peter Sellers, who was very rude. And a lovely fat Welshman who was so sweet you wanted to hug him and put him in your handbag, if indeed he had shrunk a bit. And then there was this very gauche, gangling, sexy, tall, skinny man named Spike. And I thought to myself, 'That's why he's called Spike, because he looks like a spike.' And damn it, I didn't pay much attention to him. I got my story on the Goons.

The next day the telephone rang. 'Spike Milligan here.'

'Sorry, who?'

'I think you interviewed me yesterday. Would you like to go to a party with me tonight?'

I thought, 'My goodness! A Goon inviting me to a party.' Sounded good. 'Yes, please.'

'It's at Tom Wiseman's house.' My Lord! He was a very well-known journalist at that time.

'You'll be all right. He's a scribbler and you're a scribbler, so you'll get on and I'll get on because you're getting on.'

But neither of them did. It was dreadful because, as I suspected, everybody was terribly, terribly smart, witty and drinking goodness knows what. Spike stood in the corner, very shy, humble and gauche. And I stood in the corner feeling very shy, humble and gauche, and I couldn't wait to get home and very soon that's what I did. And I thought that was the end of that, but the next day he rang again.

'Did I understand you to say you had a university degree when you were talking to someone at the party?'

'A Canadian BA, with honours.'

'Ah, well, I can't consort with you. You're educated. I'm not.'

'Well, let's try, shall we? Let's try consorting.'

Consorting meant going out to an Indian restaurant and talking, talking and talking. And for years, consorting, that was all that was involved.

That would be in the Fifties. So roll on the Sixties. I got married and Spike got married and divorced. But in between all those bits, and during them, we had our Indian meals. And finally, in about 1964, I said, 'To hell with all this. Let's go to bed!' And he said, 'Oh well. What shall we do it to? What have you got?'

'What do you mean, what have I got? I've got a Dutch cap.'

'Woman! You don't use language like that. I mean what music shall we do it to?'

'If we go to Orme Court we'll hear Ravel. Please, not the *Bolero*, because I know you're into Ravel, or the Beatles.'

'Okay. Jazz.'

'If you go to my place. You'll hear the Beatles and you'll hear jazz, but I don't know about Ravel, so let's go to my place.'

But we didn't. We went to Orme Court. The same gauche, gangly person getting very involved with the music, stopping the tape and saying, 'Did you hear that bit? That was particularly good.' And I said, 'Spike! I've got nothing on and I'm cold.' And he said, 'I think it's time we went home.' So that was our first, as it were.

I didn't fall in love with Spike, but I loved him. I thought, 'Here is a man I could spend any amount of time with.' The humour had to grow, because don't forget the surrealism that was the Goons, and was Spike of course, was something new. We're talking pre-Monty Python and pre-everything else. So I loved it because I was a great fan of Alice in Wonderland, and that was the sort of thing he was tapping into. He would talk and talk and then say, 'I'm talking too much. You talk. You're the one with the degree.' He was obsessed with people who had been to university and as a result thought he had been deprived of a whole layer of formal knowledge. He was quite wrong. 'Ah,' he'd say. 'Yes, that's what I've been missing.' Little did he know that when I was going to meet him for supper, I would bone up on the *New Statesman*, *New Scientist* and *Time* magazine. I got my science and politics all ready in a superficial way and I'd blind him with this because I knew he didn't have time to read these magazines.

No academic, but the man could put the erudite to shame with his colossal knowledge of what made the world tick. And he was no egoist. However humble the opinion you might offer, he would listen so intently it was almost embarrassing. And then say, so wistfully,

'You see, you went to university. I never did.' Silly man! Renaissance man. A hugely sensitive friend and lover.

He was someone you wanted to hold on to and listen to. I wish he'd done more with [his talent], particularly his music. I remember *The Snow Goose*. It was lovely. He was too clever by half and he didn't know what direction to really milk. He was so proud of the Goons. Once I offered to get his portable typewriter cleaned and he told me to handle it carefully because he had written all the *Goon Show* scripts on it.

The humour was obviously there, but he didn't practise humour when he was with me. He talked seriously most of the time. He didn't talk about relationships. He didn't talk about people in his life, and I thought that was odd because I rattled on about everything. I got married, got pregnant, and he put his hand on my enormous tummy and said, 'I wish this little person' – because they didn't know whether it was a boy or a girl in those days – 'I wish this little person was mine.' And I thought it was the most delightful thing he could say. Suzy was born on 16 April, which is his birthday. Spike added, 'And Hitler's birthday as well!'

NORMA: Spike always said that he and Hitler were born on the same day and it's not true. Hitler's birthday was 20 April. I told him a thousand times but he always chose to ignore it. I asked Liz if she ever had a serious disagreement with him because he could be very argumentative when he was in that sort of mood.

LIZ: Funny thing! I only remember disagreeing with him about two things. One was the shape of lines in a crazy pavement and I said to him, 'I think these are made in a kind of design although it's called "crazy". If you look carefully –' He snapped at me and said – 'You are not looking carefully. You are walking all over them.' And I said, 'No, stop! The rain is falling on them and they are shiny. They are like a piece of art and they zigzag this way and that way. It's very good.'

He shouted at me, 'IT'S RUBBISH! IT'S FUCKING RUBBISH! Workmen have been here. They've hacked the pavement to bits and you think it's arty. Typical, bloody typical.'

I remember another disagreement. He was very close to a man called Harry Edgington, an army friend. I never met him, but Spike did go on and on about him, and I think I said something very ill-conceived. I once suggested that his love for Harry was quite unusual and amazing. He said, 'What do you mean? What are you saying?' He stamped out of the room and when he got back to the office he got his revenge by tearing a leaf out of a leather-bound volume of *Adolf Hitler: My Part in His Downfall*. He'd been presented with it for selling 25,000 copies, so it was special and he sent me the page that referred to Harry Edgington. I must have hit a nerve because his reaction was so over-the-top and I could never understand why. To suggest that there was anything homosexual in Spike was absolute rubbish, although I have to say he wasn't your jumping up and down, wahey, hairy-chested lover, and that was nice, but satisfying? 'I ain't got no satisfaction.'

It was an extraordinary friendship. It certainly had nothing to do with sex at all. He seemed to know what I was going to say before I said it and, I'd like to flatter myself, quite often I knew what he was going to say. I just needed to know that he was in my life because as the years went on I thought, 'Here is a rich and famous man and he bothers with me.' That was tremendous. I remember when I was in the throes of my divorce. The divorce papers weren't yet on the table and my husband and I were trying to make one last go of it by having a second honeymoon in the Algarve, which was a disaster because he would get up early just so that he didn't have to look at my face over breakfast, and go off with his camera into the mountains. I didn't see him all day, so I would go down to the beach where there were little rocky coves and I sat in a small cave with the sea coming right up to my knees, and then it washed out. It was very nice, so I wrote in the sand, 'Spike – you are the one I love', and then I watched the sea wash it away. Then I did it again and that's how I spent a whole morning in the Algarve. I knew that the man I was married to was not a man I could be at one with, whereas Spike I could. I also think a lot of it was ego. I thought, 'This man is interested in me and I need my ego building.' The fact that he was willing to spend time with me was very flattering.

He never proposed. The only things he proposed were when he thought it was time I left or that we should have a race in our Minis. And yet when he was working in Australia or South Africa he wrote to me two or three times a week, not ordinary love letters. Sometimes they would begin 'Hi, Cowley.' I remember he once wrote, 'Some people might even say I miss you. I haven't said that.' So he was always on the defensive.

Spike never liked formal dates, though once I took him to a movie, *The Way We Were*, starring Barbra Streisand and Robert Redford. Perhaps selfishly I felt it mirrored so much of my own past and might help him to understand where I was coming from. As we left the cinema I expected some sort of sympathetic comment. What I got was, 'What the fuck was that all about?' I realised then that my part of the world, rapidly receding the longer I stayed in England, struck few chimes with him. Perhaps that's why we didn't marry. That and the fact that he never asked me.

NORMA: The film reflected West Coast, leftish academe, a world away from the tourists Spike wrote about so scathingly in letters he sent when he was doing his one-man show in Australia in 1972.

Liz, with her lovely face, as lively as a linnet, and her memories of Spike that will never fade, looks many years younger than she is. She remembers Spike's kindness and his requests to meet up in the early hours. There is no sadness in her reminiscences.

LIZ: Perhaps it's a cliché, but isn't the mark of a really great man his ability to stop and do little things to help others? When I very nervously started a short series of late-night chat shows on Radio 1, I asked Spike – by then running just to stand still – if he could possibly take part in a 'fathers and daughters' debate. There wouldn't, er, be any money in it but we could send a taxi. He agreed immediately and brought along his daughter, Laura. Thus my humble, local first programme got off to a flying start.

When I began a series for teenagers on BBC1 he came up trumps again, agreeing to sit in as an 'agony uncle', offering advice to young people alongside agony aunt Lulu. Now this was a man at the very pinnacle of his career. He didn't lack for money and certainly not for TV coverage. No wonder I loved him. But perhaps, too, there was something very Christian, in the best sense of the word, in this colourful lapsed Catholic. I once asked him whom he would most like to meet in the afterlife and without hesitation he said 'Jesus Christ.'

But perhaps what I remember most fondly touches on the magical. Here was a man you could walk with down a bleak, rainswept street and he could make it an adventure. 'Look at that outdoor guttering. Just look! It's so ill-fitting it's swinging in the wind. See up there! They're crashing about like metal cobwebs.' Or the manholes under our feet, so delicately etched, said Spike, they belonged in a museum. 'And the ones in the British Museum aren't much better.'

He was never one for honeyed compliments, however hard you'd worked at the slap and silk, and although gauche he was immensely kind and tried so hard to bite the bullet of his depressions. I visited him once in hospital with a basket of Canadian Golden Delicious apples. Years later he couldn't recall that particular episode of his 'black dog' but he never stopped talking about the apples. 'Whereabouts in Canada do they grow them? The Okanagan Valley, you say. Do they use a special kind of fertiliser? Can you find out? And to think you brought them all that way to the hospital!' [She smiled at the memory.] He seemed to think I'd made the trip to Canada to get the apples for him so I didn't explain that my sister had sent them.

I always felt I could confide in him and his response always was that if I was in trouble he would help, but not if it was boring. I was never bored by him, otherwise I wouldn't have rushed out in my Mini at three in the morning because he had telephoned and wanted to see me. I sometimes wondered how many other girlfriends he had phoned before me, but I never asked. He was married to Paddy at the time and I think Spike was looking for something he wasn't getting at home. Obviously, he didn't get it from me otherwise he wouldn't have had other girlfriends. At that time I was pretty naïve about sex. Perhaps he didn't give enough of himself to his wives. That possibly alienated them so that they couldn't give enough of themselves to him. Another thing to consider is Spike's love of experiences. If he was to give himself completely to one woman that would blot out much of the opportunity to have the experiences he was always looking for. He loved experiences. Talking, moving, shifting around and a woman tends to be more possessive than that in marriage. Perhaps he didn't want to be tied to one woman.

He was diabolically clean and I think to him the act of sex was perhaps a bit dirty, in a liquidy kind of way. I remember him saying, when we were deciding whose house we would go back to, 'I'll bring the dangly bits. You bring the juicy bits.' And I said, 'Okay.' He said, 'You are not supposed to agree with things like that.' He was constantly trying to put me back into a mould of innocence and Doris Dayism. He said one of the things he liked about me was that I was very 1950s, wore red lipstick, had a hairstyle of that period and looked like Betty Grable. That was all right by me.

Once he rang at three in the morning. Mike, my husband, picked up the phone and Spike said, 'I'm here to commit verbal adultery with your wife. Put her on.' Of course, Mike had been woken up and he wasn't a happy man. When I was producing a daily programme and needed the sleep, Spike would sometimes telephone at two in the morning and say he knew a restaurant where they were still serving curry. 'So get in your car and I'll meet you there.' And I always did. I always came whenever he asked me. He had no jealousy because I was married and I had no jealousy whatsoever about the Bayswater Harem. I knew one or two of them slightly. Lovely people. But when he was hurt or suffering it tore my heart apart. I remember silly things. Once I took a Sara Lee frozen apple pie to Orme Court because I'd just discovered them. I thought they were very good. He thawed it and ate the whole pie and then sent one of his people out to get nine more.

There were so many evenings I remember fondly. The most fun night I can recall was when he came over all mysterious and invited me back to Orme Court, nothing unusual about that, for a night-cap after a television show. He was one of the unsung heroes of the Thames mud banks at low tide. He found odd artefacts with his metal detector and dug them out with his bare hands. But this particular evening he said he had something special. He opened his 'secret' drawer and brought out an ancient, mud-caked half cask of brandy.

'Here's to Drake, Shakespeare – well I found it near the old Globe – and the Royal Navy generally.' He prised it open, 400 years old perhaps, and we scoffed the lot. Now that's friendship.

I've often read so much and heard so much about his treachery. It was a closed book to me and I never came across it at all. There was a time when I ventured into one of his black dog depressions. It was when he invited me to go to Manchester and he was doing a one-man show, all those ad-libs that I knew off by heart. He had booked me a room next to his in the hotel. He had said, 'Let me know when you arrive,' so I arrived and started to put notes under the door of his room saying, 'Hello. I'm here.' There was a big sign on his door that said, 'DO NOT DISTURB. I'M SLEEPING.'

I wouldn't dream of knocking on the door so I kept pushing notes under it and then I sent him cartoons and little poems. I was bending down with a note saying, 'It's nearly 7 o'clock and you are due on stage at 7.30,' when he opened the door and sent me flying because I was down there with my nose on the end of the door. He shouted, 'What are you doing on your hands and knees outside my room? It's theatre time, woman!' I said, 'Actually, you invited me up here, Spike, and I thought you'd be amused by the notes. And you asked me to let you know when I arrived.' He said, 'Go to the theatre. I don't want to talk to you now.' And he left.

NORMA: I asked Liz if she was ever the butt of his treachery.

LIZ: Treachery is not a word I would use, but he could and did hurt me. When he was filming *Ghost in the Noonday Sun* in Cyprus he asked me to fly out to be with him. Then he ignored me totally, went out to dinner with other people and never invited me. That was terrible. Otherwise I had a lovely trip – enjoyed the beach and the sunshine – but it seemed he didn't want to know me. It was very hurtful. I came home early.

NORMA: I told Liz my memory of her on that trip. The sun was shining, she went into the sea, lay on her back and said, 'Thank you, Spike.' So it wasn't all bad.

LIZ: No. At least I got away from the English weather.

NORMA: Spike was a strange person and Barry Humphries said he could be an absolute shit but that people forgave him. I asked Liz why she thought people forgave him.

LIZ: Because he had such a kind and sweet way of making up afterwards. He could be sweet beyond belief. This was my experience, anyway. Sweet beyond belief. I remember when I was sacked by a Fleet Street editor. I was doing television previews for him and was absolutely demolished by this. Spike was at the Mermaid Theatre doing Ben Gunn, or whatever, and I went there straight from my Fleet Street sacking to see him. I was crying and the doorman was so flustered he let me into Spike's dressing room. Spike said, 'I can't talk to you. I'm just about to go on,' and I said, 'I know. I know.' I told him what had happened. He gave me a bottle of wine, half full. He'd had the first half. He told me to take it home, drink it in the bath and I would feel better. I did exactly that and when I arrived at the house there was a huge bouquet from Interflora. How he managed to get it there before I got home I don't know. That was the sort of radiant kindness that touched me again and again. When I hear of his treachery and his racism I can't associate these things with him at all. It was silly, wasn't it, just because he'd blacked up as an Indian in *Curry and Chips*, for heaven's sake.

He was very kind in his own way and he loved my little girl, Suzy. I was talking to Suzy the other day – she's a fully-fledged shop-owner now – and she said, 'I didn't think much of him.' She had brought him breakfast in bed one day when he came to stay. She put a little flower in a vase and he shouted at her. He didn't want toast, he wanted a roll, or it could have been the other way round. Suzy was demolished. She came back and said he wanted a roll. I said, 'We don't have a roll. It'll have to be toast.' He shouted from the bedroom, 'I heard that. And make sure it has butter and strawberry jam on it.' Suzy took it upstairs and Spike said, 'Take it away. I'm not hungry now.' And that from a man who loved children! It was very hurtful. She was only about four, but she knew I adored him. That was too bad, and yet when he was leaving he said, 'Look, I'm very fond of Suzy. I didn't mean to shout at her, so take my undershirt. She can have it because the weather is turning cold.' It was one of those Wolseley knitted vests. Huge! Of course, she would drown in it, so I kept it and I still sleep in it to this day.

NORMA: There were tears in her eyes as I told Liz that I had always wanted Spike to marry her and that towards the end of his life he was unhappy.

LIZ: I wish I'd known. Perhaps I could have helped. But he never called me. I would have gone anywhere with him if he had asked me.

NORMA: He came to stay with me, he said to sort himself out. He was deadly serious. I told him he could have a room as long as he wanted to stay. He said, 'What a friend we have in Jesus, but I've got a better one in you.'

LIZ: The last time we met was in one of his favourite restaurants, the Trattoo, in Kensington. It was The Ivy of the day in the Sixties, Seventies and early Eighties, always buzzing with people from theatre and television. It was a year before he died and I could tell his health was fading. As we parted he said, 'Please. You stay alive and keep your enthusiasm. I think I've lost mine. Yes, this time, I really do.'

NORMA: Liz hasn't lost any of hers. And I'm sure her memories of Spike keep her warm in colder days. He should have married her.

Sunday. 21 March   393 Orange Grove Rd
                             Woy Woy
                          Until 13 May

Dearest 'Cowley'
              Parker 51? thats 25 years old
Parker 76 is what you need. Weather hot
72-, 80° - they've never heard of air-conditioning
in Theatres out here - and when your under
the footlights-arc lights. the temp on stage
is 90° - I almost de-hydrate with the heat!
Thank god (G) Im fit! The shows from
Melbourne, Adelaide + Sydney have been sell outs!
The astonishing thing is audience age - average
23, The critics in Melbourne wrote me off as a
'has been'... they're so out of touch'. I must be the
only writer to be writing Two series at the
same time for the BBC. I went into the Bush'
in Adelaide - looking for Aborigine kitchen
middens along the banks of the Murry River -
we found some but no artifacts. In Melbourne
it took so long to get out of the city, it wasn't
worth the journey, but now Im in Woy-Woy
I know the district, and I can go 'exploring', my
nephew Michael (9) my brothers son, found a
metal arrow head in our garden in Woy Woy -
as the Abo's never mined iron, it must have taken
place after the arrival of the White-man.
So indifferent are my family to such treasures
, my mother kept it in the 'copper' I've
retrieved it, am soaking it in oil - and will then
clean it. Im writing this - in my fathers
cabin, which I had built onto the house for him
in 1956, it is built like the interior of a log cabin
on wall adorned with his collection of rifles,
muskets, powder flasks etc - Norma is here, shes

2

Sun bathing in the garden. My time has usually been eaten up with Radio - TV - Newspaper interview - fan letters, requests to open this - or that, address the faculty etc - so I've had no time for letter writing. In Melbourne, I woke/ arose at 10.30. Write vol III of the war memoirs - answer correspondence. at 3.30 - 4.00 I played squash - in Adelaide I got no exercise at all, and I miss exercise, after a ½ hour work out I feel great for the rest of the day. Having the Sun, and clear light, makes one feel better than one does in England. The great exploitation of Australia is on at a great rate - the Conservative Government, committed to capitalism - is opening the countries Uranium wealth to America - Japan - and this would destroy large areas of Aborigine Land - even destroying "Sacred Mountains" - in their mad search for bigger profits, I help the fight against them, but I know the whole Environmental Fight is being lost -, apathy of the masses, and the heavily entrenched large firms and governments who are absolutely unconcerned, its a great selfishness to ignore the coming appalling conditions for the innocent generations to come; but come it will. I too miss you Liz, I'll be back in June - so........ . I with close now. as I have 12 more letters to write, even the world of correspondence is crowded

Love

Spike

393 Orange Grove Rd
Woy Woy
N.S.W
Sept. 12. 1968

My dear Liz,
              Its 10 at night, Im writing
this in bed, in the almost 'noisy'
silence of the water-side bush town.
Its a full moon, and the Brisbane
Waters an inland piece of the Pacific
looks like a piece of polished shining
blue steel, its really beautiful. I've
had to extend my stay here, as my
father suffered a stroke, and is
in hospital, with mild paralysis of
one side, my mother is 75 and it
would be awful if I left her to return
home, [This is starting to sound like
Peyton Place], I've been spending the
time writing a ~~novel, fact~~, book, called
Positvely the very last World War II
Autobiography, its about me and the
last war, so far I've written 22,750 words,
it seems like a bloody million, ah!
list my portable is exuding culture,
Glousenovs A minor Violin Concerto.

2

The weather is blissful, sunny. cool, temp.70.
I've been walk about in the bush - been
active in trying to save 1) Ettalong Hall,
early colonial residence, 2) Set up a Bell-bird
sanctuary, 3)stop demolition of Gosford Court
House. (Convict built 1830) etc,The song of the
Bell bird is unique. 't is like the peal of a
small silver bell). I'll record a few native
birds, and play them to you on my return.
Since leaving heaving London. I've been to
Fiji, spent 2 days on an island with only
5 inhabitants, dived for shells, and got 15 beauties,
been San Fran bloody Frisco, never saw the city
but the Forest of Giant Redwood trees,
some 300ft high, girth. 40ft (not you dear).
Talk to Hippies in Frisco, nice people, shunned by
the 'old world' of course. Barry Humphries show
in Australia a sell out. Pd Home produced
TV Variety bloody terrible -!!! I did ½ hr TV
on my own, successful. I seen a piece of
land here that is beautiful, 16 Acres. with
Bell-bird woods. a stream, lake at the bottom -
and view of the Pacific. £17,500 bloody pounds!
What to do, oh what to do. I can afford it
but will I ever live here! You know what
ABC are repeating the Goon Shows - Monday

8 o'clock, I'm beginning to hate the bloody thing!
I flew to Melbourne to see the New Art
Gallery, wiz it is Fab! This country is on the
march but good. The cealing is the biggest
glass cealing in the world, coloured, by L.
French. Fly your self and Eammon out here -
Eammon on Australia (on BBC Travel Voucher) and
see for yourself. The wine is beaut mate, I
have a bottle of Eden Valley Moselle every
evening, I rise early, about 7.30, Suns up.
I sit on the Sun Veranda, sip strong tea -
eat toast and honey, mum cooks it.
In the garden we have. Paw Paw - Orange
lemon and Bananna Trees, plus 3 Grape
Vines I planted 5 years ago (I found them
on a deserted Farm in the bush]. No more,
drop me a line - tell me all.

As Ever
Spike

-ZZZZZ

Hasty Sketch of View from my window

DENIS NORDEN

According to his headmaster at the City of London School, Denis had what was considered to be 'a fine academic brain'. His parents, no doubt, wondered which profession he would grace. I don't suppose for one moment they considered showbusiness. What a loss to this profession it would have been if he had taken the academic route.

He met Frank Muir in 1947 and together they became the successful writing partnership of Muir and Norden, with hits such as *Take It From Here*, a radio series which lasted twelve years. Other radio hits were *Whack-O* and three series of *Faces of Jim*, both wonderful vehicles for Jimmy Edwards. But I remember the brilliant radio sketch they wrote for Peter Sellers called 'Balham, Gateway to the South'. This must have been in the early Sixties. In 1980 – about two years before Peter died – Spike, Peter and I were having dinner in the Trattoo. We were having a normal conversation when suddenly, with that chameleon quality he possessed, Peter changed his demeanour and in the accent he used in 'Balham' he recited the first part of the sketch. It was amazing. Spike just took it for granted.

But I wondered how, after all the characters Peter had played over a period of what must have been at least fifteen years, he could remember the sketch so clearly. I asked him the question and with a complete throwaway he said, 'Norm, I just can.' Spike, not to be outdone, burst into 'Ying Tong Diddle I Po' and together they sang the first five or six lines of 'The Ying Tong Song'. I don't think I've ever told Denis the story of his brilliant 'Balham' sketch. I know it would make him smile, as he made the nation smile with his long-running television series *It'll be Alright on the Night*.

DENIS: I think I first met Spike at Daddy Allen's Club where everybody (and this would have been post-war, almost immediately post-war) who was just starting at the BBC then used to go, to this club in Soho, the chief benefit of it being they had a slate and you could eat on tick there. So all of us who were trying to get into radio, particularly Michael Bentine and all those people, we would take these equally young BBC radio producers there and treat them to lunch which would always be a steak because they were in such short supply. Looking back on it now, I'm sure it was horsemeat anyway but nobody knew the difference in those days. I remember Frank took somebody and took one of the producers who ordered a steak and we didn't have any money and Frank sort of indicated to me it was to go on the slate and the producer said 'Can I have an egg on it?' and Daddy Allen said 'You can have an egg yes, but Christ, the bill' which wasn't the best way to entertain. But I think that was where I first met Spike.

Thereafter we sort of interwove quite a few times because we both recorded our shows at the Paris Studios in Lower Regent Street on a Sunday and either we went in after they recorded or they came in after we recorded so there would be this interval where we'd meet in that narrow corridor down at the bottom of the stairs at the end of which there was a canteen and we would have a cup of tea together, or else we would meet in the Captains Cabin which was the local pub for everybody who recorded at the Paris Studios.

NORMA: What were you recording at that time?

DENIS: *Take It From Here.*

NORMA: Spike was recording *The Goons*?

DENIS: Yep. One of my principal interweavings with Spike was when my children were young. Spike did a Saturday morning radio programme of records and the whole programme was aimed at children. There was one record called 'Little Red Monkey' which I think actually Joy Nichols sang, which he played regularly and the kids would sing around the house. He would also recite his poems, so at a very early age we regularly got Spike Milligan verse on long car journeys, chiefly 'There are holes in the sky where the rain gets in but they're ever so small that's why rain is thin.' Now that particular quatrain which I may not have perfectly remembered – my kids grew up with that, they then had children of their own so my grandchildren were read Spike's verses and they went marching round saying, 'There are holes in the sky where the rain gets in.' My grandson (who is an architect in Los Angeles) has two small boys and they are now perpetuating those 'holes in the sky where the rain gets in'. So that's four generations of holes in the sky.

NORMA: What was your first impression of Spike?

DENIS: I think it was his audaciousness on radio, quite apart from the fact that technically he did things with sound effects which nobody had done before. Spike was the first to fool listeners' ears with his sound effects and it's never been better done than those interminable footsteps he would write in, which is now a kind of cliché but all clichés begin as novelties. He had enormous nerve in beating the censors in ways that they never noticed. We all suffered from having to have our scripts examined before they could be broadcast, but I remember Spike would throw in references, for example, 'Grant Road, Bombay', which nobody knew (except those who had either been brought up in India or had served there) was the road where the brothels were, and various other Indian expressions which he only got caught on two or three times, as I recall. He got away with murder in that respect. When he was at his best, there was nobody like him. Gaiety – that word which has now been kidnapped. There was nobody who could make a gathering more, in the old-fashioned sense, gay, or make people feel more at ease than Spike when he was on form. As everybody knows, he wasn't always on form but for a large part of the time he was and my principal memory of him is laughter.

I think people are inclined to get the wrong idea about the Fifties. They are always painted as being dull, austerity was the word. What they forget was we had passed the decade before, or at least half of the decade before, in a state of constant apprehension, boredom, grief and sometimes terror, a wholly artificial way of living – and suddenly we'd been reprieved and you can't over-emphasise the enormous feeling of relief that everybody had at that time during the late 40's and the 1950's, you know time doesn't split neatly, the 60's actually began about 1957 so you know it doesn't divide into decades so neatly. But we had what no other generation has had since, an enormous feeling like a group of people who have been trapped in a room and suddenly they're all let out and standing on the pavement outside. The whole country was like that and we'd all lived through the same inconveniences and dangers, and you only had to mention them and everybody picked up on them. We could share allusions in a way that nobody has been able to since, particularly as it's now become so multicultural that there's not a great sharing of allusions anyway. So we were very fortunate in that respect and there was a mateyness too, especially amongst those of us who had been in the Forces. Frank and I had been in the RAF, and we'd done the troop concerts, either writing or performing, and we knew that the way to make a military audience laugh was to send up the officers. You had to gauge it in such a way that you made fun of them but without inciting to mutiny. You had to know where to stop. And that is why I think that generation, Spike and so on, sent everything up but not to the point of destruction. One thing I remember about Spike, talk about a rebel without a cause, Spike was a rebel with too many causes. He was a rebel with more causes than anybody.

Radio comedy was a consequence of the war, there's no doubt about that, because prior to the war, radio comedy was very much a genteel pursuit that was cultivated by the BBC itself. During the war we all heard the American Forces Network which was broadcast not only on the BBC in Britain but also overseas. It would be broadcast over the tannoys which were set up in every parade ground and so the likes of Bob Hope and Jack Benny showed us the possibilities of radio. We had thought it was rather like *Punch*, something that was for a certain generation and a certain class, and we were suddenly shown that radio was available to our generation and our sense of humour. Because of this great pool of shared experiences, everybody – the audiences and the performers and the writers – had a lot in common.

I remember there was a kind of consensus that television arrived too soon, that if it had held off another four or five years we'd have got radio really licked and perhaps television would never have come along. But then television did come along and everybody had to get in there.

NORMA: A lot of people at the time said that they thought Spike was just an idiot, you know, and that he wouldn't last, would be a flash in the pan, which obviously is not quite how it's been. What did you think?

DENIS: I can only talk for Frank and myself but Spike had this great enthusiasm which he shared at the same time with another great enthusiast, Michael Bentine, and the two of them together were simply an endless well of invention and ideas of which it has to be said that at least fifty per cent were useless but among the other fifty per cent there was a treasure trove.

NORMA: Were you ever the butt of Spike's treachery and did you ever see him when he was very down?

DENIS: I had an experience with Spike. Now, I'm not going to use names in recounting this, but Frank and I at one time shared an office at the bottom of Bruton Street which leads into Bond Street and it was above a club called The Gay Mounties which was run by Eric Maschwitz and his wife. For some reason we always had offices right at the top of a building (only once did we have a place where there was a lift) so you had to go up all these stairs to get to us and one night

I was alone in our office, everybody else had gone. I was at the desk busy with something and I heard these feet running up the stairs and the door burst open and there was Spike. He had a knife which he flung on to the desk and it was the first time, and the only time, that I've ever seen that favourite shot of a knife quivering when it stuck in the desk and quivered backwards and forwards and Spike said, 'He's in the Grosvenor Arms and I'm going to get him.' He was talking about another writer who had a reputation for stealing jokes which were our capital at the time and Spike went on to say that this other comedian had written something which contained a full page that he had written a few weeks earlier and he had the knife and had every intention of going round to the Grosvenor Arms, where he heard this guy was, and using the knife. Luckily I had a bottle of Scotch which we always kept in the office, and I succeeded in calming him down and finally leaving with him, putting him in a taxi to make sure he didn't go anywhere near the Grosvenor Arms. Because I was alone in the office there was only one light on and the stairs were dark, so it had all the elements of melodrama, unwittingly.

NORMA: Did you have any fun times that you can particularly remember?

DENIS: When three of us turned up together on the special programme BBC Radio put on to celebrate his eightieth birthday, he greeted us with the announcement, 'It's Sykes, Speight and Norden, back from the dead for one night only.'

[For another recollection Denis pointed towards a passage from his memoir, *Clips from a Life*:]

One of my more searing memories of him goes back to 1964, when he was appearing in the West End in the play Son of Oblomov. They had given him free rein to ad lib all he wanted, with the result that no two performances were ever the same. On the night I saw it, I had the misfortune to be in a seat where he could spot me from the stage. Consequently, about fifteen minutes into the first act, he waved the proceedings to a halt, advanced to the footlights and, motioning me to stand up, introduced me to the audience. Then, addressing me, he confided, 'This next bit, it's a little dull. You're a scriptwriter, can you suggest anything I can do to cheer it up?'

When I stammered something desperately wide of the mark, he smiled encouragingly. 'Just some funny little line,' he said. 'Doesn't have to be a whole new scene. Work on it and if anything occurs, shout it out. God bless you, guv.'

He nodded me to sit down again and resumed the play. But during the rest of the evening, on at least half a dozen occasions – all of them, I must now admit, beautifully judged – he would halt the play and get me up again with such remarks as, 'Still nothing?' and 'I'm perfectly prepared to pay Writers' Guild rates,' and, finally, 'You're not much without that fellow in the pink bow-tie, are you?'

When we went round to see him in his dressing room afterwards, he was in high spirits. 'I think that worked out very well, don't you?' I could only gesture weakly at the whisky bottle.

I actually put him up for a Lifetime Achievement Award at the 1994 British Comedy Awards. He got a bit sentimental at the ceremony and he said, 'You put me up for this?' We were sitting at the table and you were next to me and then he went up and bad-mouthed Prince Charles. Do you remember that?

NORMA: Yes, I do.

DENIS: What did he say? Toading bastard or something.

NORMA: Jonathan Ross was reading out a letter from Prince Charles, going on and on and on and he just wanted to shut Ross up and he said, 'The grovelling little bastard.'

Did you ever see Spike in pantomime?

DENIS: I remember taking the kids to see him in *Treasure Island* where he just got right through to them. He was wonderful with children and his performance was brilliant. He could have gone down the pantomime route and made a fortune but Ben Gunn [the character he played] was special. The kids came out in a kind of trance, that look kids have when they've been taken right out of where they were.

NORMA: He had this quality and I think it manifests itself in all the children's books. It's a childlike quality that children seem to buy into straight away. Not childish, it's the childlike. He won the nation's favourite poem for 'On the Ning Nang Nong'.

DENIS: I'll tell you while it occurs to me. He was childlike in a sense that reminds me of Peter Ustinov. I remember Frank and I did a series with Peter where we acted more as editors than anything, and Peter, like Spike, would pour out ideas and we had to choose which ones to include in the programme, and we would say, 'We think this is the bit, I think we should edit out this other bit.' Immediately you said that, his lower lip would come out – just like children when you tell them off – and he'd mutter and say, 'Well, I rather like that' and you say, 'Yes, it's very good, Peter, but the others are better' then he would say things like 'It depends on your sense of humour, doesn't it?' You see, those little would-be spiteful things that children say when you take something away from them, and Spike was like that. If he had an idea and you said 'Yeah, it's good, you know, but,' he began to have that look of a child whose toy had been taken away. He would then start saying rude and unkind things about you. But it was part of him.

NORMA: He was petulant like that at times. Why don't you like this, what is it you don't like? Then attacking you for not liking it. Denis, do you think that he will be remembered only for the Goons?

DENIS: I don't know, I really don't know. I mean, the ways in which you commemorate people these days is only through the media, the DVDs and so on. His children's programmes have been wiped so future generations will have no idea of those. His movies, his television programmes, there's no sign of them being waved in front of people any more.

NORMA: Do you think that is because he was very, very politically incorrect?

DENIS: No, I think a lot of it is due to the fact you couldn't tape-record everything in those days. Tapes were very expensive and the heads of department had a tape budget and they had to make, I think, on-the-spot snap decisions about what of that last month's output was worth putting into the archives. You can't really reprimand anybody for making wrong choices because it's enormously, enormously difficult to know what of today's output somebody will like in twenty, forty, fifty years' time. I was a cinema manager in the West End in the days when there used to be continuous performances, not like today where you have separate performances which you book tickets for, so that at the end of the main programme they would put on a Laurel and Hardy short after the main feature and they were known as 'chasers' because they would chase a portion of the audience out. People wouldn't stay for it and you could then get more people who were waiting in the queue to come in and take their seats. Now that was the current judgement on Laurel and Hardy and of all that material that was shown in cinemas in those days what has lasted, not the big features but Laurel and Hardy. So, as for Spike's, somebody made a snap judgement that there was something else they would rather keep for posterity. I think, for quite a lot of the time, they equated that off-the-wall outrageousness of Spike with something that was temporary. They didn't feel it had anything of lasting value. Now so much of comedy consists of that kind of thing: tastes have completely swung round.

NORMA: Did you ever think at any time that Spike was a racist?

DENIS: Well, again, by today's standards he was but then so was all of England, you know. The word 'negro' is looked upon as racist today. We knew no other word: we thought 'black man' was racist back in those days. Wolf Mankowitz had a chat show in the early days, really early days, and he had Spike on and I remember Spike ran him ragged, he was particularly irreverent. Wolf finally lost his temper and he said to Spike, 'When did you give up membership of being a Blackshirt?' and it threw Spike and afterwards I said to him was that true and had he joined the British Union? It wasn't called the British National Party then, it was called the British Union of Fascists, I think. Spike said he liked the uniform, the black shirt, which was a perfectly satisfactory explanation for Spike. Well, was he a racist? I don't know. I mean, in what respect did they call him a racist?

NORMA: Well, you see a lot of people have said that he was a racist. He told jokes about the Pakistanis and told jokes about the Jews.

DENIS: Yes, the thing he did with Eric. Now that show where Spike played a Pakistani and Eric was the sort of decent foreman, what was it called?

NORMA: *Curry and Chips.*

DENIS: *Curry and Chips.* I thought that was so funny and in fact I tried to show bits of it on various compilation programmes I did. I don't think it was in any way racist. I think it was very fondly done.

NORMA: Written by Johnny Speight.

DENIS: Yep, I wouldn't in any way point to that being racist. No, racist isn't a word that immediately comes to mind when you think of Spike because so much of his background was either Indian or Irish.

NORMA: Do you think people will remember all his writings, not just *The Goon Show* but the war memoirs, for example, the seven volumes of those?

DENIS: Well now, what's going to happen to books, you see. If people don't remember I don't think it'll be down to Spike, it'll be because (a) people no longer read books and (b) they're no longer interested in the war. To anybody who was around at that time those books were essential reading and a constant joy, but of course if you've never experienced anything near to what he was writing about, as it recedes further and further into the distance, I don't know whether people will remember it.

My last thought on Spike is of the laughter, and one of the few members of my trade who deserves to have a public park named after him is Spike Milligan, the man responsible for such eternal verities as: 'Anyone can be 52, but only a bus can be 52B' or 'Some people are always late, like the Late King George.' It is also to him that we owe the proposition that Tring was named after the inventor of the bicycle bell.

MARCEL STELLMAN

'The dreaded Marcel Stellman', as Spike always called him, is very proud of the fact that there is only one *Goon Show* songs album, and 'I'm glad to say I'm the guilty one.' He should also be proud of the fact that his track record as an A & R man at Decca records is very impressive. He speaks five languages fluently, he produced Dame Vera Lynn and taught her how to sing in German. He taught Julio Iglesias to sing in English from Spanish, and Marianne Faithfull from English to French. The great Armenian singer Charles Aznavour was recorded and produced by him, and he wrote one of Aznavour's greatest hits, 'You've Let Yourself Go'.

At the Cannes Film Festival in 1981, Marcel saw a television show, *Countdown*, and persuaded Armand Jammot (the man who devised the show) that it would transfer to British television, and Marcel now represents the show in Britain.

After sharing his memories with me, we went to lunch at Scott's, and over lunch he said something to me that summed up his success: 'You need to understand these people.'

NORMA: I asked Marcel if he could remember when he first met Spike.

MARCEL: I was listening to the radio and *The Goon Show* came on. It reminded me of a show I'd seen and heard in France called *Le Canard*

Enchâiné (The Duck in Chains) and it was based on what I think was goonery.

Listening to *The Goon Show* made me think the radio show was more than just a radio show, and there were possibilities for either sketches, or, if Mr Spike Milligan (who I didn't know at the time) could write songs. My researcher tracked down Spike and discovered he was represented by ALS (Associated London Scripts). So I went along to Orme Court for a meeting with Spike. It was the strangest meeting I'd ever attended. He was sitting at his desk writing with a pencil. I remember wondering if he was writing a book or a script. Why wasn't he using a typewriter? He continued to write, but said, 'Won't be long.' The phone rang and he ignored it. I didn't think I should answer it, and it kept on ringing. It stopped. A minute later it started ringing again. He put down the pencil, moved away from his desk, pulled the phone out of its socket and threw it out of the window. I was stunned. I just sat there. I didn't say anything, but a thought went through my mind, 'God, it could have hit someone on the head.' As if nothing happened, Spike said, 'You're from Decca. Is that right?'

NORMA: They had their discussion and Marcel found out that Spike did indeed write songs. He told Spike that his idea was to make a record with Spike, Peter and Harry but that Spike would have to write the songs. 'Sure I'll write them but you have to speak to Norma, but in principle I like the idea.' He came straight downstairs and told me about the phone through the window incident.

MARCEL: The reaction I got was an explosion of laughter from you who dismissed the whole episode with, 'Oh, he's done that before.' Anyway, that was my first meeting with Spike.

NORMA: At the time, Marcel was also responsible for the international business at Decca, but he wanted to be a producer only and not be involved in the international side of things. He went to his boss with the idea to do the Goon songs on record. He bought the idea.

MARCEL: I went back to Orme Court to see you, and asked, 'What is the possibility of getting Harry and Peter?' You agreed to talk to Peter but told me Harry had a contract for records with Philips and I should talk to Johnny Franz, who represented Harry. And Johnny said yes.

Two days after that I got a phone call from Spike. He said, 'I've written a song. Come to my house in Finchley and I'll play it for you.' Another strange meeting. June, Spike's first wife, told me to go upstairs and knock on the door. It reminded me of Orme Court. As I knocked, what I heard was like a creaky door in a castle, with chains and locks, and the door opened and there standing in front of me was the maestro himself, Spike Milligan dressed in a nightshirt, bedroom slippers and a nightcap, with a pencil in his hand. There was a small table and a couple of chairs. Someone else was in the room, a writer, I think. There were no pleasantries, but Spike asked, 'Tea?' and I said, 'Please.' Spike picked up the phone and dialled a number. To my amusement he had dialled his wife downstairs. He didn't call her or ring a bell, he phoned her downstairs and said, 'June. Tea at half past two.' The tea came, and then Spike produced the first song. It was called, 'I'm Walking Backwards for Christmas'. I was taken aback as it was July. Then he produced song number two, 'Bloodnok's Rock 'n' Roll Call'. Spike performed them and I immediately said, 'We'll record them.'

Recording went ahead in the Decca studios in Hampstead. This was in the late Fifties and I could have sold tickets for an audience in the studio. Everyone who had heard about it wanted to be there, but I said no, we didn't want to be disturbed. I was expecting trouble from the three of them, but it went like clockwork. There were the usual stops and starts, mainly because Spike, with all his witticisms and nasty little ways, made people laugh when it wasn't wanted and Peter was a terrible giggler. We would get to a lyric that amused Spike. He would emphasise it, then he would start giggling at himself. I had to say, 'Please, Spike. Can we go right through? And don't make Peter laugh.' Of course they would gang up together and Peter said, 'I enjoy laughing. Don't spoil it for me.'

Finally we managed to finish the recording and after the session we had to talk about billing. I asked Spike what they were going to call the orchestra, to which he replied L'Orchestre Fromage. I pointed out this was cheese and Spike said, 'I know that, and that's what I want.' And within a matter of seconds said, 'of the Balls Pond Road.' I looked at him and Spike ignored me and said, 'That's the way I want it.' And so it was.

NORMA: Marcel went back to the sanity of the Decca office, and the head A & R man asked how things had gone. He told him the title, 'I'm Walking Backwards for Christmas'. The A & R man said, 'Oh good. A Christmas record.' Alas, he had to point out that it had to come out in July because to Spike that was Christmas, 'because that's when Spike goes to see his mum in Australia.'

MARCEL: The head A & R man said to me, 'Do what you want. You're all loony.' It became a huge success and, of course, Decca wanted a quick follow-up. Spike had already given it to me – 'The Ying Tong Song'. My A & R boss said, 'What? Say it again. Spell it.' I couldn't, but resignedly he told me to go and record it.

On the day of the recording in the Decca studios everyone was on time – the woodwind and brass sections that Spike had wanted. Ten to ten Peter arrived, charming, full of fun, and carrying a basket. In it was a cheesecake. 'It's from the shop locally. It's the best cheesecake in London.' Minutes later Spike arrived carrying a large bag with a bottle of beer in it.

Peter went first, past the woodwind and brass sections. 'Open your mouths.' The whole studio laughed with him and the boys opened their mouths. He put a piece of cheesecake in everybody's mouth, immediately followed by Spike with a bottle of beer. 'Me too. Open wide,' and he gave everyone a drink. The next thing I knew, 'Everybody play!' I said. 'They can't. There's cheesecake and beer all over the studio floor!' I had to stop everything and have the floor cleaned, but the recording was hysterical. I thought if people don't laugh at that one I'm going to stop making records. I thought it was very funny and so well put together. It went into the charts and was their biggest hit – released three times over five years.

Spike had a lovely way of doing things. If we had a hit, he would invite Jeannie [his wife] and me for dinner. On one occasion he turned up at a restaurant in Elizabeth Street and parked right outside. I couldn't believe my eyes. Spike got out of an old Rolls-Royce with chintz curtains.

NORMA: I'm not disputing Marcel, but memory does play tricks. I've never known Spike drive a Rolls. Neither have all the other people who knew him from those days. The picture is not right. Spike in a Rolls!

MARCEL: I remember my first impression of working in the studio with Spike. After about half an hour, I thought, this man is not only clever but a little over the top. I learned very quickly to give him what he wanted. I appreciated what he did and I felt, leave him alone – he knows what he wants – and I hoped it would come out okay. It usually did.

I also learned that everything with Spike was instant.

Once my phone rang at three in the morning. 'Wake up. It's Spike.' I said, 'It's three o'clock in the morning.' 'I know but I've written a song. Haven't you read the papers? The Sputnik went down and I've written a song about it. I want to record it tomorrow morning.' I told him, 'It's three o'clock in the morning. Where am I going to get a studio, an orchestra, an arranger and musicians? It's not possible. We'll do it next week.' He said, 'It'll be old news by then. Ah, well . . .' and he put the phone down. I never heard any more about it.

On one recording of 'The Ying Tong Song' Spike wanted a soprano – not any soprano, of course. 'Get me the wife of Rawitz and Landau [a double act who played piano]. Don't know which one, but one of the wives is a soprano.' After the search, which took quite some time, I brought her to the studio and she sang three notes over four bars of 'You Will Remember Vienna'. It was followed by a splash of someone falling in the water and then footsteps fading in the distance. I had them running up and down the studio, so it's genuine. It's a real sound on the record, not an effect.

One night Spike invited us to the Ritz for dinner. He arrived dressed in a black velvet jacket, beautifully togged, like a gentleman dressed from Harrods. There were other people – someone from the medical profession and a famous reporter – and there were no jokes. He was a serious and wonderful host.

NORMA: Marcel reflected on an occasion when I had rung him to ask a favour. Spike and Peter were making a film, *The Great McGonagall*. Peter was Queen Victoria, playing the piano, and he insisted on miming to Erroll Garner playing 'I'll Remember April'. We couldn't get clearance, so I rang Marcel knowing that if anyone could help me, he could. He knew, having worked with Spike and Peter, that once they had made their minds up, nothing would change them. Marcel knew Martha Glazer, Erroll's manager. He phoned her in New York, told her we had no money and did a deal, giving Erroll an on-screen credit. Spike said, 'The dreaded Marcel Stellman has come up with the goods. Tell him dinner's on me.'

MARCEL: Erroll Garner was a lovely man and his warmth shows through. A few weeks later he came to London for a concert at the Barbican. He called me. He wanted to know about Peter playing Queen Victoria. I managed to get a copy of the rushes and Jeannie and I took him to this old movie house and he sat and watched Queen Victoria miming to his version of 'I'll Remember April'. He thought it was hysterical.

Spike had heard Erroll was in town and rang me. 'Okay, the dinner's on. Bring Erroll. Peter, Norma and I will meet you at the Trattoo.' We had a wonderful evening. Spike was on top form, and when he was on form there was nobody better. You know, Spike's first love was his trumpet. He loved jazz, and Erroll was one of the greatest jazz pianists of his generation. Spike admired Erroll's playing and was always amused by the fact that he was self-taught and couldn't read a word of music, and the fact he played the piano in one key and hummed in a different key.

NORMA: Spike described Erroll as 'A giant of a man at the keyboard, who was only five foot four and wore Cuban heels and sat on a Manhattan telephone directory while he drove his limo.'

Amid all Marcel's recollections he remembered two other extra-ordinary stories about Spike.

MARCEL: Did you ever meet June [his first wife]? She was a very funny, funny woman. She couldn't refuse door salesmen and anything they were selling she would buy. Spike would go home from the office to be confronted by brooms, buckets and carpet sweepers. According to Spike, their cupboards were bulging. One night, when we were all having dinner, June blurted out, 'A man came to the door today and sold me a series of dance lessons with the Arthur Murray School of Dancing.' I heard later that when Spike was working at the BBC he used to lock June in the house and take the key so she couldn't open the door.

NORMA: Eric Sykes also told me this story. He said June used to drive Spike mad and it was the only way to stop her.

MARCEL: And I remember too, very vividly, the time when Jeannie and I were in the VIP lounge at Heathrow Airport and quietly reading newspapers. In the corner of the lounge was Spike. He was going to Australia to visit his mother. We went over to join him and we talked for a while. Our flight was called and as we said our goodbyes, Jeannie looked around and said, 'I'm sure they've called Spike's flight, all the other people have gone.'

His flight had gone but I couldn't understand why the receptionist hadn't noticed and asked him to board his plane. He surprised me. He didn't go ballistic. He was as gentle as a dove. I said, 'Spike. Where's your luggage?' 'Oh, that's gone. I'll come back tomorrow. Norma will go mad.' And he stood up and quietly said, 'Goodbye, you two. Have a good holiday.' I was flabbergasted. It's strange, but I can still see him walking out of the lounge not in the least perturbed. He'd missed his flight to Australia.

NORMA: How would Marcel remember him?

MARCEL: He always called me 'the dreaded Marcel Stellman'. I'll remember the laughter. Wherever he is now, I hope he remembers me, because I will always remember him.

GEORGE MARTIN

I know this reflects badly on Spike, but it is a fact that he had little respect for most people. Of course there were exceptions and George Martin was at the top of the list. George could do no wrong and as I was on my way to see him, I was thinking of the wonderful friendship they shared. In the latter years their careers had gone in different directions and they didn't see much of each other, but this did not dim the affection they had for each other.

Spike was convinced that without George, the Beatles would certainly have been a success – they had raw talent – but not the phenomenon they became. Peter Sellers once said of Spike: 'I was like a vase of flowers and Spike arranged me. And so it was with George and the Beatles.'

Spike's theory was: 'Listen, anyone who was a pilot in the Fleet Air Arm of the Royal Navy in 1943 AND appreciates Ravel and Rachmaninov can't be bad.'

One of the happiest times in Spike's life was when George produced the album *Bridge on the River Wye*. It included the voices of Peter Sellers, Spike, Jonathan Miller and Peter Cook. It was a spoof on the film *Bridge on the River Kwai*, loosely based on a *Goon Show* called 'An African Incident'. The film company threatened they would stop the album if the name was used, so George edited out the 'K' every time the word was spoken and renamed it *Bridge on the River Wye*. Spike's reaction was 'He stood up to the bastards and won.' I believe this was the start of his respect and admiration for George. He had kicked against the big boys.

———————————

NORMA: When did you first meet Spike?

GEORGE: Well, I started in the record industry in 1950 and we met through Peter Sellers when I was at Parlophone Records. I had to find something different because our little label couldn't compete with the big fellows. There was EMI, HMV and Columbia and they all had input from America. HMV had Elvis Presley, Columbia had Frank Sinatra and Doris Day, people of their eminence. Poor little Parlophone had nothing except Humphrey Lyttelton and eventually John Dankworth, people like that. It was a jazz label. I knew I would never find a Frank Sinatra but I had to find something different and I decided to make comedy records.

My first effort was with Peter Ustinov. He was quite an expert in baroque recording and so was I. We had that in common. He did a party piece and all the different voices were his. It was almost a Spike Milligan thing. It was called 'Mock Mozart' and it was a spoof on opera. On the B-side there was a love story of a man in Russia who made love to his tractor, very Spikeish. I wanted to make an album with Ustinov but he was so ephemeral – all over the world writing things. Then I heard about this fellow Peter Sellers, who did funny voices as a stooge to Ted Ray, the comedian. We met and I suggested we make a record. He jumped at the chance. The first was 'Boiled Beef and Carrots' and ''Enery the H'eighth, I h'am', and it was through him I met Spike because, of course, they were the Goons. I met Harry too, but he was already under contract as a singer. Spike and Peter went hand in glove, side by side, so to speak.

When I met Spike I wondered how I could possibly capture his humour on a record because he was such an off-the-cuff character, a complete original. He was a lunatic really and I had to make his lunacy work. Whereas I had to suggest ideas to Peter, who would work on them, Spike didn't need them. They poured out of him. To Peter I would suggest he do a Ukrainian accent as the star of a new production of *My Fair Lady* touring India and he would work on that brilliantly. With Spike it was a question of 'What have you got?' One day he said, 'How about this?' and produced an auction catalogue. Now how can that be funny, I wondered. But he made it hilarious, intoning odd articles for sale such as 'A set of brass candlestick holders, engraved P. Hodgson Esq.' and that sort of thing. To make it more surrealistic I wrote a piece of music, kind of Debussyish with a wafting effect in the background. Spike loved that. I think it's my favourite track of his. Then, of course, he did songs with Paddy, whom he eventually married. He met her when she was in *The Sound of Music* and got her out of the habit. She had a lovely voice but he recruited her as a kind of straight man to his lunacy and had her sing something that he would interrupt with crazy stuff. But I had to be very careful. You never quite knew where you were with Spike. You had to capture the moment. It was impossible to rehearse anything with him because the next time it would be quite different. He was like a brilliant bubble that you could try and grasp but must never touch, because then it would burst.

We had enormous fun together but I don't think we ever sold too many records. In fact I earned a reputation in EMI [where George went after leaving Parlophone] of being a madman too. But I didn't mind that because Spike was such an extraordinary man, incredibly talented and, as I've often said, a complete one-off. Without him we would never have had the humour that followed with *Monty Python*. *Monty Python* came out of Spike Milligan. Without Spike it wouldn't have happened.

But making records with him wasn't all wine and roses. If I didn't like something and told him so he would go off in a huff. But it was necessary. I thought to myself: 'It's okay. It's Spike. He'll come back.' And when he did he was like a child, very contrite, to tell me I was absolutely right. Then we would start again. Once we agreed on where we were going he wasn't difficult in the studio. He knew what he wanted and I tried to provide it for him. In those days recording was primitive. You flew by the seat of your pants. We didn't have multi-track recordings but bits of tape we would chop up and try to make into something sensible. [He smiled as he reflected.]

I remember on one occasion when I was asked to do something for Yorkshire Television and decided to have Spike as the star turn. I had an orchestra and introduced people and Spike sang something but he wasn't content. He thought the show needed brightening up, so I asked him to do a visual interpretation of something I had done with Peter Sellers, which was singing 'All the Things You Are'. I suggested we would have a close up of him shaving, just his face and him singing. I told him the camera would pan back to show him in full evening dress sitting in a bath full of water. Of course the water was freezing cold. Poor Spike. I don't think he ever forgave me. He went along with it because he knew he could make it very funny and he did. He got out of the bath and asked me, 'Why didn't you heat the bloody water!' We had Pan's People in the show. He was dancing around with them, knocking over the scenery.

NORMA: Did you and Spike ever have any serious discussions?

GEORGE: Well, we talked about life. We talked about people and certainly about women. He had loads of serious ideas because he thought the world was a crazy place and it certainly was to him. He was normal and the world was mad. And, do you know, from what I've seen since I'm inclined to agree with him. The world is crazy. He didn't trust politicians and neither do I. Underlying his humour was this enormous charitable streak. He regretted he couldn't do more to change the world, and grieved. He could see so much that was wrong with the world, that so many people were in a bad way. He would try to help them and he certainly did. Spike was an extraordinarily generous person – a sucker for a handout, that's for sure. But he had great foresight. He realised what was happening to the Amazonian rainforest long before any other lay person and started the campaign to save it. Way back in '66 I didn't realise how right he was. Sting has taken over that particular campaign and the world now realises how important the forest is to the planet but Spike saw its importance long before anyone else. Actually, the future isn't very bright and he knew that. He wanted to help to save the world and was so frustrated when people thought he was exaggerating the threat.

NORMA: You've always said how much you admired Spike's devotion to children, haven't you?

GEORGE: Yes, that's right. I think he had an extraordinary ability to see into the mind of a child. He was sensitive to their likes and dislikes and, like them, could be hurt easily by remarks that most people would shrug off. I remember the weeks he spent repairing the Elfin Oak – a fascinating attraction for children in Kensington Gardens – after it had got into a terrible state. He wanted children of future generations to enjoy it and he worked on it for weeks. He repaired and painted the little figures of fairies, owls and wild creatures. He was alone, working on it one day when an old lady said to him, 'I've been watching you. You've taken months to do this work. Do they pay you good money?' He was destroyed by her remarks, that she could be so unkind when he was doing something worthwhile. I believe he went back to the office, just across the road. That's how a chance remark could depress him – perhaps for days. The world isn't fair and it wasn't on that day for Spike.

NORMA: Did you find him reliable?

GEORGE: If you were his friend he was reliable. He would never desert you and if you were in trouble he would be the first to help. Very devoted. I never had any problem with him. If I asked him to turn up for a session he'd be there on time.

NORMA: What if he didn't like you?

GEORGE: I can't answer that because he did like me. But if he didn't like someone he would have no time for them. He would dismiss them and say, 'Go away! I don't want to know about you.' On the other hand I don't think he was ever consciously unkind. If he didn't like somebody he would move out of the scene and leave it to somebody else.

NORMA: What about his girlfriends?

GEORGE: Spike loved women. I know somebody started to spread the rumour that he might be a closet homosexual. It's laughable. He adored women and adored them in the nicest possible way. Yes, he had quite a few girlfriends but strange though it may seem I wouldn't describe him as a philanderer. When he met someone he fancied he was in love with the affair. It wasn't merely a question of getting them into bed as quickly as possible. There was always a great deal of affection. And remember this: he was the target for a lot of women because he was enormously attractive to the opposite sex. They literally queued up for him. [He laughed.] And that made Peter Sellers extremely jealous. In those days we called Spike 'Golden Balls'. Now Peter never really made it to first base with any of his leading ladies whereas most of Spike's fell for his charms fairly quickly. There was a rumour about Sophia Loren and Peter. They had worked together and made a record and that was it, but there is this story, no doubt propagated by Peter, that they had an affair. I can assure you it never happened. Now Spike was an absolute charmer, you know – when he wanted to be.

But not always. When his first marriage to June was reaching breaking point, that was a terrible time in his life and he didn't make it easy for her. He didn't want the marriage to break up but he told me he couldn't go on living the way things were between them. He found it unbearable, but it must have been terrible for her because he could behave atrociously. Once when they weren't on speaking terms he locked himself in his bedroom. In those days we didn't have things like emails or mobiles but we did have telegrams. They were delivered by a boy in a pill box hat who rode a bicycle. Spike had picked up the telephone in his bedroom and sent a telegram to June. The boy knocked on the door and you know, in those days telegrams often meant something disastrous had happened – a death of a close relative or something like that – so June opened the door and must have thought the worst when she saw the telegraph boy. She tore the envelope and the telegram said: 'I would like a boiled egg, two slices of toast and a cup of tea. Thank you very much. I'm upstairs. Spike.' To put it politely, she didn't take too kindly to that.

NORMA: It was a devastating part of his life and later they were divorced. He won custody of the children – very unusual – and brought them up on his own. He had an affinity with children, and his brother, Desmond, said he had always had a childlike quality about him.

GEORGE: Yes, there was something endearing about him. I remember you asked me about Spike being unreliable. Well, on one very important occasion I let him down very badly, quite by accident incidentally. The occasion was Spike's second marriage to Paddy and he did me the honour of inviting me to be his best man. Now Paddy came from this very formal West Riding family so it was morning dress for us and full nuptial mass and so on. I had to get him there on time and do all the things a best man is supposed to do. For instance, I brought his cufflinks, made sure his shirt was okay and got the tickets for the train from King's Cross to Leeds in ample time to get to his in-laws' house, a good half-hour's drive from Leeds station, for the pre-nuptial dinner. At King's Cross I presented the tickets to the man at the platform gate and he asked me for our Pullman tickets. Well, I didn't know this particular train was a Pullman and that reserved seats were necessary to get on it. I didn't have any Pullman tickets! The railway man was adamant. Without Pullman tickets he wouldn't let us on. We'd have to wait for the next train, an hour and a half later. Fortunately, Spike hadn't heard any of this. He was like a lot of men immediately before their wedding, on edge and hoping that nothing would happen that would upset his ultra-formal future in-laws. Yet unless something drastic happened it looked as though I would be responsible for the non-appearance of the bridegroom. Can you imagine?

As nonchantly as I could, I turned to Spike. 'Change of plan!'

'Really,' said Spike.

'Yes. We don't want to go on that silly train. We'll go in my car.'

Spike was over six feet and I was two or three inches taller but we both squeezed into the front seats of my Mini.

In those days there weren't any motorways and we rattled along at 70 mph in this little tin can, our knees up to our chins, the noise deafening. He didn't say anything throughout the whole journey, just gripped the dashboard for dear life for about four hours. We arrived there only about three-quarters of an hour late. Spike got out of the car, stretched himself to his full height and said, 'Don't ever ask me to get in a car with you again – not for the rest of your life!' With that he strode off. He was furious and had every reason to be, poor bastard. He recovered in time for the dinner, though he was a bit nervous the following day, because on one side of the church the pews were crowded with Paddy's family and friends, hundreds of them, and on Spike's side only him and me. I was feeling terribly self-conscious. Spike leaned over and whispered, 'Are we in the right place?' I said, 'I think so. You're due to get married.' The atmosphere was very tense but everything was saved when we heard very heavy footsteps clonking down the tiled aisle. I peeped round. It was Harry Secombe and he had flown in by helicopter from Llandudno where he was in panto, or something like that, specially to be with Spike at his wedding. Wonderful! Harry knelt in the pew behind us and before saying his prayers he said to Spike, 'I've been making a record. It's a wonderful song called "Leatherthong".' Spike asked, 'Leatherthong?' and Harry nodded and sang, quite loudly, 'Leatherthong in my heart.' Everyone on the bride's side wondered what the hell was going on but it broke the tension and Spike was much happier after that.

NORMA: Do you remember an occasion when he wasn't very happy?

GEORGE: Spike was deeply embarrassed when he forgot to turn up to be godfather for the christening of my son Giles. He wanted very much to be there. The ceremony was at the church at Hyde Park. The other godparents turned up but Spike was missing. I wondered what had happened to him and about an hour after the service finished when we were back in the house for drinks, there was a knock on the door. I opened it and there was Spike, very contrite. He said, 'I'm very sorry. I hope I am still his godfather.' He put a present in my hand and I asked him to come in but he was so ashamed he couldn't face me or the other guests. The present was a napkin ring and somehow he had found the time to get it inscribed: 'To Giles Martin on his christening from his nearly godfather.' Giles is terribly proud of it and tells everyone that Spike was his godfather. But Spike was so ashamed at letting me down he couldn't face people at the drinks party. That was the nature of the man. I imagine he went back to the office and shut himself away for a while. He was very sensitive and because he had failed a friend, in his eyes something he would consider indefensible, he found it difficult to face me.

NORMA: What do you think will be his legacy?

GEORGE: I'd like him to be remembered for his originality. He had a different way of looking at things and his humour stemmed from that. Of course the black dog plagued his life, I'm sure caused by his wartime experiences. It would be called post-traumatic stress now. He did a great deal to help other people suffering from it. But for me his legacy is his originality, not only his performances but his writing. He could see something that wasn't what it was to everybody else. It was startlingly different. He had a fresh outlook on the world that other people didn't have. He could see things that we couldn't see and when he described his world to me I understood what he was talking about. He was able to think outside the box. He taught me to think about things other than what was in front of your bloody eyes. That was part of his genius. He would not accept the ordinary. He would always look beyond it. Interestingly, the Beatles also were able to do that. They were always looking for something that wasn't the obvious and so when I made records with Spike, with them or other people, I looked for something that was different.

NORMA: I always thought John [Lennon] was like Spike.

GEORGE: Well, John was like Spike but Spike was a much kinder person, a much nicer person. John could be very dismissive of people, quite hurtful. He had a lovely side to him but there were times when he wasn't very kind, whereas I don't think Spike was intentionally unkind to anyone.

I had heard that he told people he was proud of me and what I had achieved, and that we had been together at the very beginning. Well, we were and he encouraged me to leave Parlophone, which eventually became part of EMI. It was 1962 and I was under contract to them as Head of Records on £2,800 a year, no perks and no car. I told Spike and he said, 'What a lot of bastards. You don't need them. You're good enough to go on your own. You're very talented.' So I told them I only wanted to work on records if I had commission on sales. Their sales people got it at Christmas and I was making a fortune for the company and getting nothing other than my salary. Because I had a wife and was poor I stayed for another three years and then the Beatles came along. I was producing their records on a salary of £3,000 a year, no perks and no royalties. I had to give a year's notice in writing to terminate the contract and I did that at the end of 1963. Spike had told me how he and Eric Sykes had set up a co-operative of writers, Associated London Scripts, with Alan Simpson, Ray Galton, Johnny Speight and others, so I decided to do something similar with three colleagues. I formed Associated Independent Recordings – AIR – and stupidly divided the shares equally between the four of us, though I set out the rules. We could each get ten thousand a year no matter whether individually we had earned more or less. Kind of communist really. Well, great in theory, all the participants are imbued with zeal and high principles, but fraught. It was not only fraught but stupid as it turned out. At first it was very successful and we were able to plough back a great deal of money into expanding the company and building studios, but then two of the guys got delusions of grandeur and we split up, just like ALS. That was terrible but the real tragedy was to follow. When we parted our lawyer told me I had signed the rights to the Beatles recordings, with their royalties, into the company and I would never be able to get them back. I think he was wrong but I accepted his word so I lost all the Beatles recordings. Eventually, the company was sold to Chrysalis.

NORMA: Obviously you liked Spike. Was there anything you disliked about him?

GEORGE: I don't think so, though he could be dangerous. When you were with him you were never absolutely sure of your ground, no matter how well you knew him. There was always an element of danger that told you it could end in disaster. Either that or it could be absolutely bloody brilliant – and generally that's how it was. But that danger was always there because it was part of his make-up. Having said that, there was nothing to dislike about him because of his childlike air. I know he raged at people but I never saw too much of that, thank God. [Then he smiled.]

I remember him with great affection and one of the stories I'll always remember about him sums up his unique and wonderful sense of humour. He had been lunching with Harry Secombe at Bertorelli's, a restaurant that in those days was round the corner from his office in Orme Court. They got thoroughly pissed and as they walked back Spike noticed a funeral parlour. Spike grabbed Harry and pulled him through the door. He saw a piece of purple cloth on display, grabbed it, lay down and covered himself with it. Then Harry shouted 'Shop!' They giggled helplessly. But what I find so charming about this is that it wasn't a performance for an audience. It was done entirely for their own amusement. That was one of Spike's endearing traits, and how I like to remember him.

GROUCHO
(ALAN MATTHEWS)

Groucho has become part of my family. He was writing fan letters to Spike before I arrived at Orme Court in August 1966. I got to know and admire this determined Tynesider. I have lived his life with him. The ups and downs could only have been shouldered by someone with immense character and courage.

As a boy his sight had been damaged when a pellet from an air rifle struck the optic nerve and he was in hospital for several months. A nurse, seeing how he seemed to be so alone among older patients, gave him a guitar. He was a natural and in his early teens became a session musician. But then bravery turned to tragedy. When he was a teenager he saw a young boy struggling for his life in a heavily polluted River Tyne and dived in, pulled him above the surface and was swept downstream. Eventually, he fought his way to the river bank where helpers pulled them to safety, but the boy was dead and the toxic waste in the river had burned more of the sight from Groucho's eyes. The worsening of his sight had, of course, severe effects on his career as a musician. He just stopped going out, stopped playing and sat at home, unable to cope at first. Now he is totally blind. Spike was often fond of saying 'Eric Sykes has the courage of a lion.' Well, so has Groucho.

I was travelling on the train to Newcastle to meet him, reflecting on the way our lives have been interwoven because of Spike. I was anxious to see him again, to share his memories, and there was a warm anticipation because after the 'memories', my partner Jack and I would be having dinner with Groucho and his wife Dee, and I was so looking forward to the laughter.

My life has been enriched knowing Groucho and I'm thrilled to be able to call him my friend.

———————

GROUCHO: I was a reasonable musician, not yet sixteen, and one night in the Marquee Club in London – it would be around 1966 – I met Peter Sellers. He was a very famous person by then. He liked musicians and made quite a fuss of me. I didn't know it at the time but apparently at the drop of a hat he would tell someone who interested him that he was a genius. It turned my head, I suppose, but suddenly Peter didn't exist. I saw Spike! My hero! Today people can have no idea what he meant to millions of people who tuned in to *The Goon Show* every Sunday. Even now the delicious smell of Sunday lunch being prepared in the kitchen reminds me of the Goons. There had been nothing like it before. Yes, there had been great comedians: Max Miller, Tommy Handley, Robb Wilton, Arthur Askey, Jimmy James and others who kept people chuckling during the Depression and the war but Spike was revolutionary. Brilliant, original and, above all, hilarious. And there he was, in close conversation with a very attractive busty young lady. I suppose Peter could see the worship in my eyes and thought it would be very funny to introduce this formal young man and put Spike off his stroke. He took me over to Spike's table. I wanted to say something original but I did that awful thing when people are introduced to their heroes – I was lost for words. I put my hand out and said, 'It's a great pleasure to meet you, Mr Milligan.' Spike turned and said, 'Fuck off!'

I had nowhere to go. I stood there with my hand out but Spike turned away and was chatting up the girl again.

NORMA: Weren't you offended?

GROUCHO: Not at all. There he was, the great man himself. Out for an evening's relaxation and chatting up a busty young lady. And I'd spoilt it. Peter must have thought it was very funny to break in on Spike but when I looked round he had buggered off. And there I was faced with the long walk back to my table with, as I thought, everyone in the club looking at me. It's like when you are very young and ask the best-looking girl in the room for a dance and she tells you to get lost. Then comes the lonely, humiliating walk back across the floor to your friends. The people I was with were laughing their heads off. It was such a shock and yet I didn't dislike Spike for being like that. Despite what had happened I was happy that I'd met him. And I wasn't offended at his language. There are people who can swear with humour and there are those that can't. Take Billy Connolly. He is very good at it and it's funny. And when Spike told me to 'Fuck off!' there wasn't any malice in it. I've heard Spike dismiss people like that a number of times but never in a bad way.

Well, I can't tell you when I returned to Newcastle how many people I told that I'd actually seen my hero. And almost shaken his hand. You won't believe it, but I actually wrote to him and apologised for intervening. Of course there was another side to Spike as I was to find out.

NORMA: Tell me why you became known as Groucho.

GROUCHO: One day I saw a much older session musician, very experienced – he had worked with the National Variety Orchestra, the one based in Manchester – collect his fee. He opened his shirt and put a ten pound note in a small leather bag hanging round his neck. He could see I was curious.

'Get yourself a grouch bag like this, son,' he said. 'When you get paid put enough money in it for your train fare back home. In this business you never know what might happen. Gambling, girls, too much booze. Then you're broke, but in your grouch bag you've always got your fare back home.' So I took his advice. Why he called it a grouch bag I don't know. But I soon became known as Groucho because of it.

NORMA: After the initial fan letter, how long was it before Spike started to help you?

GROUCHO: Oh, very early early in our correspondence. My first marriage was breaking down, that brought me to my lowest ebb. Over the years I'd kept in touch with Spike – sent him a tape of my songs. They were dreadful but he wrote saying how wonderful they were and told me to keep plugging away. I think by then I knew I was going blind. The encouragement he gave me was out of this world. A fiver and sometimes just a note saying he was thinking about me. Remember, back then a fiver was almost a week's wage. Then one day he telephoned me. How was I? I told him my marriage was breaking up and I didn't know what to do about it. Then came a bit of vintage Spike.

'Tell her to fuck off,' he said and put the phone down. Just like that. Well, I took his advice, but not literally. He would have got away with it, being Spike.

On the telephone he was always friendly but brusque. It was never a case of 'Hello, Groucho' or 'Well, I must be going now, so goodbye.' He didn't need to introduce himself. I knew that voice so well. He went straight into the conversation, listened to what I had to say, responded and put the phone down. He was always like that. Our marriage ended and soon I met my wonderful Dee. How she could be bothered with me I'll never know. A blind musician! With no hope of any gigs.

Soon Dee and I had our first child with another on the way. By then, Norma, you had been his manager for some time and you would ring me so you could tell Spike how I was doing. I didn't dare say how bad things were. We were completely broke and the larder was literally empty. Occasionally we could afford to buy one egg which we shared. We visited friends at meal times in the hope that they would invite us to join them. That sounds terrible, maybe pathetic, but we were in dire straits. I was at my lowest ebb and Christmas was coming. As they say in all the best stories my guardian angel was about to ring.

I answered the phone. Again no preliminaries.

'Are you strapped for cash?' I probably mumbled something.

At the other end the phone was replaced.

Two days later a Christmas card arrived from Spike and inside was a ten pound note and a message: 'Make sure Dee gets a Christmas present.'

That speaks volumes about Spike. He would make a gesture like that but never made a big thing of it. I can't tell you what that ten pounds did for us. I suppose today it would be worth fifty or sixty pounds. And Dee got her Christmas present. Spike gave us a Christmas but more than that he gave us hope.

NORMA: But Spike rang again in the New Year, didn't he?

GROUCHO: It was another typical call, brief and very much to the point. He said, 'Groucho, get off your arse. Tomorrow will be different. Get a job. Beethoven was blind but he wrote great music.' Down went the phone.

You know, I felt privileged to get those phone calls and letters. Although I was in a bad way at the time, either in a letter or in conversation, he would let something slip that made me feel sorry for him, so much so that I wanted to put my arms round him. And then he could say something so awful that I felt like strangling him. That was Spike. I genuinely loved him – and I miss him. He gave me a life I would have never had.

NORMA: But you believe that despite his kindness and encouragement Spike never thought of you as anything other than a devoted fan.

GROUCHO: Yes, but he became more than a star to me because I saw the human side of the man. I know, I know, I know. One day he could make you feel important to him and the next dismiss you as if you didn't exist. I think that happened when something had upset him, possibly in his personal life. And there was another factor – he hated the notion that he was public property. But, he was always there for me.

NORMA: So you eventually returned to Tyneside?

GROUCHO: I thought something would come along, but it didn't. Quite early on I realised I hadn't the talent to make it as a musician. The only talent I had was as a producer. I'd done some production work for the BBC and Tyne Tees Television so when licences were issued for commercial radio I was able to earn a living. I did that for a few years but it coincided with the time when my sight was getting much worse and jobs dried up. Nobody would touch me with a barge pole. I actually gave up. I wouldn't say I was close to suicide but the thought wasn't so far from my mind. Due to my eye injury I had been in constant pain since childhood and after diving into the Tyne it got worse, much worse. I was sick of taking drugs to relieve the pain. It was ever-present. I had a young family but I had nothing to offer them. Then Spike phoned and reminded me about Beethoven. He turned my life round and Dee knew that in him she had an ally. She would read his letters to me. Then came Spike's ultimate threat. 'Get out and do something or Norma will be after you.'

NORMA: But you were never blind to his faults though, were you? (Excuse the pun).

GROUCHO: Call me naïve but one thing I disliked about Spike was what you called the 'Bayswater Harem'. I was really surprised when I became aware that, although he was married, he had other women. Here he was, married – for the second time – with two families, but he seemed to believe that the usual mores didn't apply to him. He was so open about them I could never understand how he got away with it without the press crucifying him. He said he loved them all and they were all aware of one another. Can you believe it? And yet it was true. They did. With him it was the old adage. He was a one-woman man – one woman at a time. But that was Spike. Whoever he was with would be the object of his total affection. Then he would walk away. And then there would be another. [He shook his head but smiled, rather like a younger brother forgiving a talented but erring sibling.]

Once when I phoned Spike, he barked, 'You're not my fucking pet, you know.' Bang went the phone. End of conversation. Perhaps that was what I needed because soon afterwards I applied for a job constructing beds with the Institute for the Blind. The atmosphere was almost Dickensian. Monotonous work for basic wages. But it was a job and it put bread on the table.

Spike continued to telephone. We talked frequently. He was always kind and had time for me. He had great sympathy for those who were suffering. He had some wonderful qualities. I've never known what Spike saw in me, but we clicked. Somehow we came together on the same level.

NORMA: After monotonous years making beds you became a consultant when Gateshead Council started a scheme to train handicapped people to take a role in the workplace, didn't you?

GROUCHO: I helped the council set up recording studios and then developed audio-taped national newspapers for the blind. It was really satisfying work and I enjoyed it. But eight years ago the scheme was dropped when it was decided it was costing far too much money. By then I had realised that there was huge scope to train handicapped people for the workplace. Either I did something or I would be out of a job again. I was happily married, I grant you, but with two children to feed. I knew companies needed to comply with government legislation to employ handicapped people but someone had to train them. And then Spike rang. I told him I believed there was scope for someone to train handicapped people and, in the process, give them a life. But I was terribly nervous about committing our small savings into a company that could fail. He said, 'Go for it, Groucho.' So I did.

By then Dee had saved some money. I'll never know how but I shouldn't be surprised because she is a miracle woman. By borrowing from relations we scraped together five thousand pounds. A colleague from the council scheme did the same and with that small amount of capital we started M.P.H. in a dilapidated building on a council trading estate. That was eight years ago. Now the company has a hundred full-time employees, some handicapped, and is the biggest of its type in Europe.

NORMA: So instead of getting the bus across the Tyne Bridge to your job with Gateshead Council, you're picked up from your country house at five a.m. by the chauffeur and walk into the managing director's office while most of the staff are still in bed.

GROUCHO: It was touch and go but Spike was always there with encouragement. I didn't want money from him but every now and again he would ask 'Are you you all right for bread, Groucho?'

NORMA: [The stature and dedication of the man, as well as the disadvantages he has had to overcome every day of his life, are known only to his intimates. Constant pain caused by his blindness is made tolerable only with the strongest of painkillers. But the company's studios now cover most of the Gateshead trading estate and are in constant use as handicapped people are trained to live a useful life in commerce and industry. Alongside them executives are shown how to make the most of the skills now offered by the disadvantaged.]

GROUCHO: The saddest thing for me is that Spike never found out what a success we made of it and as much as he would have hated what I had done he would have been proud in a way, proud of the achievement.

I remember I never cried about Spike when he died. What I do remember is a programme about when he went to see Harry Secombe who was recovering from a stroke. I hadn't seen Spike for a long time. Dee was watching this programme with me and his opening line was 'I see you have had a gas range installed.' It was the piano in the living room. Dee went really quiet and I think it was the first time I realised how ill Spike was after his heart bypass. It was the first time I cried about Spike because I realised that at some point he was going to go out of my life. What nobody will ever understand is that he gave me a life that I wasn't going to have. I had been willing to sit down and do nothing. I would have lost my wife. She couldn't have put up with what I was becoming. Spike never gave up on me. He could annoy me, he could tell me off, he could tell me I was a waste of whatever he wanted to tell me, but he never stopped telling me, and that's the difference.

[He took off his dark glasses and dabbed his sightless eyes. A smile crossed his face].

I know what he would say if he knew I was a fifty per cent shareholder of a multi-million pound company.

'You fucking capitalist!'

There was a kind of leprechaun about him. I remember when Prince Charles was going to his house for dinner. Spike was determined that Charles would do the washing up. I can't remember whether it happened but the idea really amused Spike. There was always that element of mischief about him.

I miss Spike being in my world.

BARRY HUMPHRIES

Dame Edna Everage is an intellectual. Well, perhaps not Edna or the disgusting but fascinating Sir Les Patterson, but their creator Barry Humphries most certainly is. And a charmer. But that, I hope, will become obvious. At one time he dressed with a certain theatrical flamboyance – a fedora and a cloak – but now he is more reserved, a deep-thinking man. He came to my office at 9 Orme Court in Bayswater for the first time in almost forty years.

He looked round and with the presence so typical of the actor that he is, said, 'Nothing has changed.' And then with the wave of a hand, 'And the atmosphere is the same. I sense Spike's presence and I wonder if I go up the stairs whether his Keep Out sign will be on the door. Will it be a case of being greeted by my genial friend, with a joke, always with a joke, or will it be "What the fuck are you doing here without an appointment." He chuckled. 'One never knew.'

BARRY: Spike and I go back a long way – to the late fifties. I was doing my first one-man show in Sydney in a very small theatre, now demolished, when one of the cast said Spike was in the audience. I'd never met him but of course I knew of his legendary radio show. I looked through the hole in the curtain and sure enough, there he was. It made me terribly nervous but throughout my performance Spike's laughter was the loudest in the house. In fact I thought he was laughing a little too loudly, so much so that people were laughing at Spike's laughter. Afterwards he came backstage and was very flattering. I was awe-struck.

We met again over lunch. Now, in Australia there was a bit of a myth that Spike was Australian and he never denied it, just as many people like to pretend to be Irish, and at one time I actually believed he was an expatriate Australian. His mother lived in Woy Woy, once a country town that was being absorbed by a growing Sydney, and he often travelled to Australia to see her.

We didn't meet again until after I was cast as the undertaker, Mr Sowerberry, for the original 1960 London production of Lionel Bart's *Oliver!*. [Later he played Fagin in two revivals of the show.]

I had been in New York in the cast of the Broadway show of *Oliver!* and came back to London to do something in Peter Cook's new club, The Establishment. I was very nervous about it and went to see a for-tune teller. She warned me that I wouldn't go down very well at the club but not to worry because I would get a telegram that would change my life. Those were the days of telegrams, after the telephone the quickest way of transmitting a message. Well, the fortune teller was right. The Establishment audiences relished impersonations of people like Harold Macmillan, and my Australian monologues weren't to their liking. Well, my contract ended a bit sooner than it should have done. I wondered what on earth I would do next. Then the fortune teller's prophecy was vindicated. A telegram arrived. 'Come to the Comedy Theatre in Panton Street and see me. I think you're good anyway. Spike.'

That was a reference to some of the rather bad reviews I had received for my Establishment show. So I went to the Comedy Theatre and Spike said, 'Look! I'm doing *The Bed-Sitting Room*. I've written it with John Antrobus and I want you to play the lead.' Now just about everyone got the same line. Spike, of course, was the lead and the rest of us were bit players, but actually my part was quite big. Now I knew the show had been at the Mermaid Theatre but I didn't know the history of this particular production or that my part had been played by Graham Stark, who left quickly after Spike threatened him with a gun. I had no idea of any of this history of supposed violence on the part of my employer but I went to the Comedy to see a performance from a front row seat. Now I saw Spike in action on the stage and anyone who thinks he was no more than a radio performer and writer can forget it. I was totally convulsed with laughter. Spike had an incredible stage presence. I had listened to The *Goon Shows* but was never a huge fan so I had tended to be rather grudging in my praise of them. But this was an incredible show. Half of it seemed improvised. I do believe Spike was putting on a particularly good performance because I was fully lit sitting in the front row.

I couldn't believe my luck and went straight into rehearsals. Sometimes Spike would appear but generally he let me get on with it. It was quite an experience. For example, one night he did the first act but didn't appear for the second. It was very puzzling for the audience, who had paid a fair bit of money for their seats, when they came back after intermission to find a different person playing Spike's part. They seemed to assume that it was a Milligan joke, except that he wasn't even there for the curtain call!

The cast had some genuine personalities. There was Valentine Dyall, a sort of tragi-comic figure, Bob Todd, Johnny Vyvyan the dwarf and John Bluthal, another Australian who slightly resented me because when I left the cast of *Oliver!*, having understudied Ron Moody who played Fagin, I applied to Donald Albery the producer, to see if I could replace Ron when he left the production. To my amazement Johnny Bluthal got the job and he was a very good Fagin. He was a brilliant actor – still is – with a healthy self-esteem and he reminded me at every opportunity that he had got the role of Fagin when I had wanted it. At the time it pissed me off that another Australian had got the part but I soon realised that one of the reasons Lionel Bart chose him was because he was Jewish and that would probably take the anti-Semitic edge off the role. But that apart, Johnny was always a good mate and when I joined the cast of *The Bed-Sitting Room* he took me aside and said, 'This isn't like an ordinary show. Sometimes, depending on his mood, Spike doesn't appear.' The lead didn't appear!

But I was to discover it turned out to be true. Sometimes Spike would open in the first act and then disappear, leaving an understudy to take over. Or he would fail to turn up for the opening and pop up in the middle of the second act. Very disconcerting but we got used to it. And somehow the audience forgave him. Now, I liked Spike but he could be cruel. For instance, to Bob Todd, a well-known film actor, along with Valentine Dyall, who was known to the public for his magnificent mellifluous voice and to actors for his addiction to alcohol.

Throughout showbusiness Bob had a nickname, a cruel one but justified, and Spike used it at curtain call when the actors took a bow. 'Step forward Borrowing Bob Todd,' or sometimes 'Bob hide the silver Todd.' Bob would look sort of sheepish having been so publicly outed. Then it was Valentine's turn to be humiliated because as he introduced him Spike would turn to the audience and make drinking gestures. Not very nice.

After my first performance Bob took me aside and said, 'Look, you're new to the show so you probably don't know that we don't get paid until next week. If you find yourself short I can always lend you a fiver.'

I was amazed and thought it disgraceful that everyone in showbusiness gave Bob such a bad name. However, by the end of the week I was so short I rather nervously asked him if he could oblige me. He couldn't have been more charming and said a fiver wouldn't be enough and he more or less forced me to take ten pounds. Of course I paid him back as soon as I got my money, which wasn't much more than ten pounds or so. Now a week or so later, one Saturday morning, Bob called at my house in Highgate to see if I could cash a cheque because he had called at his bank a minute or so after it had closed. He wouldn't have bothered me but he needed the money urgently. I immediately tried to cash his cheque. But I waited a long time to be paid back and discovered that more than one publican had wads of Bob's dishonoured cheques. Eventually his agent got the money for me. I'm afraid Bob was shameless. Then I saw a news content bill outside a newsagent's shop that said 'Actor disappears'. Sure enough it was Bob and there were reports that he had gone to Ireland, presumably to escape his creditors.

He was a man who was not only addicted to booze but to sailing very close to the wind. Later he turned up and was given work by Benny Hill. And then there was poor Valentine Dyall who, at the time of the *The Bed-Sitting Room*, was having desperate conversations with his wife on the box office phone, which Spike imitated. But then Spike was also very generous and there were often drinks in his dressing room after the show or he would entertain the cast to dinner.

Sometimes they went to The Light of India where Spike delighted in embarrassing suburban diners. He tipped the waiters in advance so that he could insult them, all because he delighted in watching the shocked reactions of other diners. Or he would invite strait-laced friends to dine with him to make them feel embarrassed. Now this was in the days when racial sensitivity wasn't as acute as it is now. When everyone had taken their seats Spike would clap his hands and shout, 'Woggy boy!' for the waiter, who would come obediently to the table. Of course there was complete silence with the other diners absolutely incredulous. It was outrageous but he liked to shock people.

NORMA: Particularly people he considered to be middle-class bigots. But there was nothing racist about Spike. I'll bet the waiters entered into the spirit of the thing and enjoyed it as much as he did. He had an infectious sense of humour and would somehow make them feel that they were equal participants in his attempt to discomfort other guests. That was Spike, but in all the time I was with him I never heard him say anything that was genuinely racist. In fact, Indians in particular thought he was marvellous because he used to share jokes with them in Urdu.

BARRY: I knew Spike's second wife, Paddy. She was an extremely warm-hearted woman and very tolerant of him. Once he came round to my place in Little Venice, when Paddy telephoned and asked whether I had heard from Spike. I said, 'Well . . .' But Spike was making frantic gestures that said I shouldn't tell her he was with me. Then she added, 'I just wondered because he's in Australia and he hasn't called me.' I didn't like to say that he was sitting in an armchair in front of me. But that was Spike. He was a frequent visitor to my place and got on very well with my wife, Rosalind. I don't know how well he got on because he was sometimes there when I came home! All I can say is that when Rosalind and I finally broke up he was very angry with me. He was shocked and showed great moral disapproval. Can you believe that? I was amazed to find that he was so puritanical about other people's marital difficulties. And this was the man whose wife thought he was in Australia when he was in my house in Little Venice!

I remember Spike introduced me to one of his Australian actor friends, Bill Kerr. A great actor. He doesn't seem to have altered in appearance since the early Sixties. Spike introduced me to him when they were both raiding derelict houses and business premises that were to be demolished. Can you believe that! Bill would get up a ladder – more adventurous than Spike – and strip the roof of lead which he would then sell. Spike rummaged around and occasionally found some rather good watercolours which he hung at the office. He had a very good eye for such things, particularly if they had an Australian connection. At that time I still laboured under the delusion that he had an Australian connection!

I remember sensing there were occasions when Spike was sheltering behind his depression and using it as an alibi. He was on a lot of prescribed medication which, inadvisedly in my opinion, he mixed with huge amounts of rosé wine. Mind you, at the time I drank a great deal of wine or whatever I could get my hands on. It seemed to me that if Spike took pills for depression he shouldn't drink so much wine. If he phoned me I could tell by the thickness or fuzziness of his voice whether or not he was medicated. Sometimes when I called at the office I could see that he had slept there and I knew that everything wasn't rosy with Paddy, but I assumed she took the rough with the smooth.

A couple of years later I was cast in another Lionel Bart musical, *Maggie May*. I had quite a big part which unfortunately was cut in the try-out in Manchester so that I ended up opening and closing the show with nothing in between. I was a sort of commentator, a balladeer with a drum on my back and cymbals between my knees.

After my appearance at the beginning of the show, I had to sit in my dressing room from about 7.45 until 10.15, so I took to going out. I would take the costume off and perhaps go to a movie, then

I started to go to parties, some distance away, in Kensington or Hampstead and once even as far away as Putney, where I had great difficulty in getting back and just made it. The management warned me never to be late and they were obviously very worried.

Then Spike telephoned to tell me he was opening in a show called *Son of Oblomov* that became a massive hit.

'Come along,' said Spike.

'I can't,' I said. 'I'm in the West End myself.'

I soon realised that Spike had done his homework.

'Now, Barry,' he said, 'I know your show. You can leave the theatre by ten to eight and be with us for our eight o'clock start. You're at the Adelphi and I'm at the Comedy. I'll have a ticket at the stage door for you. My show finishes at ten and you can get back to your theatre in plenty of time to go on.'

I thought that sounded reasonable so I changed out of my costume after my appearance, hailed a taxi and found Spike waiting for me at the stage door.

The first thing he said was that I should try a new vitamin pill his doctor had given him. He was forty-five or forty-six, which was then quite old to me and I must say he looked absolutely marvellous.

'It's given me a new lease of life,' he said, then gave me one of the pills. 'You need to take it with a drink,' and handed me a glass of rosé. I downed it with the rosé and then went to my seat. I was sitting there looking forward to the show. And then I saw Spike and others in the cast bowing. That's unusual, I thought, but typical of Spike, opening the show with a curtain call. Then I noticed that the audience were leaving the theatre and I knew the pill had knocked me out and that I'd slept throughout the play. I'd left my watch in my dressing room so I grabbed the wrist of a man next to me and saw I had only five minutes to be on stage at the Adelphi. I rushed out of the theatre, grabbed a taxi and there outside the Adelphi, standing in the middle of the street, was my dresser holding my drum and cymbals. I jumped into them, smudged some burnt cork on to my face and went down the staircase to the stage with the drum bashing against the wall and creating a terrible racket. As I got to the wings I saw the whole cast were waiting for me – in silence.

It was supposed to be a key moment in the play after the actor Kenneth Haigh fell from some scaffolding on to the stage with his leading lady, Rachel Roberts, sobbing, and the rest of the cast, dock-workers, stunned by what had happened. That's when I should have walked on, in costume of course, banging the drum and the cymbals and singing a lament. Instead I kept the whole cast waiting.

They were really pissed off and afterwards didn't speak to me. Instead of coming on in costume I arrived on stage in a suit with some black marks on my face, one cymbal round an ankle and a drum hanging off my shoulder. As I sang the lament the cast ignored me. The impresario, Bernard Delfont, said my job was on the line. I realised, of course, that Spike had given me a powerful sleeping tablet. Evil! I could have been sacked.

The next day Spike telephoned and asked how I had enjoyed the show. I had expected the call so had checked on certain things in *Son of Oblomov*.

'I loved it,' I said, and extolled Spike's performance, mentioning some of the highlights.

Spike was baffled. 'You saw the show then.'

'Yes. You were brilliant.'

'And did you get back in time for your own appearance?'

'It wasn't a problem.'

Abruptly, Spike put down the phone.

I realised then that there was another side to this guy. I could have been sacked. He must have thought that missing my appearance would have been a huge joke. But not for me. I never gave him the satisfaction of knowing that he had knocked me out for Oblomov.

After Spike's final marriage I saw him infrequently. He had moved to some remote place and in any case Spike disapproved of me.

NORMA: Whatever for?

BARRY: Because I was no longer married to Rosalind.

NORMA: He adored Rosie.

BARRY: She was adorable. But then after I married again I invited him to have dinner with us. He was very disapproving because of my marriage! It was odd for such an eccentric man who expected the world to adjust to his foibles to be so intolerant of someone else's. There was a kind of Catholic Puritanism about him. And there was another trait that wasn't all that attractive. He was very angry when Harry Secombe was knighted. Success of certain other people really riled him. I remember once in Australia how annoyed he was when he saw that quite mediocre radio actors and rather third-rate entertainers had very large houses with tennis courts and swimming pools. 'I'm still working and look at what they've got,' he said.

NORMA: Well, he had houses with tennis courts and swimming pools and he gave away thousands upon thousands of pounds.

BARRY: Yes, he could be envious and yet very generous, definitely a split personality. There was a very sweet, lyrical Irish poetic side to him and at the same time a demon at work. I don't think he was helped by the uppers and downers that were prescribed for him. It might have been all right if he had stuck to the recommended dose but he took them by the handful. If he had been taken off everything he might still be around now. I looked up to him and at the same time I was disappointed at some of the things he said and did. You know, he had a very keen perception of the world and what was happening to it and his saving grace was his compassion. Above all, I'm so glad I knew him.

RICHARD LESTER

'An American with a sense of humour,' is how Spike described Richard Lester when I asked him, 'What's he like?' Richard had directed Spike in *A Show Called Fred* and *Son of Fred*, two of the very early television shows that Spike had written. I believe Spike won his first television award for *A Show Called Fred*.

I think this is nostalgia, but Spike said *The Running, Jumping & Standing Still Film*, directed by Richard, was the happiest time he and Peter Sellers worked together.

'We found a field, Peter had a camera and Dick just shot what we were doing, nobody to bother us. Dick instinctively knew what we were trying to do, he never tried to clip our wings.' I wondered 'What about *The Goon Shows* and the "happiest time of my life".' I suppose it all took place in the Fifties when they all had dreams, and life had yet to sour some of Spike's dreams.

More than twenty years later, in 1973, when Richard cast Spike as Raquel Welch's husband in *The Three Musketeers*, they were filming in Spain and I had yet to join Spike on set. So I was making nightly calls to him after the day's filming – 'Is everything all right?', 'How did it go today?' – the usual 'keep him happy' conversation. And to my relief, 'Raquel is lovely. She's a tiny little thing and Dick is so good with everybody, he cares about the actors, a bloody rare thing.'

So, Richard still was not 'clipping his wings' and everything was 'Love, light and peace'.

Richard Lester is tall, slim and as animated now as he was when at the age of twenty-one he arrived in this country in 1953 from the US to work for independent television companies that were desperate for experienced directors. Only the BBC transmitted television and they guarded their staff as carefully as a Victorian chaperone protected the chastity of a debutante. Dick had been something of a child prodigy and started his studies at the University of Pennsylvania when he was fifteen. At eighteen he got a job in television and in less than a year rose from stagehand to director, so when he arrived in England three years later he was that rarity – an experienced television director and much in demand.

He remembers a telephone call in about 1954 from Peter Sellers who was keen to translate *The Goon Show* into television. The result was *The Idiot Weekly, Price 2d*, followed by *A Show Called Fred* and *Son of Fred*.

RICHARD: The one statement that summed up my two or three years with Spike and Peter came from Bernard Levin, a famous columnist, who wrote a long article about *A Show Called Fred* for the *Guardian* or the *Observer*. It was about a three-thousand word piece, very eloquent, and he said something which summed up the whole experience: 'I went down and watched the rehearsals and the director was a young man who looked like he had just gone into the lion's cage and realised he had forgotten his whip and his chair.' And I thought he had got it in one. That's how it was all those years ago.

NORMA: Do you remember when you first met Spike?

RICHARD: Yes, before work could start on any of these projects I had to meet the writer, Spike Milligan. Peter took me to Spike's office and there he was, lying on the floor with his head, not in a noose, but in a huge halter rope. He never looked at me, just said, 'Comedy will never work on television. If I feel like writing for radio I can have two Eskimos go down a hole and come up in Oxford Street. You can't do that.' I said I could try. I thought our relationship was going to be very brief. He was convinced that I was wasting his time, you know, 'Please go away because I'm very busy.' That was his attitude. But Peter was determined to carry on so Eric Sykes became script editor and all the young people in the office contributed – Muir and Norden, Johnny Speight (writer of the Alf Garnett series), Dick Barry, John Junkin, Terry Nation (the Dalek creator), Lew Schwartz and Dave Freeman. Everybody wrote little bits and Eric put them all together.

After the first transmission [of *The Idiot Weekly*] Spike rang me at nine o'clock the next morning to say he had the running order for the next show. There was no mention of whether the first show had been okay. 'Does your secretary take shorthand?' he wanted to know. Yes, she did. 'Right. I'm coming over.' He arrived with a piece of Bob Godfrey [a famous animator] film. We put it on. Now I may be romantically minded but I'm convinced Spike had never seen it before. He then ad libbed a four- or five-minute commentary, funny, building up, marvellous. And then he dictated the running order. My secretary took it down and we did the show. That would be in 1956. I believe we did seven shows and they were sufficiently successful for us to be given another series of seven more. That was *A Show Called Fred*. And then they gave us thirteen of *Son of Fred* but pulled it after four or five shows that were most extraordinarily difficult to do.

We had a small budget and four cameras, no tape or telerecording. Spike had done the earlier programmes and made them work. And I think he wanted to try something better, different. I was totally for it. 'Let's do it,' I said. We had nothing more than plain flats for sets with nothing on them except a number or a letter. Someone would ask, 'Now tell me how it all began,' and Spike would say, 'Well, it all began in a small place called D3.' Then they all walked over to the flat with D3 on it. Everything was pared down so that there were no pay-offs and no gags. He would refuse to do the joke that ended the sketch and there's something about that sort of Brechtian alienation that loses the audience and they go home. I think that Spike had achieved that by the middle of the third series. For instance someone would ask, 'Captain, what's our course?' and the reply was 'Prunes and custard.'

You know, I think that Spike worked on the principle that we were all idiots and that some people were wilfully being idiots because they couldn't be that stupid unless they wanted to cause trouble. Now that was far from the truth because we were working under the constraints of doing a live half-hour show with only three or four hours' rehearsal time. I remember we had a back projection which worked in the rehearsal but someone forgot to re-wind it so on transmission it went the wrong way round. Fortunately, as Spike was involved everybody thought that was how it was supposed to be and nobody mentioned it.

I remember a sketch with Graham Stark and Peter Sellers sitting on a park bench, one in seventeenth-century costume and the other a city gent with rolled umbrella and a bowler hat. They were both reading newspapers, one a seventeenth-century broadsheet and the other *The Times*. *The Times* man, without looking up, says 'It's awful. This is terrible. The cost is disgraceful. Do you know how much I have to pay for a flat?' The other character looks at him. He asks, 'A flat what?' They start to look at each other and they both begin to think that they are having a dream and that the other has spoilt the dream. The pay-off was that there was a St Bernard dog asleep next to the park bench and they were part of the dog's dream. It worked beautifully in rehearsal. The dog belonged to Derek Roy but when it came to transmission the dog must have decided he didn't like the mood. He probably thought, 'I don't like the mood here. I'm going home.' Now the dog is chained to this rather hefty park bench but he is a big, strong dog and when he moves off he takes the bench with him. Peter and Graham fall on the floor and the dog drags the bench with him and starts to whine and scratch at the door. So I've got a backdrop of a park, no bench and two actors on the floor. I shout to telecine, 'Take me off the air, please.' They said, 'It's only 8.24. We can't do that. Tell them to ad lib.' There was still some time to go before we were due to go off air. So I tell them to ad lib. Poor things. No matter how clever they were they stumbled through it. It was a disaster.

NORMA: Did you ever have any major disagreements with Spike?

RICHARD: No. I just tried to fight my corner. I didn't want to say 'This isn't funny' or 'This is funnier than that.' That's not what I do. I try to make what you want possible. If I can do it I will do it. If I can't do it I will offer you something as close to the spirit but I'm not going to censor you. And I believed that what we were doing was good. I worked on the principle that Spike knew more about comedy than I did and I was grateful to be able to learn. But at that time he was still involved in word play and to make a contribution I wanted to see if I could do it visually. There was always tension because Spike was single-minded and this affected others in the cast. I think it was the third show when somebody decided, after the last rehearsal, that what Peter did wasn't funny. He sent out for a bottle of brandy and drank half of it. Incredibly, he gave an absolutely word-perfect performance but instead of it running twenty-seven minutes it ran thirty-four. It was just that bit slow so we had to chop the end off. It was the only time it ever happened and I wasn't very happy about it.

Spike was always very focused and knew what he wanted. If he wasn't striving for something better then we were having serious trouble producing it. But that's why he was so good. He didn't want to compromise and live television is a knotted mass of compromise. It has to be. He should have been involved in film right away. He shouldn't have been involved in television. Film for television was very expensive and could absorb our whole budget.

NORMA: Do you think he was disciplined?

RICHARD: I think that's a word that's almost irrelevant. Considering the body of work he produced it's inconceivable that he wasn't discip-lined. It proves that he must have been but I wouldn't say his running order was the same as that of other people.

NORMA: Once, when Spike was asked whether his thought process was different from others, he said, 'No, I don't. I just think sideways.'

RICHARD: Well, after all, that's almost another classic definition of a surrealist. It is looking obliquely at something that is the norm. You know, the idea of Spike relaxing is one of the oxymorons of our time but, you know, when we went to the Trattoo, his favourite restaurant, with Alan Clare playing the piano, he could be in a desperate state of mind, didn't want to talk and didn't want to look at anybody, but by the second bottle of his favourite Italian wine things would warm up and the rest of the evening would be such a pleasure that you forgot the first hour or so. His mood at the beginning could have been because of genuine problems, but as everyone says Spike had one layer less of skin than anyone else. But the joys of the good times and his perception, his insights on humanity, made it all worthwhile. Absolutely! I've always said that three people in the world have influenced me and he was one of them. The others were John Lennon and Buster Keaton. I've had the great privilege of working with all three.

NORMA: We know that Spike could be very nasty, but why is it that everybody forgave him, no matter how badly he behaved?

RICHARD: The same with John Lennon. They were very similar. John suffered fools very badly. He got very angry with things that he thought were unjust. He could suddenly turn against people he thought were absolutely useless. Spike wasn't nasty. He was a delight and he produced moments of sheer joy for the rest of us. Those moments might have come out of tortured anguish but they're things that you will always remember. One I will never forget is when we were shooting *The Musketeers* in Spain. In the film the cast were arriving at a castle for a fancy dress ball in seventeenth-century costumes. We had a seventeenth-century castle, seventeenth-century-type horses and carriages and seventeenth-century music. It was a scene where Spike was to look through a telescope to see his wife arrive at the ball. I was doing the rounds to see that everyone was in position before we started to shoot and there was Spike sobbing as he held his telescope.

'What's wrong?' I asked him. There were tears running down his face.

'It's so beautiful and they're all dead.'

Nobody else would have thought of that. They would be thinking 'What's my cue?' Not Spike.

A week or so earlier I remember I had taken him out to dinner. We were sitting outside the restaurant having a bottle of wine and some shrimps.

Two or three drunken Scottish louts from Glasgow rolled up. 'It's fucking Spike Milligan,' we heard. They sat down and one of them started to roll this huge joint and this was Franco's time in Spain and we're right on the street with police about. But Spike was wonderful and calmed the situation. He was terrific.

NORMA: Was he reliable in his work?

RICHARD: Yes. I have no memories at all of him being anything but disciplined. He was always there on time and there to work. I don't have any memories other than that, certainly not with the films I did with him. I know he didn't like the way *The Bed-Sitting Room* turned out because he thought it was far too serious. But that's the way I saw it and he accepted that. I know it wouldn't have been the way he wanted it but he didn't want to write the screenplay so I had to do it the way I saw it. When we were filming *The Musketeers* every scene he did was a delight. He couldn't have been better. He was inventive, wonderfully inventive, ad libbing bits of business with Christopher Lee which I thought were a delight. I can't fault him in that way at all.

NORMA: Do you think he was a generous person?

RICHARD: To me any comic performer is generous. I don't see how a comic can be selfish. He has to go out and expose himself. That's an act of generosity. The thing about Spike was that he could bring out a kindness in people that was unexpected. One of his first scenes in The Musketeers was with Charlton Heston. When I introduced them I could see what was probably going through Spike's head, about Heston's politics, his later life idiocy. But this is what I mean about bringing out the best in people. Heston shook his hand and said, 'I've been so nervous and so thrilled at the chance of being able to do a scene with you, Spike. I've been so in awe of you.' It was very gracious and they got on very well. I have confessed to using Spike as a weapon. With Raquel Welch, who starred in the film, I told her I had cast her husband, someone very famous – and then Spike turns up! But she realised we weren't trying to do her down. I think she'd had some very bad times in the business. I couldn't give her any directions on the set. She had to have her own costumes brought over from Hollywood. They were all Lurex! When I saw them I asked, 'Didn't you do any research?' 'Yes,' she said. 'We got *The Three Musketeers* costumes that Lana Turner wore!' She was a bit like coming on to the set, throwing in a hand grenade and asking, 'Why doesn't everybody like me?' But she got on with Spike. On the set she didn't get a lot of the humour and in the end we would do things where she was playing straight, which is the only way to do that sort of comedy. God help us if she had thought she could be funny! There was no problem between Spike and Raquel but there was a problem between Raquel and Faye Dunaway. They couldn't stand each other. The odd thing about film is that you always think of Raquel as being this extraordinary physical creature and yet she is tiny with the tiniest hands and feet, an exquisite little doll-like creature with large breasts. Now Faye was always Bonnie and Clyde, a bruiser who disguised it very well. In a fight scene Faye changed all the rehearsed moves and threw Raquel on the floor and dislocated her elbow. We had to cut the moment she hit the floor and then had to shoot around it until she could do it again. And the funny thing is we had a special photographer called Terry O'Neill, who was assigned to photograph Raquel for the film. As she lay on the floor screaming in agony Terry rushed forward, pushing everyone out of the way, and started photographing her. I grabbed him and said, 'Terry! For Chrissake! What are you doing?' He said, 'Faye will kill me if I don't get these.' Darn me, within a year he had married Faye Dunaway.

NORMA: I was worried that Raquel might upset Spike and then there could be problems because he could be very nasty and then he would take her to the cleaners, but I found it was completely the opposite. I telephoned him and he said he'd had dinner with Raquel two nights running. 'She's very nice, you know, and she has a lovely daughter. I want you to send some books out for her children, *Silly Verse for Kids* and *Little Pot-Boiler.*' Good, I thought. No problems.

RICHARD: Everybody on the set loved Spike. He was wonderful and very, very funny. I suspect it wasn't too long and he wasn't having to hang about. It wasn't on his shoulders. It was scripted for him. He could come in and add that little bit of magic which lifted everybody's spirits and then he was off and back to England.

NORMA: What did you think about his demonstrating?

RICHARD: We lived though a time when everybody was demonstrating about something. You were either marching on an embassy or trying to get a war stopped or fighting about universities being fascist and one thing or another, and Spike was trying to save some trees. I became embroiled in the 1968 May riots at the Cannes Film Festival when Truffaut and Godard tried to burn down the curtains of the festival. They dragged them down so they couldn't show the films and we had to cancel everything. That was on a Thursday. Demonstrators were throwing stones and there was a police battle charge. Everything came to a halt. There were no trains, no planes or buses, not even taxis and no petrol. Yet on the Monday I was due to start shooting the first day of *The Bed-Sitting Room* at Cobham. We found a small boat and paid a fortune to get to Italy. There we hired a car and drove through Germany and Belgium, and finally got back on a Sunday afternoon. There was a sense that society was collapsing, genuinely collapsing. In the States the National Guard had killed four students on a university campus. It was at that time I went back there for the first time in sixteen or seventeen years to make a film, *Petulia*. There was an edginess and anger at the height of the Vietnam War in a society that was losing its way. The review of *Petulia* came out, as it does, three or four weeks after it had been written and on the cover is the body of Robert Kennedy. That review was in the same edition as the report of Bobby Kennedy being assassinated, and only a couple of months before they had killed Martin Luther King. This is the time that I knew Spike and what Spike was doing didn't seem odd at all.

NORMA: Have you a favourite story about Spike?

RICHARD: I have a lovely memory of Peter Sellers' house in Elstree. This may not be right but my memory is that everybody was sitting in this rather posh new living room. There was an open archway and the stairs came down into the room. All of us, except Harry and Spike, had our backs to the stairs and I think it was Harry who started, very quietly, doing a commentary about burglars who were coming down the stairs and taking things through the door. Then Spike picked up the commentary and they kept it up. It was beautiful, the invention of what was being carried down, drum kits and that Mini with the basketweave, all disappearing, with Peter not seeing what was going on behind. It was just very sweet.

I remember evenings with Spike at the Trattoo. Alan Clare (the pianist) would take a rest and have a drink so I played the piano and Spike his trumpet. It was lovely and a rare treat for me.

Spike taught me a great deal about what is possible in comedy and my life has been enriched by that and by knowing him. It is inconceivable that my life and career would have developed the way it has if Peter Sellers hadn't made that phone call about the Goons. Ultimately, Spike was the driving force and the first thing the Beatles knew about me was that I had done those films with Spike and then *Running, Jumping & Standing Still.* That was the calling card that enabled me to have the first meeting with the Beatles in 1963 and led to those films with them that helped me to develop a career way beyond where I thought it would go. My life would have taken a totally long and different path without Spike, so gratitude is the very least I can say.

NORMA: I remember George Martin talking about John Lennon and I thought, 'Wait a minute. He's talking about Spike.' Neither of them could ever say sorry.

RICHARD: John really hurt people. The worst thing in the world is to treat badly someone who can't talk back to you and I've watched people in our profession do it. I never saw Spike being unpleasant to a waiter, for instance, or anyone who couldn't speak back. He was never condescending or imperious towards those that couldn't fight back.

NORMA: John really liked Spike.

RICHARD: Yes, I know that.

NORMA: But Spike could be very hurtful.

RICHARD: I don't think so. It hurt me when he was intolerant with people on the set and thought they were all against him and trying to sabotage a brilliant idea. Peter Sellers was very hurtful and made me angry, because Sellers would get people fired if they wore the wrong sweater and I would think, 'This poor kid!' I am thinking specifically of a case I knew. He had got to pay his gas bill and he'd just lost sixteen weeks of decent wages because he wore the wrong sweater that morning.

NORMA: I don't think Spike was like that.

RICHARD: No, he wasn't. The sad thing is remembering Peter in the days of Tetherdown and the two little dogs and the kids with Anne. We had a lot of laughs together. He used to come to see me when we first moved to Chelsea. We had drunken evenings and good times, but Peter and I went separate ways, fairly early. We kept trying to find something we'd like to do together, but by the early Sixties when I was having some success, Peter got resentful and I never knew what it was but he turned very nasty towards me. Shortly before Peter died we met by accident, coming back from New York on Concorde. We were in the lounge and fortunately we had a good time together. Not long after that he died.

NORMA: [As I left Richard, I looked around his office at Twickenham Studios, the walls hung with posters of his work:]
    Juggernaut

How I Won the War
Petulia
Help!
The Knack
A Hard Day's Night
Robin and Marian
Superman II
A Funny Thing Happened on the Way to the Forum
Superman III
Cuba
Royal Flash
The Three Musketeers
The Bed-Sitting Room
Get Back
The Four Musketeers
The Ritz

I was mindful of your comments on Spike's 'body of work'. Two talented young people who met over fifty years ago with a dream and an ambition to be laughter makers: you succeeded, your 'body of work' speaks for itself.

RICHARD: What did you miss most about Spike?

NORMA: The laughter and the flowers he used to send me.

RICHARD: He never sent me flowers but we drank a lot of very good white wine together and, what is more important, he gave me years of laughter.

RICHARD INGRAMS

As a general rule, the role of an agent is to successfully negotiate contracts for their client, get the best deal they possibly can and make sure the client gets paid for the work he or she has carried out. The role of the manager is to advise on their career, be their doctor, nurse-maid, psychiatrist, mother confessor and 'Get me out of it' friend.

When I became Spike's agent and manager in 1967 he had already thrown away the rule book. I realised my first task would be to sort out his finances; I had discovered he had received neither statements nor royalties for quite some time on his first poetry books, *Silly Verse for Kids*, *A Dustbin of Milligan* and *The Little Pot Boiler*. The conversation went something like this:

'Spike, you haven't been paid any royalties for over two years.'

'I know, he's [the publisher] got no money. Do you know, I went round to see him and his kids were eating jam and bread.'

'What's that got to do with it? If you go on like this *your* kids will be eating jam and bread.'

He laughed as he walked out of my office and said, 'Right on, Norm.' Only a matter of weeks later, I found out he had been sending cartoons and titbits to *Private Eye* and again the conversation went like this:

'Spike, these cartoons are very good. You should be getting paid for these.'

'They haven't got any money. Richard is my friend and I have to help him. Do you know, he plays the organ beautifully.'

So jam and bread and playing the organ beautifully made it all right. The illogical world of Milligan.

He loved *Private Eye*, he enjoyed the fun of it all, especially when they were being sued for libel, which was often in those days; he treated it all as a huge joke. Until one day in 1976 when Sir James Goldsmith sued them for criminal libel. Spike couldn't understand how 'this giant of a man' could possibly take it all so seriously. He wrote to him asking him to drop the case and pleaded with him to 'treat them like sixth-formers having their usual pranks'. Unfortunately it didn't do any good and on that day, in Spike's eyes, the giant of a man became a pigmy.

Of course, Spike's loyalty to Richard strengthened and he contributed to *Private Eye* most of his life. He was immensely fond of Richard and their friendship lasted until Spike's death. Mind you, if Spike rang Richard and he didn't return the call immediately, or if he disagreed with something Richard had written, it would be 'What do you expect, and anyway he's a bloody awful organist.'

RICHARD: I first met Spike in 1961 when I formed a theatre company after leaving Oxford. We managed to get the Marlowe Theatre in Canterbury for a two-week run but we needed a play. Someone rang up Spike and asked him whether he had anything we could put on. He and John Antrobus had written a play called *The Bed-Sitting Room* but I believe Spike thought it wasn't much good. So when he got a call from a bunch of young graduates he said we could put on the play. I don't think we paid him any money for the privilege, and it was a big hit and got good reviews from critics such as Kenneth Tynan. Spike didn't come to the opening night but after the reviews he did come down to see it. If we'd had a proper business manager we would have had some cut because the play went on to become a huge West End hit with Spike as the star, but we were very young and inexperienced. Willie Rushton was the star of our production and was spotted by Ned Sherrrin, who put him in *That Was The Week That Was*. I appeared in the play as the Plastic Mac Man, a very small part. However, I met

Spike and found him to be very charming. He had no reason to be nice to us but he was. Now, John Antrobus was more interested in the play than Spike, presumably because it was his idea, but Spike had the necessary discipline to write it, alongside John of course. That might surprise people who didn't know him but Spike was very disciplined. People thought he was this kind of crazy, anarchic character but in fact he was very professional. Later, when I worked with him, I saw it for myself and also saw the strain.

I didn't really get to know Spike until I started *Private Eye* with other old boys of Shrewsbury School – Christopher Booker and Peter Usborne. That was later in 1961 and I think the first time he got in touch with us was when we were sued for libel. He wrote to me and said he wanted to be libelled, so I put in this piece saying 'Spike Milligan is a dirty Irish poove.' He issued a writ because we called him Irish. [He chuckled.] Very Spike.

After that episode, Spike became a very good contributor and when the magazine was sued for libel he always appeared when we needed to raise money to defend the action.

I remember the time Roger Graef, a well-known documentary film-maker, was waiting in my office for Spike and Peter Cook to turn up to be interviewed for a documentary about *Private Eye* for Canadian television.

Spike and Peter got incredibly drunk and were filmed in that state. Spike was so drunk he couldn't go on stage for that evening's performance of his one-man show – there was no understudy, so that was it – and the documentary was never shown. I'd have loved to have seen it. But Peter Cook was a terrible boozer. It killed him in the end.

NORMA: He used to come to Orme Court about ten thirty in the morning. He was a very nice man . . .

RICHARD: Yes, he was a nice man and I know Spike admired him.

NORMA: . . . and Spike would say, 'Not now! I can't start to drink at this time.'

RICHARD: Fortunately, he had the discipline and Peter didn't.

I recall seeing *Oblomov* in the mid-Sixties. Spike made such an impression on me when I first saw him in that play. I think *Oblomov* was the funniest thing I'd ever seen. Miles Kington and I were talking about it not long ago. He remembered that the clock struck and Spike said, 'One o'clock.' And then it struck once more. Spike said, 'One o'clock again.' Very funny! In the play Spike stayed in bed all day. There was a woman who was in love with him and she sent him a letter. He got it out, read it to the audience and asked them, 'Shall I reply to it?' There was a big shout of 'No!' 'Right!' said Spike. 'That's it! That's the end of the play!' The curtain came down and the whole cast lined up to take their bow.

NORMA: I saw it three times before I went to work for Spike.

RICHARD: I suppose it was different.

NORMA: Every night. I think it drove Joan Greenwood mad. She said she'd have to leave because Spike was turning her into a maniac.

RICHARD: Because she couldn't cope with him.

NORMA: And the ad-libbing. And he used to ask 'What's wrong with her?' But he adored her voice, very distinctive. She was a wonderful actress, known as the sexiest voice in the business. John Bluthal, the Shakespearean and television actor, remembers that Spike used to look through the curtain every night to gauge the audience and change the show accordingly. John enjoyed the challenge but some actors didn't.

RICHARD: I remember when Spike and Peter Cook were on the *Eamonn Andrews Show*. They were both sending him up and it was so funny. Eamonn had no idea what was happening. Can you imagine these two men, one on either side of him. Spike and Peter together! I think of those two as the great comic geniuses. It was so spontaneous with both of them. And they both respected the other's talent.

We worked with John Wells on Spike's Q series for BBC Television. It was Q5. John had an acting part but then he was and is a performer. I wasn't and my role was to read the announcements. What was evident to me was Spike's discipline and all the sketches were very well rehearsed. They were done with a live audience and when Spike had weighed them up he would sometimes change the script at the last minute. When that happened there would be a fair amount of panic among some of the actors. And occasionally the recording of the show would stop and Spike would shout abuse about the audience to a man offstage they couldn't see. I realised it was all part of the show. Humphrey Lyttelton said when Spike used to laugh at his own jokes it was so infectious. But then all the best people do. I thought Q5 was very, very funny, much funnier than *Monty Python*. Spike had this joke in Q5 which wouldn't be permitted now. It went something like this. 'Are you Jewish?' 'No, a tree fell on me.' If you mentioned 'Jewish' now you would be banned. And then there was a sketch with a dwarf, Johnny Vyvyan. Spike was a door-to-door salesman selling this kind of blow-up hunchback. The idea, he explained, was that if you couldn't get a seat on the Tube or a bus you would blow the thing up and someone would offer you their seat. You'd never get away with that now. And there was a wonderful sketch where John Bluthal – he was later in *The Vicar of Dibley* – did a marvellous imitation of Huw Wheldon in this very English voice interviewing a guru called Guronoteeth, played by Spike. Wheldon says, 'I seem to hear chanting.' Spike, as the guru, says, 'No. That's a lot of Pakis next door.' Then he picks up a tin of cat food and throws it through a hole in the wall. They'd never put that on now. But it was very funny. Some people might say it is unpleasant but I never thought of it like that. It certainly made me laugh.

I remember taking my children to see Spike in *Treasure Island*, appearing with Willie Rushton and Barry Humphries. We went two or three times because they loved that show and so did I. I remember visiting Spike in his dressing room. At the time he wanted to write a play about heart transplants. He was very taken with the idea and wanted me to collaborate with him. We wrote so much in his dressing room but then he lost interest. But when he was focused on something nothing else mattered. For instance, Ian MacNaughton was the BBC's producer-director for *Q5* and Spike got very annoyed with him because he thought he didn't see his jokes. He didn't. He wasn't a very funny man. And yet he went on to do all the *Monty Python* series. I met him some time later when he was doing a programme about *Monty Python* because they wanted someone who didn't think it had been funny. I never thought it was funny. Well, he did the programme but it was never shown.

[He paused and reflected.] Do you know what happened to Ian?

NORMA: He married a German girl, went to live there and worked for German television. He had a very bad car accident on the autobahn. Some lunatic who wanted to commit suicide was driving the wrong way and crashed head-on into Ian's car. He was in hospital for months but afterwards he was immobile. We talked about the old days on the phone. He loved that. He never recovered from the accident and died soon afterwards. Talk about being in the wrong place at the wrong time.

RICHARD: I started the *Oldie* magazine in 1992 and remember the times Spike turned up uninvited to *Oldie* lunches. He always sat at the top table. On one occasion he had his lunch and left before the speeches. On another, when he was in one of his morose moods, a man came up to him and said, 'I've got to shake the hand of the very funniest Englishman.' Spike stared at him and said, 'I'm not a fucking Englishman. Now fuck off!' You should have seen this man's face. He didn't know what to do, then laughed, Ha, ha, ha, as if Spike had made a funny joke, but Spike meant it.

NORMA: How many times have I sat through scenes like that, cringing and toes curling!

RICHARD: But I'll always remember his spontaneity. Once at an *Oldie* lunch he was sitting next to me and asked, 'Richard, why are we having this bread and butter pudding?' I said, 'Because it's Lent.' He said, 'Well, when do we have to give it back?' It was so quick. That was the way his mind worked. I saw him being nasty to other people but he was never nasty to me. Once Barry Cryer was at one of the lunches and, I suppose, trying to be funny, said to Spike, 'Do you realise there are a lot of paedophiles here today?' Spike asked, 'Why do you hate us so?' It was said immediately, without a second's thought. Peter Cook was like that.

NORMA: Spike didn't like Barry Cryer.

RICHARD: Barry makes out that he's every comic's best friend. That was an Oldie of the Year lunch and was the one that took place after Spike had insulted Prince Charles, calling him 'a grovelling little bastard'. It was because of that remark, completely spontaneous again, that he was made Oldie of the Year.

I'll always treasure a meeting I had with him when I was doing an interview with him for the *Independent*. He was living temporarily in an oast house at Ticehurst. Now this is a typical Spike story. He told me about something that happened to him when he was doing a Gay Byrne show in Dublin and was staying at the Shelbourne, a very posh hotel. He wanted room service before he went on, and when the dinner arrived it was for two people.

'Well, there's only me,' said Spike and invited the waiter to join him. Ah, now that was a bit unusual, but he did join him and tucked into the wine as well as the food. When they had finished, the waiter asked whether Spike would mind if he said something to him. No, Spike wouldn't mind at all. Said the waiter, 'I would have thought that somebody with all your money could afford a better fucking dinner guest than me.' Spike loved to tell that story.

I remember visiting him with John Wells at his house near Rye. Spike loved Wells, a very funny man. Afterwards I wondered what he was doing in a modern house like that. It was so incongruous. He didn't fit in with it and it was so out of the way.

NORMA: His dear friend, Eric Sykes, said about that move from London: 'Spike is a North London man. What's he going to do about Ronnie's?' He lived at Ronnie Scott's.

RICHARD: So why did he go there?

NORMA: Spike told me his wife wanted to live near her mother. But Spike had a beautiful old house in North London, a real folly with towers. He loved that house.

RICHARD: He seemed so out of place in that one near Rye.

When Eric was one of the speakers at an *Oldie* lunch in 2003, I remember he had just written his autobiography because he didn't want someone else to record his life in an uninformed manner as had been the case with Spike. The book about Spike had been particularly scathing, a character assassination. I never read it. Funny, really. That's what happened with Peter Cook. There was a very nasty play about him on television. I can't remember what it was called. Everybody said it was a wonderful play, but it's the same thing. It showed Peter to be a very nasty person and he wasn't. Not at all.

NORMA: Did you ever see Spike when he was depressed?

RICHARD: I do remember there was one day on the Q5 show when he was seriously depressed and he just sat in his dressing room all day. That was the first time I had seen him like that. I don't remember Spike being unpleasant. I had experienced the same thing with Peter Cook. When he was drunk he could be very cruel to Dudley Moore, but that is because I think he resented the fact that he relied on Dudley. He didn't like the idea of that, so he took it out on him. I don't remember Spike being unpleasant at all.

NORMA: Did you trust him?

RICHARD: Yes. In many ways he was very old-fashioned, particularly with women. My wife and I had dinner with him in the Trattoo and he was very, very attentive to her, very courteous. She was Irish so they had that sort of bond but I'm afraid she was a bit of a boozer.

NORMA: Do you think Spike was reliable?

RICHARD: Yes. I know there's this thing about him sometimes not going on stage, but as a friend, yes, he was very reliable, such as when he used to send cartoons to *Private Eye*. I think it was Peter Cook who named him 'The Millionaire Prankster'. It has the ring of Cook about it. I'm sure it was him. An advertisement appeared saying that Spike Milligan would like to meet a wealthy widow. Intention: Murder. And would you believe there were a lot of replies.

NORMA: Did you know about his girlfriends?

RICHARD: Yes, I did, but I didn't know the details. Actually, I knew about Liz Cowley. I remember her coming round a couple of times – maybe it was when we made that film with Roger Graef – and I knew there was something between them.

NORMA: Yes. Forty years between them. She was there when I arrived at Orme Court and he was still taking her out about eighteen months before he died. A real love affair. He should have married her.

What about his involvement and campaigning for the environment?

RICHARD: Spike had this terrific indignation, which was quite genuine, about all kinds of things that were going on in the world, the sort of things that most people shrug off and think there's nothing they can do about it, but Spike got really worked up about them. I didn't go along with it. I heard that towards the end of his life he was still going on demonstrations – with Carla Lane to protest about veal calves – and I know for the sake of his health you tried to persuade him not to go and to leave it to others because he had done his bit. It was typical Spike. He said that the bastards wouldn't go, so somebody had to do it.

My abiding memory of Spike is his generosity. If we had appeals for funds when I was running *Private Eye* Spike would always put on a show for our benefit. He was a strange man in many ways. His humour could be cutting and he was very much a man of the times, yet, as I have already said, he had an amazing old-fashioned courtesy with women, very attentive and most polite, standing when they left or joined table at dinner. And he shared one characteristic with Peter Cook. He knew who the goodies were, a marvellous judge of people. He was fond of Joan Littlewood and Muggeridge and so was I. And I always trusted him. A good friend.

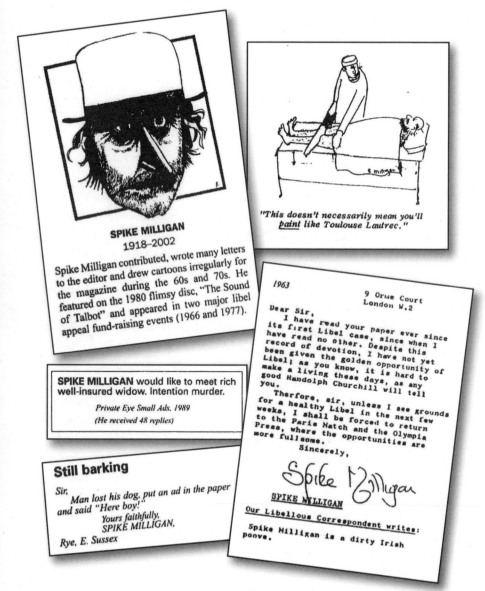

SPIKE MILLIGAN
1918–2002

Spike Milligan contributed, wrote many letters to the editor and drew cartoons irregularly for the magazine during the 60s and 70s. He featured on the 1980 flimsy disc, "The Sound of Talbot" and appeared in two major libel appeal fund-raising events (1966 and 1977).

"This doesn't necessarily mean you'll *paint* like Toulouse Lautrec."

SPIKE MILLIGAN would like to meet rich well-insured widow. Intention murder.

Private Eye Small Ads, 1989
(He received 48 replies)

Still barking

Sir,
　Man lost his dog, put an ad in the paper and said "Here boy!"
　　　Yours faithfully,
　　　SPIKE MILLIGAN,
Rye, E. Sussex

1963
　　　　　9 Orme Court
　　　　　London W.2

Dear Sir,
　I have read your paper ever since its first Libel case, since when I have read no other. Despite this record of devotion, I have not yet been given the golden opportunity of Libel; as you know, it is hard to make a living these days, as any good Randolph Churchill will tell you.

　Therfore, sir, unless I see grounds for a healthy Libel in the next few weeks, I shall be forced to return to the Paris Match and the Olympia Press, where the opportunities are more fullsome.
　　　　　Sincerely,

　　　SPIKE MILLIGAN

Our Libellous Correspondent writes:
Spike Milligan is a dirty Irish poove.

JIMMY VERNER

'You'd better tell Jimmy I'm ill and I can't go on tonight.' I can't recall how many times this happened over a period of seven years. Jimmy Verner was the impresario staging the tours of Spike's one-man show. The first tour was in 1973. It opened at the Adelphi Theatre in the Strand. He survived, I think, because over that period the tours were intermittent, twelve weeks in a year, and then perhaps six weeks in the next year and so on. Jimmy would go away, lick his wounds for a week, recharge his batteries and, masochist that he is, stage a tour of Marcel Marceau in his one-man show. He hardly gave himself an easy ride, two equally difficult men, but different. One wonders how he got involved with two eccentrics, coming from a classical background as he did, although he had started his career in television working on a programme inspired by Sid Caesar, one of America's greatest comedians.

In 1958 he moved to the Old Vic as stage manager, quite a leap from Sid to Julius. He stayed there until 1962 when the general manager of the Mermaid Theatre (founded by Bernard Miles who worked unceasingly to get it established) approached him. They needed a good stage manager/stage director and Jimmy fitted the bill. His first production was *The Bed-Sitting Room* starring Spike Milligan. 'In the world of contrasts there's Mark Antony saying, "O, pardon me, thou bleeding piece of earth . . ." and Spike running round his dressing room blowing raspberries in my ears.'

JIMMY: My first introduction to Spike was in his dressing room at the Mermaid Theatre. I was setting up a tape recorder which he had requested, when he walked in blowing raspberries, extended loud raspberries! He casually informed me they were nuclear explosions and then a short, louder raspberry saying, 'That was an atomic bomb going off.' What a baptism! He wanted a new tape of sounds for the show and whenever the atomic bomb was mentioned the raspberries came over the speaker system and he ran around with a fly swatter. So, he locked his dressing room door, turned on the tape recorder and practised blowing raspberries for the entire afternoon.

After four years at the Old Vic with Ibsen, Chekhov and Shakespeare, I found Milligan very strange but how was I to know it was about to get curiouser and curiouser. This was my first day so foolishly I thought I had better tell Bernard Miles about Spike's behaviour only to be told that Bernard was locked in his dressing room and couldn't be disturbed. His trick dagger wasn't working and he was practising the plunge. Apparently the actor or actress who plunged in the dagger couldn't or didn't handle it properly and the 'blood didn't come out'. At that moment Bernard walked out of his dressing room and said to me, 'If I hear you have left home for three days because you've heard there's the most amazing trick dagger maker somewhere up in the Northern Hebrides, I shan't be worried, because I'll know when you get back you'll have one that works,' and walked away.

When I put Spike locked in his dressing room blowing raspberries and Bernard locked in his dressing room with his trick dagger together in my head, I thought, 'I don't think I can stay here very long, I think I've got to go to save my sanity.'

NORMA: His sanity was saved when he was invited to be the manager for the Royal Shakespeare Company at the Aldwych Theatre. The classical again and the madness of Peter Hall. You know, there's always a comic somewhere with a slightly crazy attitude. I asked Jimmy what was his impression of Spike when they started to work together – apart from raspberry blowing and the fly swat.

Right: Florence and Leo performing *Fun Round a Sentry Box.*

Below: Florence and Leo – 'Equestrian Tricks'.

Below: The Lamanian Army. Spike was in charge. Nothing changed.

Above: Florence and Desmond. She was a good pianist.

Below: Desmond, Florence and Spike. She's in charge – that's where he got it from.

Spike, Norma (Grandma's adopted daughter) and Grandma. Spike's 58th birthday in Woy Woy.

Desmond's portrait of Spike. He captured him brilliantly, even down to the crooked finger and the pens.

Eric and Spike. 'My boys arriving' – working in shirts and ties.

Eric and Spike. 'My boys have arrived' – despite the lack of shirts and ties.

Alan Simpson, Spike and Ray Galton. Not only shirts and ties – waistcoats and all.

Sexy Liz Cowley and Spike. 'He should have married her.'

Above: Denis with Sammy Davis Jnr. One of the world's greatest entertainers.

Below: Peter Sellers and Marcel Stellman after the recording session – and still friends.

Marcel with the gang. Listening to the playback obviously went well.

Spike and George Martin. Spike said, 'George Martin canonizing me'.

George conducting the Hollywood Bowl Symphony Orchestra. No wonder Spike used to go around telling everybody how proud he was of 'Gentle George'.

George, Spike's best man. How can they look so composed after the nightmare journey?

Spike presenting George with an award. Just two old mates.

The Elfin Oak tree in Kensington Gardens, lovingly restored by Spike in 1962.

Above: 'Groucho' not too concerned about the initial meeting with Spike.

Right: 'Groucho' after so many years. He really was Spike's number one fan.

Below: A formidable trio. Spike, Barry Humphries and Willy Rushton in *Treasure Island* at the Mermaid Theatre.

Left: Spike, Richard Lester and Harry on the set of *The Bed-Sitting Room.*

Above: With Richard Ingrams. Why are they both looking so respectable?

Left: With Richard. He loved to go to the *Oldie* lunches.

Left: Jimmy Verner having been told the Milligan tour was a sell-out.

Below: With Terry on *Wogan* in my favourite red braces. 'Da daaa!'

Bottom: Keeping the devil away. Terry thought he was already there.

Left: With my gorgeous hunk Peter Medak on location in Kyrenia filming *Ghost in the Noonday Sun*.

Below: 'Spikey baby'. Trying to teach Peter Medak how to direct. The other Peter is rehearsing to look like Quasimodo.

Left: Keith Smith and Alan J.W. Bell (right). Spike trying to convince him he's not really Adolf Hitler.

Above: With Joanna. Truly one of his favourite human beings.

Left: Doug Dickless Boyd and his missus, albeit worse for wear.

Above: Throttling Des O'Connor.
I just love this photo of both of them.

Below: With the Python boys on location
in Monastir.

Lecturing Stephen Fry in the BBC's *Gormenghast*.

Eddie Izzard's turn to lecture Spike.

JIMMY: I think what I liked about Spike as a performer was he knew what he wanted and went out to get it and he made certain he did get it. He may have driven you, Norma, a bit barmy, as well as various other people, but he got what he wanted and he needed to express to the audience what he wanted to get over. I thought Spike sometimes lacked discipline but his anarchy made him who he was, an incredible comedic performer. He wasn't a comic or comedian, he was more than that. He was an extraordinary anarchic actor, with tremendous humour and depth. But retrospectively you see people in a different light and looking at Spike now I realise he was a very extraordinary human being as well as a performer.

In 1967 David Conyers, another impresario who worked at 9 Orme Court, asked me to be co-producer of a revival of *The Bed-Sitting Room*. Masochism took over once again and I agreed, forgetting some of the downside of the last production. I presented it at the Saville Theatre [which is now a cinema] having met with Brian Epstein of Beatles fame [who owned the Saville at that time] to discuss Spike appearing there. I took the opportunity to discuss with Brian about also using the same theatre for Marcel Marceau. Here we go again, I thought to myself. A fairly young producer dealing with these two extraordinary talents, Marcel with his worldwide fame and Spike who had huge fame in this country. I had to balance those two different types, and the answer was to try and stay out of the way and this is where you came in. You were of great assistance at the outset when you said to me, 'You should always come to me first,' and I said, 'You know, I think I'm going to do that,' and that's how it was.

NORMA: After the success at the Saville Spike wanted time away from the theatre to concentrate on his writing, and Jimmy became involved in bringing the production *Hair* from America to the West End. It became a huge success. Spike enjoyed his holiday away from the theatre and wrote *Adolf Hitler: My Part in His Downfall*, the first of his war memoirs, published in 1971. After a period of two years, Jimmy heard, via the theatre's Chinese whispers, that Spike was thinking of returning to the theatre to do a one-man show.

JIMMY: I remember I was beating you, Norma, over the head for several lunches to persuade Spike to say yes and out of the blue one day you rang and simply said, 'He's ready to do it.' I remember the first-night opening at the Adelphi Theatre. Peter Sellers wanted to see his old mate and wanted to hear Spike play his trumpet again. After the after-show drinks party Spike wanted a quiet dinner with Peter, so I invited them to Rules, the oldest restaurant in London, where I was a regular. It was next door to my office. It was an extraordinary dinner. Peter turned up with two fairly attractive blondes – twins – it was bizarre. The show had been great, Spike received a standing ovation and Peter, carried away by the euphoria of the evening, said he wanted to appear on stage.

That was all I needed and I persuaded them to sign a contract on the tablecloth. I wrote on the cloth, 'We agree to perform on stage for Jimmy Verner. Signed Spike Milligan and Peter Sellers.' They both signed the tablecloth, and after probably a glass or two or more they left the restaurant. The following morning I went to Rules to pick up the tablecloth to confront Spike and Peter. Alas, cruel fate; the table-cloth had already been sent to the laundry! I insisted on seeing the tablecloth when the laundry was delivered to the restaurant, but the writing was barely visible. To handle Peter and Spike together would have probably finished me off.

NORMA: Having taken Spike on tour over a period of seven years with *The Bed-Sitting Room* or his one-man show, Jimmy has a myriad of memories. I asked him if there is one which has stayed in his mind.

JIMMY: Yes, there's one I will never forget because it was the definitive description of Spike on tour. I had received a call from my company manager. They were performing *The Bed-Sitting Room* in Leeds. One of the jobs of a company manager is to report to the producer on the behaviour of the crew, actors and actresses. On this occasion all had not been running smoothly.

I arrived at the stage door to be met by little Johnny Vyvyan who was about 3′8″ tall and Spike had employed him for years. So Johnny knew me well, and Spike had always taken care of him. I asked him,

'Well, what's happening? How's everything this week?' and with all the acceptance of someone who knew Spike very well Johnny said, 'Well, you know, the usual days of wine and neurosis.' I thought it was such a classic line.

NORMA: Although Jimmy liked the money he was taking at the box office from Spike's performances, he wasn't enthused about taking Spike out to dinner every now and again.

JIMMY: I wasn't quite sure that Spike enjoyed my company, so I decided to send Spike a crate of his favourite wine, Gewürztraminer, bottled by Hugel, every Monday morning. That was the first job of the week for the company manager. So when I visited Spike I could have a glass of wine with him in his dressing room rather than take him out to dinner. And we could be lovely to each other, and then I could go home and everybody was happy and he made some more money. Thank goodness.

NORMA: The thank goodness was for a vivid memory he had of a production he was mounting, a musical, *The Black Mikado*, and the money Spike made was being funnelled straight into paying the *Mikado* cast their rehearsal salaries.

JIMMY: In the early days of my touring activities, I employed a chap to go to the bank to pick up the salaries for the cast, and wherever they were appearing, drive to the venue and pay their salaries. One day when I was in the office the chap walked in with a carrier bag and I asked where the money was, to which he replied, 'Under the Brussels sprouts. I'm carrying all this money and I don't want anybody to steal it and nobody would look for money under the Brussels sprouts.' This made me laugh because the same chap was going up to Bradford where Spike was appearing to collect the box office takings to bring them back to me in London for the *Black Mikado* rehearsal money. I thought that going to pick up money from Spike Milligan with a carrier bag full of Brussels sprouts might have been going too far so I gave him a shoebox. 'You get it in cash. I've arranged for the theatre director to give you the advance and put it in this shoebox.' And that's what happened.

NORMA: I reminded him of the night in Bradford when Spike didn't go on and the takings were down. His reply was typical of the attitude that endeared me to him.

JIMMY: Ah yes. Well, so you just have to get by in this life, don't you. That's when there's the call to the bank manager for a few thousand – who incidentally was called Borrett – and he always obliged.

NORMA: Jimmy's sang-froid and acceptance deserted him on a trip to Dublin with *The Bed-Sitting Room*. Dublin had always been kind to him in terms of box office takings. The Irish loved Marcel Marceau, so he knew Spike in Dublin would be a bonanza week.

JIMMY: It's well known in theatre circles that there are very few advanced bookings in Dublin, and hardly a pound is taken at the box office before Monday morning of the opening week. First-night takings weren't brilliant but healthy. As Spike was leaving by the stage door there was a scuffle, no one knew what had happened, but it ended up with Spike attacking the local paper's photographer and, of course, that was front page news the following morning. The Irish didn't like it, and not too many came for the following week. This was a big blow because I had to pay all the cast's air fares and expenses.

NORMA: I asked him whether he felt very let down.

JIMMY: I did feel a little, but again I don't suppose Spike ever let anybody down in a close personal sense. It seems to me he was always willing to help people; he helped me.

NORMA: Moving on from Dublin, I reminded Jimmy of a bizarre incident that occurred in Nottingham when Spike was appearing in his one-man show.

JIMMY: We opened Monday night to a great reception from the audience and there was a huge advance at the box office. It was going to be a sell-out, everything was lovely, but on Tuesday morning I had a telephone call from you. 'He's not going on tonight. Sixth row from the front, the third seat in is squeaking, it's stopping his concentration.'

NORMA: The silence on the other end of the phone was palpable.

JIMMY: The mind goes into freefall, but then you just have to plug in and think 'How am I going to handle this?' You don't worry about the lunacy of it, you just think 'How am I going to handle this?' I knew Ted Gollop, the theatre manager. It was a Moss Empires theatre and they were the most ordinary people you could wish to meet, lovely people, though they weren't theatrical people, but Ted had been there forever and had dealt with every big star coming from America. I called him. 'What is it this time?' I explained it was squeaky seats. Ted had no idea what I was talking about. Who would?

'I've got to have a crew of men and women oiling the seats in the auditorium. Spike's coming in between 12.00 and 12.30 to have an inspection, I want him to see people oiling seats. Make certain they are down in the front area, so they are immediately visible, and everything he has asked for is happening. You had better take this seriously or he won't be there tonight.' I clearly remember saying this, like it was ordinary. It must have been because half an hour later the resident staff were oiling the seats and checking for squeaky seats. [He laughed.] 'Have you checked your seat for squeaks lately, Madam', it's almost Milligan – well, it is Milligan. It's extraordinarily ludicrous on the one hand, but there's also a kind of insane sanity – who wants to have squeaky seats interfering with a performance? And incredibly he was right, it was the sixth row from the front, third seat in.

I had perfected working with Spike, and used to put my mind out of gear and never query the stupidity of things, because for Spike it wasn't stupid and if you met some of his bizarre needs, there was always the guarantee Spike delivered in terms of his performance. He was very particular about his props, and they were the most unsophisticated props of any performer, as long as they worked Spike didn't give a damn about the quality of them. If everything was right for him, he could make it work. His favourite prop was a large black hat, the brim was about three feet wide and when he put it on his head he twirled it around and shrivelled up underneath it. He had perfected this trick so he would end up on the floor and Milligan almost disappeared underneath it. He loved it, but it was only about a 20-second sequence in a two-hour show. He was appearing at the Mayfair Theatre in London, and who knows why but he had gone into the theatre at lunchtime.

NORMA: Then came one of Spike's dreaded phone calls to me. 'Someone has nicked my black hat, it's the most important part of my show, I can't go on tonight without it.' The company manager had informed Jimmy – no hat – no show. Not wanting a confrontation at the theatre Jimmy dashed to 9 Orme Court, to ask me to go to the theatre and persuade Spike that a 20-second sequence out of a two-hour show wasn't that important. That would have been a moment of insanity and in what has now become folklore in our office Jimmy walked through the door only to be told I'd gone to the hairdresser. 'Does she know his black hat has been nicked and he's talking of not going on, people at the box office wanting their money back and we have a sell-out?' He was told 'Norma knows all that, she's gone to the hairdresser.' Resigned to the situation Jimmy replied, 'There's one thing I like about Norma, she always gets her priorities right,' and that statement has been repeated 100 times over the years.

JIMMY: The culprit, a member of the stage crew, who'd nicked the hat for a keepsake, heard of the 'No show tonight' and stealthily returned it to the stage when no one was looking. So I didn't have to stand at the box office doling out the money for a 'No show'.

The happy times, dinners at the Trattoo restaurant, with Alan Clare playing the piano, sometimes it was like being on eggshells: Relax, sit back and enjoy – No. Pay attention – Yes. Other nights were truly memorable: a wonderful atmosphere, laughter, wine and great company – but that's how it was with Spike.

NORMA: I asked Jimmy if, after so many years of touring and seeing Spike at close hand, he thought Spike was disciplined as a performer.

JIMMY: He was anarchic, but does that mean he lacked discipline? No. Any performer has to be disciplined. All the books he wrote you can't write without discipline; it was a gift not to appear to be disciplined. I don't think this was calculated or that he had worked that out. It was just the way he was.

NORMA: To my amazement we couldn't discuss Spike and his women simply because Jimmy had not seen any evidence of them. I mean, all those tours, the times Liz Cowley came up to Birmingham or Edinburgh or wherever Spike was appearing. He was adamant that it wasn't just him who had not seen the evidence.

JIMMY: Nobody working for me would have seen it, because had they seen it I would have known. People you employ to take care of the shows, it's part of their job to keep you informed about what's going on, so you are able to handle whatever might crop up, including the press, particularly when it's a big name, and Spike was a big name.

You have to be forewarned. There was never a whisper on my front and therefore there was never a whisper on the theatrical side.

NORMA: How many years? How many tours did he do? Are we talking about another Spike Milligan? God forbid there should be another one. We had a break and over coffee Jimmy was telling me how weird it felt, after so many years, to be sitting in my office again. He thought nothing had changed and for him there was such a feeling of security. I was bemused, equilibrium was never the order of the day, and for an office that had witnessed more ups and downs than the lifts in the Empire State Building security seemed an unlikely choice of word and yet, and yet, strange as it may seem it touched a nerve and I could relate to his feeling. Maybe Spike had finally got to me, and I was going mad. I suppose we all have our fantasies and with a quick jolt I was back in the real world listening to Jimmy theorising about people born in India.

JIMMY: In my life, I have met four people born in India, and there is something different about them. My wife of thirty-seven years, a master carpenter who I employed for the tours, an actress and Spike. Every one of them distinctive, they are all nuts and have complexities, and they all have a curious side to them. All lovely people. They all had mood swings. Some people said it was somehow connected to the moon, but I thought the moon stuff was garbage, they were just born in India.

NORMA: Time, and our minds, play tricks on our memory. He had no recall about Spike's depressions.

JIMMY: All comics are always terribly sad. I think all the comics I've known have had certain problems, because they are totally dependent on themselves, and they have to get the laughs. This makes them focus on themselves, and that's a bad place to be. They all have an over-developed sense of self awareness. Then there is the adulation they receive, making them feel special, all this helps their complex to come out. Then comes the responsibility to meet people's expectations, and that's not easy because at the end of the day, they are just ordinary human beings, except Spike who was born in India. But he had to meet people's expectations and then his expectation of himself was what drove him to the brink because you can't meet that expectation continuously. That's why some of his performances suffered and I was thankful for the number of performances we got from him. At the time I didn't look at it with this kind of logic, but what we did was right. You and I just ploughed on, we didn't allow the difficulties to drag us and the situation down. We ploughed on and made it continue and then he joined us again, and that's what happened, think about it. He might have expected to see all the tractors stop in the furrows, but he didn't and we just chugged on and then he got back on to the tractor and we continued on. We could have cancelled but we didn't, we waited for him to come back. He always did. The normality helped him to come back.

NORMA: After each tour it would be 'This is the last one, I ain't doing it again' then a few months would go by and Jimmy would be on the phone, 'Does he want to do another one?' I would remind Jimmy of Bradford or Southsea where he was being sued for breaking the contract for a No show, and his reply was always the same, he preferred to remember the nights at the Trattoo and the laughter.

JIMMY: We got through what was going on and the good times came with your 300 roses and me getting another tour. But there was always one thing shining through, and that was Spike's generosity of spirit. He cared about things and people, he looked after all his friends. He wasn't generous in the sense of lavish 'let's all go to the Savoy', he'd rather take his friends to an Indian, sit round, eat his curry, drink wine and talk, he was very generous of heart. Spike was like a diamond with many facets, and every facet was different which is what is being put together in this book. I don't want to call Spike a diamond, he was a diamond in the context of British humour, he's in the Pantheon, he's not half-way down, he's up there. But with all his facets you're only getting one view. Your view is completely different from mine, on two counts, he was intensely close to you for obvious reasons, and secondly everything came at you because you were the point of contact with everybody else, so your view isn't necessarily rounder, it's just deeper. Everybody has their own view of Spike and everybody had a Spike Milligan story.

NORMA: I asked Jimmy what he thought would be Spike's legacy.

JIMMY: His legacy will be his writing. Certain people do say he influenced their humour but his potent legacy is his writing. His writing was truthful, and his children's poetry was absolutely brilliant and, for me, his funny drawings which are now cards – they're wonderful. I'm not sure if people will remember his charity work and the campaigns, in particular the street lamps in Constitution Hill and the passion he showed fighting to keep them instead of the concrete iron fingers they had already erected. He was successful, the iron fingers came down and were replaced with the original lamps.

I'm amazed the BBC don't repeat his television shows. Other shows are repeated ad nauseam but why is his Q series not shown because without them being shown who's going to take it up and learn from Spike, as he had learned from the Marx Brothers?

NORMA: I asked him if he had a favourite story or memory of Spike.

JIMMY: I loved going to see him and being at the back, laughing. Go round afterwards, do I have to? Oh, all right, I'll have a glass of that Gewürtztraminer wine I paid for.

PETER MEDAK

I can't imagine Spike allowing anyone to call him 'Spikey baby' except Peter Medak, the film director. Spike had such great affection for Peter and it manifested itself in one particular way. Much to the amazement of most people, Spike was very punctual. If he said, 'I'll be there at 8 p.m.', he would be there at 8 p.m. prompt. He was very unforgiving, intolerant and volatile with people who were bad timekeepers.

Now, Peter didn't know the meaning of time. When we had meetings at 9 Orme Court I can honestly say Peter never turned up at the appointed time. Not once did I hear Spike complain. Normally it would be, 'If they can't turn up on time, there'll be no bloody meeting. I'm off.' And he would go. All I heard when Peter was late was, 'Where the hell is that Hungarian refugee. I've bought him some warm doughnuts.'

When there were script meetings, sometimes three or four a week, Peter would, as usual, arrive late and breathless. 'I couldn't get a taxi,' or 'Sorry, Spikey baby, my car wouldn't start,' or 'My ex-wife kept me on the phone for half an hour.' Instead of Spike raging as he would do normally, he said to me, 'He's running out of excuses. I'm going to make it easy for him. Wait until you see his face.' He tore up several strips of paper and wrote a different, ludicrous excuse on each piece. 'Gone to the moon. Back later.' 'Visiting Valentino's grave. Will be half an hour late.' 'Having breakfast with the Queen. She's a slow eater.

Will be back A.S.A.P.' He folded each strip, placed it in his corduroy cap, and we sat in his small office waiting for Peter to arrive, late as usual. As Peter opened the door and before he could offer any excuse, Spike jumped out of his chair and said, 'Peter! To save time just pick one and we can get on.' Such was their relationship.

To contemplate a book of memories of Milligan without Peter Medak as a contributor would be, for me, like thinking of Scott Fitzgerald without Zelda. So my search for Peter began. He didn't reply to my fax to his home in West Hollywood. Not like him. We have remained friends; as Spike used to say, 'They're best mates, those two.' Then I discovered he was directing a commercial in Mexico, where I tracked him down. 'Oh, darlink, I miss Spikey baby. Of course I'll write a piece for you. I'll ring you when I get back to California.'

Knowing Peter, that could mean one week, one month or one year, and time was running faster than I wanted it to and my editor, Louise Haines, was getting to her 'angsty' stage. She knows I don't do pressure, but she also knows that I don't like to get into her bad books. There was no alternative but to hassle Peter.

A phone call from California: 'Oh, darlink! I can't do it for a week or so. My friend is opening on Broadway and I promised I would be at his first night.' So while he was jetting from West Hollywood to opening night on Broadway, I'm standing in the bus queue waiting for the 328 to take me to the office to tell 'angsty' Louise that I hadn't got the interview with Peter, but I had persuaded him to write a piece of his memory about 'my lunatic friend'.

Back from New York, Peter phoned me. To hear his voice always gives me a warm feeling. 'I finished my piece last night and it's gone in the post this morning. I do hope it's what you want.'

It is exactly what I wanted, so much so that the following is as he sent it to me, together with his letter.

April 24, 2010

Darling Norma,

Finally here are my haphazard memories of darling Spike. I know I am
rambling on sometimes but I beg you to use your editorial mind and just
make the best of it. I promise when I come to London I will call ahead of
time. I send you and the entire building lots of love.

Love + Kisses

Peter

PETER: I first met Spike in a Chinese restaurant on Kensington High
Street in the early Sixties. This was one place among many others
where all of us used to hang out, with Michael Caine, Bryan Forbes,
Peter Sellers and Peter Cook. Spike was always pulling my leg about
not speaking English properly. 'You bloody Hungarian refugee, eating
our Chinese food, how dare you?' Then he always blew a raspberry
(making the noise of a fart) on his arm and got totally hysterical with
laughter, mostly falling off his chair on to the floor. He thought
blowing a raspberry was the funniest thing on this planet and he used
to do it after each sentence to punctuate a joke – Spike the Phantom
Raspberry Blower.

Everybody knew him who was around in those wonderful days of
Sixties London – King's Road and Kensington High Street, Soho,
Mayfair, *The Goon Show*, the Beatles, the Stones, the Ad Lib Club,
La Trattoria Terrazza in Soho, the Trattoo in Kensington, the best
of Italian wines, the fish'n'chip shops and the millions of Indian
restaurants on every street corner.

I remember well Spike at the opening of my film, *The Ruling Class*, in 1972 and the party afterwards when he again attacked me. 'How can a bloody Hungarian like you, who we allowed in my country, criticise our aristocracy? How dare you!! Go back to bloody Budapest, you pest!' Then another raspberry and then he hugged me and told me what a brilliant movie I had made, despite myself.

Soon after *The Ruling Class* I was in New York having some meetings with United Artists about making my next film, Death Wish. In my great wisdom I decided to try to cast Mr Henry Fonda, but the studio didn't agree with me and, of course, I quit and ran back to London into the arms of Peter Sellers on the King's Road. 'Come on, baby, we got it all ready for you, you can start shooting this incredible comedy,' which was *Ghost in the Noonday Sun*, starring Peter Sellers, Spike Milligan, Peter Boyle and Anthony Franciosa and many other of the most brilliant English lunatics. Peter supposedly had been developing and working on the script for several years, but as I later on discovered to my horror he had never read any version of it. It was too late to foresee the disaster I was about to enter into as I had agreed and signed my contract with Columbia Pictures, with John Hayman, Tommy Clyde and Ben Kadish producing it. The original script was written by Wolf Mankowitz, which was later re-written by Evan Jones and finally it had additional material by Spike who, of course, played one of the main parts in the film.

My first task was to try to put some sense and logic into the script, which was impossible as it was written in Spike's Goon-style humour. Spike was a comic genius and I truly believe that he created Peter Sellers and all those various voices and characters while doing the *Goon Shows*, which Peter then used for the rest of his life and career. This was the first and only time Spike and I worked together and I must say it took a little while to be able to get into his routine and the inner workings of his brain. I used to come to his wonderful office building in Orme Court off Bayswater Road, which he shared with all the rest of the great British comedy writers of the Sixties. It was an amazing joke factory, the front room controlled by Norma Farnes who was Spike's agent, manager, secretary, mother confessor, and who basically tried to run and organise his entire life.

I think Spike's office was on the first floor. Needless to say it was the tiniest room in the building with the famous 'Keep Out' sign on the door. There was a military camp bed in case he was too tired to go home, or he was running away from his various wives or girl-friends. There was, of course, a writing desk and lots of wooden bookshelves and books surrounding the walls. The windows were always open and one day I asked him to please close, as I was freezing to death, which he refused to do, saying, 'They will be here any minute. They always come exactly at three in the afternoon.' And lo and behold three little sparrows flew in through the window straight to his desk where he kept water and food for them . . . of course, this was their daily routine, typical of Spike. He loved animals, trees and most people.

Working on the script was a total nightmare as Spike wanted to kill everybody on every page of it, and it mattered not that some of them were already dead on the previous page. He kept saying, 'Don't worry, Daddy. We'll kill him again.' We continued working for several days intermittently with great luncheons at an amazing Greek restaurant at the back of Orme Court, and dinners at the Trattoo.

I remember one night Peter came with Liza Minnelli as they were very much in love at that time, and Spike and I were each other's date (plus his trumpet in a blue case which he seemed to carry everywhere with him). During dinner, just when they served the delicious pasta, both Spike and Peter started to tell a joke, but every time it came to the punchline they both started laughing hysterically, staring into each other's eyes, turning red in the face and finally falling under the table and disappearing from our view, leaving Liza and me staring at each other not knowing what to do while they were still screaming underneath. Finally, as they came up for air and trying to continue the joke again, they collapsed in a hysterical fit and were never able to finish. After two bites of the pasta Spike suddenly jumped up, pulling his trumpet out of its case, and he rushed to the front of the restaurant where he played brilliantly with his great pianist friend Alan Clare. Half an hour later he returned to the table and made yet another hopeless attempt at that joke.

On another occasion while we were working on the script, I remember Spike being late for our afternoon meeting. He came back soaking wet and covered in mud, holding this thing in a brown paper bag and saying this is an architectural item proving the several layers of ancient London, which became his treasured possession for days. When I asked him what it was, he pulled out of this bag a very, very old half pair of shoes all curled up with age, him being convinced that it was several hundreds of years old. He retrieved it from a dig in the embankment when they were still pulling down bombed-out buildings from the Second World War. I wouldn't be surprised if it was still somewhere in Spike's old office now.

After several days, I realised that there was an unsolvable problem with the script, as it just did not make any sense, which was most typical of all the pirate movies ever made. Spike still continued to want to eliminate everybody to the point where there were no characters left in the film except himself and Peter. I tried to talk to Peter S. on the phone about it, but finally decided to visit him on a Saturday and actually force him to read through the script with me, to point out our problems. Bert, his driver, let me into the mews house in Belgravia and said Peter would be down in a minute. So I sat and waited in the living room listening to the phone constantly ringing, and the three answering machines that I had actually brought back from New York for him a few days earlier as they were answering the calls in a rotating manner with Peter and Spike's voices in their various Goon characters. After twenty minutes of this I went upstairs, knocked on the door and found Peter standing on his head, completely naked in a yoga position. I leant down towards him and pointed out my watch and the time which we had left to try to read through the script.

Finally, he came down and we opened the script and started reading to each other and after about fifteen pages the phone rang again and it was Ms M. very upset on the other end of the phone from Chicago, as she was coming to London where Peter was going to pick her up later on. Realising how upset she was, Peter asked her to close her eyes (3,942 miles away) and as he started counting to ten he told her that she is going to see everything more and more pink and everything was going to be okay. He kissed her and told her how much he loved her and hung up the phone. He looked at me. 'What a woman!' and broke down and started to cry. I felt most uncomfortable as I put my arms around him, and we walked to Mimo's, another famous Italian hang-out of ours during the Sixties. When I told Spike about this incident his only comment was that 'they' were obviously both totally bonkers, 'and so are you, thinking that Peter could help with the script.'

A few weeks later I arrived in Cyprus and started to film on real boats in the Mediterranean, which no other motion picture has ever done. Peter S. on the first day of shooting faked a heart attack and thereby started the most insane, indescribable experience in forty-seven years of my directing life. By the time Spike turned up on the island, Peter had missed ten days of the film with fake heart attacks, fired the producers who were his partners, fired a wonderful camera-man, Larry Pizer, who was his and my friend, and then started turning on me. I desperately needed an ally to help me control Peter and Peter needed Spike to keep him sane and also to tell him whether the film was brilliantly funny or not. Needless to say, Spike's verdict was that the film was a disaster, which was the last thing I needed at that point. I knew the film was a disaster before I started it because of the script, which I could never get fixed because of Peter and Spike. However, Spike and I had become great friends and the next three months we were together we desperately tried somehow to control his lunatic friend and somehow complete the film so we could all become free from his madness and continue on in life.

Needless to say there were some incredible and wonderful, mem-orable moments of high comedy in the film such as when Spike and I decided to have seven brothers for the character he was playing (Billy Bombay from Bombay) turn up on set looking absolutely identical where they all copied Spike's walk and physical manner to the degree that amongst the eight of them it took me several minutes to find the real Spike. On another occasion, in a scene with Peter and Spike, there was a palm tree leaf in between their faces, and Spike kept hitting the palm, with his eyes maniacally following it.

Yet another day – I think it was Peter's seventeenth faked heart attack – he was rushed to hospital in Kyrenia. We stopped shooting for a couple of days, but the next evening, while all of us were sitting in a bar overlooking the Mediterranean, I picked up the *Evening*

Standard from London, and there was our friend and star of our movie, not in hospital in Cyprus, but in San Lorenzo's restaurant in London having dinner with Princess Margaret. When I showed this to Spike he was so outraged by seeing his lunatic friend in London that he jumped up and did a ritualistic dance around the table, cursing his friend, poking and pointing his shaky fingers at the newspaper, screaming that he will never speak to him again. Which only lasted until Peter returned to the island and Spike embraced him and said, 'I hope you had a lovely dinner with the princess.'

They were both totally insane but Spike's heart was filled with total goodness (most of the time), but Peter's, sadly, was not, despite the genius he was. I started prematurely going grey during this film and there were times when I thought I was never going to come out alive from this experience. Peter and Spike literally drove me insane but for some reason I didn't mind Spike, although Peter at times was evil. I still loved them both, which only proves that I was more insane than the two of them put together.

Towards the end of the film Spike and I hardly spoke to Peter, apart from being on the set, and one day Peter came to me, like my best old friend, saying that Spikey and he had been asked to do a Benson & Hedges commercial and they both would love me to direct it on a weekend, which was our only rest day in ten days of night shooting. It was a very simple story where they break into a customs shed and steal the gold bullion. We decided that Peter should be dressed as the Clouseau character from *Pink Panther*. At one point I had to ask Peter to shove the Benson & Hedges box to jam the alarm bell so it didn't ring when they broke in, but Peter looked at me blankly and said, 'Didn't Dennis [Selinger, his agent] tell you I am not allowed to touch the cigarette pack?'

'Why?' I asked, and he said, 'Didn't you know, I am the chairman of the Anti-smoking League?'

'You mean you're getting a new Mercedes and £25,000 and you won't touch the pack?'

He said, 'That's right, I can't touch it.'

I said, 'Don't move,' while I went to Spike and said, 'Your lunatic friend won't touch the pack.'

Spike backed away from me, took a step too far and fell over the edge of the harbour, straight into the boat that was ready for filming the last shot of the commercial. He had broken the boat. He looked round, ignored the broken boat, and shouted, 'Don't talk to me about it. I can't touch the pack either.'

'Why?' I asked.

He replied, 'I am the deputy chairman of the Anti-smoking League. Please don't ask me to do this because I'll have to say no, and I don't want to say no to you.'

I thought I was going insane. 'You mean you're both getting all this money and you're doing a cigarette commercial and you won't touch the pack?'

'That's right,' he said.

I said, 'What about Peter smoking pot all the time? Isn't that smoking?'

Spike just looked at me and said, 'Don't ask those logical questions to me.'

I went to Jimmy Villiers [another actor] and said, 'Those two lunatics won't touch the pack. Can you fucking believe that?'

'Give me the pack and I'll do it,' he said.

That commercial has become a legend and Benson & Hedges went on making them for several years.

We somehow finished the film and after thirty-seven years, thank God, nobody remembers it but me. Spike and I stayed great friends and one of my last conversations with him was from a phone booth in Baltimore where I was shooting a film and Gary Oldman and I were trying to write a script about the making of *Ghost in the Noonday Sun* and all the fuck ups. I was insane enough to ask Spike if he would write it. Spike, of course, blew three raspberries from 3,000 miles away and agreed the making of the film would make a much better film than the film. Needless to say, we never made it, as I would have to go back into the same nightmare which I had done once, and never again.

The final shot of the film is the pirate ship pulling away from the island leaving Dick Scratcher (Peter Sellers) buried up to his neck in the sand while next to him on a rotten tree trunk, tied half way up with huge ropes, is Billy Bombay (Spike Milligan) covered up to his neck so neither of them could move, leaving them marooned forever, screaming at each other with all six cameras shooting.

All the while Norma is standing next to me on the boat taking in this incredible sight. I turned and said, 'There are your two lunatic friends. They're both insane and as bad as each other, with one huge difference. That Spike has the heart of gold.'

I will never forget him, and just thinking of him still makes me smile – forever.

TERRY WOGAN

Terry was always a favourite of Spike's. He would say, 'Terry is always full of bloody mischief.' I wasn't sure which Terry (Spike's real name) he was talking about. In my opinion, they were both full of mischief. I remember on one occasion Spike was appearing on *Wogan*. I can't remember which one because he appeared on so many. The taxi was waiting outside the office to take him to the BBC studios in Shepherd's Bush. I phoned him (I'm on the ground floor, his office was on the first floor): 'Get a move on, you're running late,' and I put down the phone. One minute later he popped his head round my office door. 'Okay, Norm, I think I'll go and annoy Terry.' It was said with such affection, but full of mischief.

I think Terry understood Spike more than most people. He seemed to know how his mind worked. My God, that's saying something, but he was in tune with Spike's illogical thinking. Spike could turn something completely illogical into logic. I think this understanding was born out of the affection and respect they had for each other.

It was demonstrated when the BBC wanted to put on a programme to celebrate Spike's eightieth birthday, *A Tribute to Spike Milligan*. On stage with Spike would be Eric Sykes and Johnny Speight, his two 'old mates', and the BBC wanted Clive Anderson to host the show. I completely disagreed. The bullying producer insisted. Stalemate. I knew Anderson was wrong for the show: in my opinion, he would try to compete with this line-up and it would turn into a Clive Anderson show.

I insisted on Terry Wogan. I knew instinctively whatever this awkward/quick-witted/mercurial trio threw at Terry, he would be unfazed and bounce back with a smiling quip.

I was right. Of course, Spike knew nothing of the Anderson saga, but when I told him I'd got Terry to host his birthday show he said, 'Thanks, Norm. You got me the best.'

TERRY: I have a vague recollection that I met Spike for the first time due to John Lloyd but it's lost in the mists of time. He was a great television producer but before that a radio producer in Light Entertainment. He had a slightly esoteric kind of quiz on radio in the days when everyone wanted to be on the panel. They were recorded in the Paris Theatre [BBC recording studios in Lower Regent Street], God bless it, three blind people, a guide dog and a lot of people with no teeth. A very distinguished panel apart from me: Ian McKellen, Anna Ford and Spike Milligan. I can't remember the content of the quiz but I know Anna Ford was on it because John Lloyd fancied her – and who didn't fancy her because she was a glamour girl. Now Spike, who was not known for going behind the door when it came to women, was very, very keen. But I walked Anna home, I'm proud to say, in the face of what can only be described as extremely powerful opposition. There was no question of hanky panky or anything like that because I was a happily married man – still am. But dear old Spike forgave me and we formed a friendship after that. Occasionally I would join him at the Trattoo, very popular with showbusiness people then. It's not there any more. On more than one occasion we'd get in touch and he would say, 'Okay, I'll see you in the Trattoo on Tuesday evening. There was a very nice manager there, Pasquale, and he'd meet me at the front door. I would ask what sort of mood Spike was in and if it was bad he'd warn me off. 'Don't go up there today,' he'd say, or alternatively it would be, 'Oh, he's great.' Then we could have our spaghetti bolognese in peace and quiet and have a bit of a laugh. But of course sometimes, he was a famously difficult man. There's no point in pretending otherwise, but everyone loved him. He had an extraordinary quality. He was a great old fake in lots of ways. He liked to say he was Irish. He wasn't Irish at all. No more Irish than Peter O'Toole – another one who tries to pretend he's Irish.

NORMA: He was proud of being Irish.

TERRY: He was, because he became a naturalised Irishman, didn't he?

NORMA: His father was Irish and Spike took out an Irish passport because a British one was denied him as he was born in India.

TERRY: Well, my father was Irish but that doesn't make you a fantastic person. Anyway, we sort of formed a mutual regard. When I first met him he was wonderful to me. I had grown up a little boy living in Limerick, really a rain-soaked island, and I speak that honestly. I've just come back from a rain-soaked island, which is why I have this lovely soft moisturised complexion. I was born moisturised in Limerick. Now I've lost the track of where I was at this point. That's right, as I was saying, much is made of his volatility but he was never anything other than really nice to me so I was nice to him, though yes, I was tremen-dously aware of how his mood could change but he had a quality people loved. There are people who are difficult and everybody shies away from them. He was difficult but everybody was drawn to him.

When I was a boy in Limerick I didn't listen to Irish radio, instead I listened to the Light Programme, which, I suppose, is part of the reason I was able to slot in, reasonably successfully. As I was saying, as a boy I listened to *The Goon Show*. I loved it and could do all the Goon voices. Nobody else in my class at the Jesuit college in Limerick knew what the hell I was talking about when I came out with 'He's fallen in the water', 'Hello, Neddy', and 'Mister Moriarty!' It revo-lutionised how I looked at things. There was an immediate response in me to the kind of thing I heard on the *Goon Shows*, the taking of an idea sideways, instead of straight up in the air.

Now I'm not a great star person, which, being a showbusiness interviewer, is, I suppose, completely wrong. I'm not really a fan of anybody. I mean, I like people or I don't like people but I was a fan of his. By any standards he was a genius, with all the trappings of genius, unpredictability and volatility. I don't know any really great comedian who isn't eccentric because I think they have to be eccentric to do what they do. It's such a painful thing. I think Spike used to feel that pain. When he went out on stage he suffered. They all suffer. I think they have some compulsion to suffer. When they start at the bottom of the bill at Clacton and work their way up it's a suffering process to walk out there in front of people who couldn't care less. Now, I can't do that. I don't need their approval. I never really needed their approval. It's about wanting people to love you. Everyone wants to be loved, of course, but comedians have it in spades and comedians are the people I most admire in all the world, because it's something I can't do. If I walk out in front of an audience and they don't respond my reaction is to walk off. I'm not going to make them love me, but comedians have to get hold of an audience and Spike had that quality.

NORMA: Eric (Sykes) has it.

TERRY: But in a more conventional way. Spike didn't think like other people, which was part of his genius. He had sheer eccentricity. The esoteric nature of his comedy was similar to those surreal painters. He was a surreal comedian so if you were on that wavelength it was unbelievable, but sometimes he would take off too far. I think he would see he had lost his audience and he would be hurt by that. He would tend to go into his shell or start to curse them. I remember once when I interviewed him with Harry Secombe, whether he was ill, I don't know, or maybe it was the way he was with Harry, he was very difficult. Harry made up for it. After we had finished doing the interview Harry said, 'That bastard does that to me every time!' That was the other side of Spike. But I also remember another show when he was particularly difficult. I could see him waiting to come on and he was in a wheelchair, which he would often use for whatever reason. He was like the anti-Christ. He really bullied the female floor manager and used terribly bad language. That was his bad side. Then as soon as he came on he changed, you know, Doctor Footlights, so in an interview he rarely showed a negative side.

I remember going to an *Oldie* lunch some years ago when Spike turned up. He was in great form. Everybody loved him. He'd been sitting with people, although he wasn't crazy about being around people he didn't know. He wanted to be around the people who loved him. That was when he was at his funniest, a bit like Peter Cook, the funniest man in the world, but Spike's real genius was to sit in front of three or four people, like Peter Cook. It was a kind of personal thing. Spike needed to be able to see your eyes in order to know that you were following every bloody word he was saying. That was Spike. It's a very rare thing that he had.

Remember the Spike Milligan tribute we did?

NORMA: I had to fight the BBC to get you.

TERRY: Great gal! And it was terrific. The band came out and marched up the centre aisle. The public loved Spike, absolutely loved him. It wouldn't matter what he did, he was universally loved by the public who didn't know him for the occasional shit that he was, but they loved him, would have loved him anyway. We had tributes from the great and the good, from America as well as here. It was a really well put together programme. A tribute to Spike Milligan. About three-quarters of the way through the programme there I am, as presenter, with him sitting next to me and everyone paying tribute to him, all huge stars and he says, 'How much longer is this going on? I've got a table booked for dinner at the restaurant.' He's not called Spike for nothing, because spiky he certainly was. Nobody can do enough for him, all that attention and love, but there is something there that makes him reject it, so often. That's what I say, he was a surreal person. He took a view of life that was surreal. The evidence is there in every cartoon that he drew. Nobody else thinks like that. I try to encourage my listeners in the morning not to take life vertically in the conventional manner because anyone can do that, but to take it laterally, take the idea outside the boundaries. Of course that was Spike's strength and what he brought to the Goons. The Goons would have never succeeded, even with Sellers' genius and Harry Secombe's bonhomie, without Spike's extraordinary ability to take an idea to outer space and to create characters that were completely surreal. He was the surrealist and he was so influential, like Jonathan Miller, because Jonathan Miller was like Peter Cook. Jonathan was a brilliant academic as well as being a theatre director and doctor. He was another one. Absolutely brilliant in one-to-one small group conversations. They were all of a type.

NORMA: Spike could behave atrociously yet people invariably forgave him. Why?

TERRY: He was manifestly a genius, a comic surrealist genius and had no equal. There are comedians but there's nobody like Spike Milligan. Incidentally, like everybody else, he wasn't funny all the time. I mean, Monty Python were about as unfunny as you can get for most of the time and they were the ones who were influenced by him more than anyone else. Spike only hit home about one in three, which makes him about the best striker. As to why people loved him I think they recognised his talent. He could be rude to other actors and comedians and they may tell you they forgave him but probably they didn't really like him. He wasn't easy to like. He could like you for a short period and then grow tired of you. Maybe his attention span was limited or maybe to be the kind of genius he was you have to be a completely selfish person. I'm sure Van Gogh was completely selfish. Geniuses have to be completely focused. Now people professed to love him but there are countless stories of how bad tempered he could be and those who acted with him on the stage tell you how at times he could be completely unprofessional, yet he was loved. Now I didn't love him. I liked him but there are very few people in the world you can love, perhaps only those in your family. The people I really love are in my family. The people I really like I work with. That's the way I have to be. People who worked with him and were hurt probably forgave him, but it wouldn't lessen the hurt. He was a selfish performer, there's no question of that, and like every other comedian he'd kill you for a laugh. I never met a comedian who wouldn't. If they thought they could get a laugh by sticking a small knife in your ribs they'd do it. It's a fact with all comedians. However, with Spike there was an anomaly

– his compassion. He seemed to respond to everything, the plight of the whale, the disappearance of the elephant and the white rhinoceros. He had an extraordinary heart. I think one of the things that is easily forgotten is that he would give up his work for things like that. He was one of the most emotional men I've met in my life. He wasn't in control of his emotions. Maybe he didn't want to control them.

NORMA: What did you think about his womanising, his girlfriends, those I called the Bayswater Harem?

TERRY: I think that happens when you are not content. Most people, like me, don't womanise because we are content and are afraid to threaten it. Spike was completely unafraid. He didn't care and he was reckless. I think womanising is an attempt to prove something to yourself and you're not content.

He liked women. Maybe it's too harsh to say most womanisers are inadequate, too simple.

NORMA: He was very kind to them, almost Victorian. He'd take them out and there would always be a little corsage on the table for them and then he'd come in the next morning and be an absolute shit.

TERRY: There are massive contradictions in the man. Most of us need people to be the same so that we can get on with our lives. He was never the same two days running. Again you forgave him because you knew you were in the presence of someone who was extremely talented. It's sometimes hard to keep that in mind. You say that he was very vulnerable and that it hurt if people didn't like him. But that's the comedian wanting everyone to love them, but everybody wants people to love them. It's perhaps more marked in some people than others. One of the things I learned in my early days of Irish television is that not everyone loves you. For everyone that does there's somebody that can't abide you. You learn very quickly not to try to have everybody to love you. This is a lesson that everyone has to learn as they go through life. In fairness to Spike he didn't want everybody to love him. He didn't give a shit whether you loved him or not. I think he cared whether audiences loved him but socially, if he walked into a room, he wasn't going to change his mood for the mood of the party, he was just going to say exactly what he thought. And then there was his reliability – or lack of it. He'd agree to do a talk show and then on the day he'd phone and say he didn't want to do it. Then you'd have to break every bone in his body to get him up there. Reliability was not his forte. Some people might want to please you and say he was reliable but perhaps they don't want to appear to be shits so they'll tell you he was lovely. The public perhaps weren't aware of that side of him. Not everybody got his sense of humour, particularly women. You see, I'm pretty certain that the audience for a *Goon Show* was entirely male. However, women were attracted to him. He was famous, he was good-looking and charming but did they think he was funny? I'm not sure about a woman's sense of humour. I don't want this to sound sexist (but I don't care whether it sounds sexist or not) but a woman's sense of humour is different. I know, I've been married to the same woman for forty-five years. It's different from a man's. A woman's sense of humour is based more on emotion and indeed it's a more basic sense of humour, whereas a man's is lateral and a woman's vertical. It's only my opinion. Intelligent women may think that statement is too sweeping. For instance, I don't think a female audience would fall around at Tommy Cooper and wouldn't necessarily think that Spike or Eric Sykes was funny, but then again Eric did sitcoms and his humour does appeal to women. Spike never did sitcoms. I'd love to have seen Spike in one. Wouldn't that have been fantastic?

NORMA: No.

TERRY: He would have been great.

NORMA: He'd have driven everybody mad.

TERRY: He would but wouldn't he have been wonderful in *Dad's Army*? God! He would have been terrific. If Eric Sykes had written for him it would have been fantastic. In a sitcom he wouldn't have wanted to upset everyone so much because he and Eric were such good pals. It's such a shame it never happened. Again, the man was an enigma. For instance, why was he so gratuitously rude to Prince Charles? [When he called him a 'grovelling little bastard'.] He knew Prince Charles would love it and he wanted to show people he didn't give a shit.

NORMA: He wouldn't think about it. It would just come off the top of his head.

TERRY: Anything for a laugh. He was prepared to skewer the heir to the throne who was his biggest fan.

NORMA: As you've already said – anything for a laugh. I didn't tell him he was going to get an award. If I had he wouldn't have gone, so the remark came off the top of his head. When I told him about the invitation he said he wasn't going there just to be a dressing. I said we hadn't had a night out for a long time and that changed his mind.

TERRY: That was a risky one. Maybe if you'd told him he would have had something to say ready in his head, but then, on reflection, he never had anything ready in his head. Now Eric is difficult to interview. He wants to embarrass you. You ask him a question and he looks at you, and looks at you, and you think, 'For God's sake, man, why are you trying to kill me?' And I know why you are trying to kill me. You are a comedian and you want to get a laugh. But Spike wouldn't think about it that way. He would do it because he was very mischievous.

NORMA: I know what you mean about Eric – a very funny man. I had a fall last week and went head over heels. I told him about it and his immediate reaction was 'Did it get a laugh?'

TERRY: Just like Eric Morecambe. I did a couple of *Morecambe and Wise Shows* and on each occasion endless bloody rehearsals, which I hate, so that they are all word perfect, and as sure as hell, half-way through the sketch he'd slip in an ad lib that would throw you. Like most comedians he'd kill you for a laugh.

NORMA: How will you remember Spike?

TERRY: For his generosity, not merely because he always insisted on paying for a meal, but because if you were on hard times he'd give you everything he'd got. You set store on those things. If you want to know why people forgave him it was because his virtues outweighed the single disability that he had, which I don't think he was completely in control of, which was the manic depression. He was always conscious of the fact that he wasn't as other men. Sometimes the moods would fluctuate. You could have dinner with him and he'd be fine, then during it something would happen to him. He'd stand up and say, 'I think it's time for me to go now.' And disappear.

NORMA: He was generous spiritually, not just financially.

TERRY: We come back to compassion. Was he a lapsed Catholic?

NORMA: Until he was dying, then he became a Catholic again.

TERRY: Why wouldn't you? Looking for the exits. It's interesting, you know, that throughout his life he didn't take any prisoners. He didn't see why he should. I'm interested to know where that came from.

NORMA: From his father. He was very like Spike. When he was about thirteen his father told him how he had shot a tiger. Spike told him that was a lie. His father said, 'Now listen, son, and remember this all your life. Would you rather have the boring truth or an exciting lie?' How about that to make an impression on a boy? Spike told that story a thousand times.

TERRY: Sometimes I'm asked for a favourite story about some well-known person. I don't have one about Spike. He never did anything silly around me. I remember the good times we had together. The weird thing is I can see his face vividly when I think about him. He will always look the same to me. Wonderful memories.

JOANNA LUMLEY

In the early Seventies, long before Jennifer Saunders thought of the title *Absolutely Fabulous*, Spike and I were going to some function – I can't remember where it was but I do remember he said, 'Joanna Lumley will be there. You'll like her, she's absolutely fabulous!' And so she is.

She's blessed with a wonderful smile that lights a room. At an age when many of her contemporaries think that sexuality is for a younger generation she glows with it. She came to my office in Orme Court on a beautiful sunny autumn morning dressed in navy blue jeans and a short bright yellow jacket with a navy and yellow scarf elegantly thrown over her shoulder. You may think that no woman can possibly have it all – meet Joanna!

She has such a love of life. She's one of those women – don't you hate them? – who are naturally glamorous, in her case no doubt helped by a course at the Lucie Clayton Finishing School in London.

Now of all possible friendships you might think it inconceivable that Joanna and Spike had a close and happy one. But they did and it grew out of admiration and respect for each other, and lasted over thirty years.

———————

JOANNA: I was a fan from the *Goon Show* days in the Fifties. I'd arrived in the UK from the Far East where I was born and spent my early years. My father was a major in the Gurkha Rifles but returned to England when India gained independence in '47. We were staying at my aunt's house in Kent on a farm, I was about eight. There were no such things as television sets, we would listen to the Goons and it was listening to shows like that and the fact that you listened rather than watched that made it even more concentrated, and so everybody would remember the names of the characters – Bloodnok, Eccles, Moriarty and Minnie Bannister and all the ridiculous catchphrases like 'He's fallen in the water'. I used to imitate them but I never thought then that one day I would meet him – and become a friend.

Well, the first time I didn't really meet him, I was just near him. I was at a 'Save the Whale' rally in Trafalgar Square where he was one of the speakers.

NORMA: By then Joanna had modelled clothes for Jean Muir and become famous as Purdey in *The New Avengers*.

JOANNA: After Spike had exhorted the crowd to join the campaign he was besieged for autographs. He took several minutes to deal with each fan. Most unusual. And then after he had finished the autographs he walked across the Square towards the Mall. He didn't have a big car waiting for him. He just sloped off and obviously he was going to catch a bus or walk to the office. I thought, how thrilling. I was terribly impressed that my huge hero was so helpful, modest and humble. I loved that.

Soon afterwards our paths crossed again when I was co-presenting a programme with Terry Wogan connected with *Children in Need*. Spike was on the show.

It was a very early show, live in the studio, before it had become so polished, as it is now with the whole evening propped up by episodes of *Coronation Street* or whatever. In those early days they had people coming on and doing things and Spike had been asked to read a poem. Being Spike, he had sorted out one of those really touching childhood poems he had written, you know, one with the innocence and sweetness of long ago, and he had chosen a really beautiful poem. 'Next guest, Spike Milligan!' Scream, scream, scream! On he came and I suspected it was one of those days when he had been depressed. I know 'the look' now. There's a sort of strange set of the eyes; a darkness. He began to read his poem. But of course the public only knew Spike Milligan as Spike the Goon and they began to roar with laughter. He looked at them bewildered and a lightning shock of pain crossed his face because it was his own precious little creature, this beautiful baby poem, and they weren't listening. What he got was 'Oh, Spike! Ha, ha, ha.' He read on and gradually they stopped laughing as they realised it wasn't funny, by which time they'd lost the point of the poem, so he finished by folding it up and putting it back in his pocket. I thought 'God! we get things wrong when we get them wrong.' We hadn't briefed him properly and the audience hadn't been told. All it would have taken would have been for one of us to have said to them, 'You know Spike as a Goon but this is his serious side.' There are so many links we're missing in this world, great gaps, where if we could have just two sentences how life would have flowed on. After that I loved him dearly but sort of from afar. Each time I met him I came to know him better.

NORMA: I asked Joanna did she remember when he sent her a telegram saying 'Please will you marry me?'

JOANNA: It was enchanting. But once he sent me a telegram asking 'Where were you when I needed you?' I was absolutely terrified and I rang him. I think it was probably a mental health charity which I hadn't been able to go to, but I rang and asked him what had gone wrong? What had happened? The urgency of the telegram made me think that something drastic had happened but all it was, I hadn't been there. He would have liked me to be there. That's all. It absolutely threw me. For a day I was beside myself with anxiety. He needed me. I don't think he did but he felt he did.

I remember a day about twenty-five years ago when I attended a meeting with Spike about mental health and schizophrenia at Syon Park. In those days those things weren't really discussed openly for fear of some stigma attaching itself to you like a limpet mine and then you would be branded for life. One could never come out as gay or lesbian either: you had to keep everything locked up because otherwise the Press would brand you forever mad or sad or dangerous. So he was very brave to do that.

I can remember that odd day when everybody in their seven layers of skin were down to about four. For Spike, it was very daring and very frightening, actually, to be with a lot of people and although on good form that day, it wasn't a favourite thing for Spike to do. He was managing it but in a most scowly, rodacious way, quite scrimpleshanks about it all, being there and resenting it. That was quite an extraordinary day. But because I loved him I knew I could sit quite near him and prop him up if he began to growl or grumble. I could fill in and steer him around a little, just say something that would stop him being quite so troubled by people. If people didn't say exactly what he hoped they'd say he could be quite furious. He predicted how he hoped it would go and if suddenly somebody came up and said 'Oh, Spike, sign here please' sometimes he'd do it and sometimes he'd walk away – you could never tell. That's the only thing you could be certain of – that you couldn't be certain what the hell was going to happen. But having said that, I think he was constant. You know, he had a sort of constancy about him.

NORMA: Joanna looked around my office and glanced at the many photographs on my sideboard. There was a sad smile on her face as she started to reminisce about her days when she had stood in for a fortnight on *Wogan*.

JOANNA: I think probably Terry had gone off to the Algarve to play 143 rounds of golf. It was the last night of my stint and I'd gone to the studios quite early. I had done all my research because I'd had a heavy bunch on the night before. I knew Spike and Harry Secombe were on the show and Spike was promoting a book he had written on the Goons.

I got there and Harry came straight to my dressing room. I knew him, only in the way I know everybody, Norma, because I'm so old

I've been banging around the skirting boards for so long. I'd met Harry a hundred times, he's the sweetest man on earth. But Harry was the bearer of bad tidings – Spike was not on good form. He was not contactable, he had locked himself in his dressing room. He had decided to go on the show in a wheelchair and had demanded one the moment he had walked into his dressing room. I was slightly bemused by the news, and asked Harry how it would work, where would he sit. Harry, as usual always the calming influence, assured me that we would get through it. 'We will ride it along, rely on me. We can always tell a few funny stories.' I decided to go to Spike's dressing room and knocked on his door. 'Spike! it's me, Joanna. I've brought you some felt pens.' The door opened and I saw that as well as wine he had a supply of anti-depressants on his dressing table. He was not in good shape.

'You never give me your phone number,' he complained. I gave him the number and the large black felt pens I knew he liked. He took the pens and wrote my number on the dressing room wall, in his inimitable large black flourish style. I was absolutely amazed and I bent over to give him a kiss. 'That's it, see you soon – all my love.' I thought possibly I'd got through to him. He rose from his chair to give me a hug. 'Don't get up, Spike, see you later.' I thought he had calmed down. Big mistake. The show started and first on 'Special guest stars Spike Milligan and Harry Secombe.' Spike had been wheeled from his dressing room and kept waiting in the corridor, something you could never do when he was ready to 'go on'. His adrenalin was high and if they weren't ready when they said they were ready – he would walk. He came on looking really malevolent and Harry started his usual machine-gun delivery of jokes.

I knew we were in for a difficult time. Spike was in a mood and didn't give a fuck about the book he was supposed to publicise. And then suddenly out of the corner of my eye I saw a young man with a paper bag which he was carrying like there was something special in it. He dodged up behind the cameraman and he began to walk across the stage towards us with his hand in the paper bag and I thought, 'Oh my God, he could have a gun in there or some acid spray or something like that. And I could see it in slow motion, the cameras were turning, a floor manager began to move towards us far too late. The man had walked up from the audience, no security at all, he just walked on stage and now suddenly he's in front of the camera with this thing. He said, 'I-I-I just' and I said, 'Hello, how can we help' or some stupid remark like that. Spike suddenly snapped out of his reverie and this boy pulled out a T-shirt saying Save the Planet or something like that.

Suddenly Spike was animated. 'This is a lot more important than the fucking book,' but the boy was bundled off the set and dragged into the stalls.

'Bring him back,' demanded Spike. 'I want to talk to him,' and then to me, 'I don't want to talk to you.'

Harry had managed to calm the situation to a certain degree, trying to make the situation look like a set-up. Spike was awful, just awful. I burst into tears: it was the shock of thinking Spike or Harry might have been killed by this madman and Spike being so awfully frightening. I was frightened of him, you know, he wouldn't look at me and he wouldn't look at Harry. He just wouldn't play ball.

Immediately the show finished Spike had left the set and gone, apparently not speaking to anyone. However, the next day he sent me a huge bouquet of flowers accompanied by a note – 'I love you – I love you – I love you.' He knew he had behaved badly and something had gone appallingly wrong.

But I was frightened because there was no way of reaching that human being at all, there was no way anybody could get to him.

NORMA: Joanna had been commissioned by the Imperial War Museum to write a book on 'Forces Sweethearts', the theme was love and romance in times of war. There was to be a launch to which Spike had been invited. He was always at the top of the list of invitations from the Imperial War Museum because of his war memoirs and his interest in the army and Joanna wanted him to be at the launch, but as soon as she saw him she knew it wasn't a good day.

JOANNA: I could see by his posture, his eyes, everything about him – the agony. I looked at him and thought you didn't have to come out when you are suffering. I love you so much but go away, you are going to be pestered with 'Oh, Spike, you are so funny, you are my favourite person, can I have your autograph?' – you can't stop them.

NORMA: I reminded her of the time – same mood, different venue – when someone came up to him and said, 'Spike, can you do an Eccles?' His remark startled the fan: 'No, I fucking can't.' Joanna gave a roar of laughter. Quite rapidly her mood changed.

JOANNA: I remember an occasion towards the end of Spike's life. I'd gone with Stephen [her husband, Stephen Barlow, an internationally known conductor] to visit my parents who lived near Spike. We decided to call to see him for a cup of tea. By this time he was frailty frail. He came into the room and was so pleased to see Stephen was with me. He loved the idea that Stephen was a musician and he wanted to play a piece of music for him. The piano was completely out of tune, and it broke my heart, but he didn't mind, he just wanted to go on playing for Stephen. And then he sat there full of wistfulness, longings and beauty, with an air of childhood and memories of India, back to his dog. That dog was haunting him – his boxer.

After we left, Stephen told me Spike was a good musician with an instinctive musical flair. He would have loved that.

My father had read all of Spike's war memoirs and had said they were an extremely perspicacious account of the war seen through the eyes of a soldier in the ranks. Spike had a way of getting into people's lives because there was a darker strand attached to all those people in the war. Today's comics often are off-the-wall. We haven't really had any conflict; we bounce along unless somebody has done something like lurch back from some terrible drugs situation or depression or something. Most people have lived pretty well. Maybe their careers have gone up and down a bit but there is something about chaps who were in the war. They have been in intense situations that put quite a different spin on life as well as the quality and dimension of their humour, tragedy, whatever. That brings out a quality and perception that is denied to us younger ones.

NORMA: Joanna looked at a picture of Spike on my office wall. It was taken by Lord Snowdon in 1972 at the rehearsal of *The Last Goon Show of All.*

JOANNA: It's wonderful – such a sweety, sweety face.

NORMA: I asked her, Do you know what he's written on it?

JOANNA: No.

NORMA: 'Pissed again. Love to Norma.'

JOANNA: It's a beautiful picture – great melancholy and humour all rolled into one. I remember when my aunt went to see *Son of Oblomov* with her son, both being great *Goon Show* fans. She sat in the front row and Milligan – who was so jolly attractive and my aunt was jolly attractive; she was one of the raging beauties, and like him, was ridiculously young and thin – directed quite a lot of the show at her. He leaned over from the stage with those blazing blue eyes and said, 'I'll see you later in my dressing room.' She asked her son, 'Do you think I should? He seemed to be looking straight at me. I think I'm going to go.' I do hope she did.

    Many, many years later I invited my aunt to attend the 'Forces Sweethearts' book launch at the Imperial War Museum and as soon as she saw Spike she wanted to go over to him to remind him of the night of *Son of Oblomov.* I knew this was the wrong moment and said, 'Aunt, please don't do that because it's not going to work today, he won't know what you are talking about, today he is just managing to walk upright and be here.' I'd heard him telling several people to fuck off. It was ghastly, sweetheart, and I didn't want her to be hurt. She thought he was the bee's knees.

NORMA: I told her Spike liked the company of women and it was strange how he did like to look after them but it didn't fit in with his persona. She disagreed with me.

JOANNA: He was an incredibly old-fashioned gentleman, one of the most distinguished-looking people you could meet, in the mould of George Martin, lean, elegant and rangy like a kind of wolf. [Earlier she had been looking at a photograph of George I have on my sideboard, young and handsome, conducting the Hollywood Bowl Symphony Orchestra.] But I think it does fit in with his persona. He had bipolar – you know, the two poles pulling him in opposite directions. The one side which is extraordinary, nostalgic, almost sentimental, beautifully behaved, tender, inventing fairy stories, writing poems about his boxer dog, and then the other a raving maniac with bad manners and cruel with it. Just insane, that kind of swing pulling away inside him.

NORMA: But she loved him because of his love of animals and that was a very strong bond between them because she also had a great love for animals.

JOANNA: I remember writing a column for *The Times* newspaper about a city farm in North London, where I wrote that Spike was the last of our free range spirits. It was called College Farm, just north of Golders Green. I had been asked to attend an open day and when I arrived Spike had turned up out of the blue. He just loved the idea that children could go to the farm for a day and see the animals in their natural habitat and be close to them. Here was this famous man, and he had somehow got himself up there, no palaver. He would have shamed Elizabeth the First, he was going around shouting, 'Buy the raffle tickets, help the farm' and talking to people. He was on very good form that day, so he could cope with it. He was just the sunny saint, the king of free range spirits because nothing and no one could tie him down. If he wanted to support Animal Welfare he would just go and do it, he didn't have to see if it was an OK cause or wonder if there would be enough people there or who was going to be on the committee. None of that seemed to matter. That was one of my happiest memories of him.

One thing I did admire about Spike, he wasn't afraid of people. I think that quite a lot of people, as they become famous, grow afraid.

Many people say to me, what if people talk to you, and I say, what do you mean, of course they talk to me, I'm on their television sets. I go back home on the Tube and people talk to me as if they know me. The greatest compliment in the world is people treating me as a friend, what could be nicer. So many people put on dark glasses, run into hotels – well, that's their life and that's fine, but that's not mine, and it wasn't his.

NORMA: Joanna wondered had I heard any news about the proposed memorial statue of Spike to be erected in Finchley. She had become a patron and, typical Joanna, had organised a fundraising dinner and sent them a cheque for a thousand pounds. She had seen the plans and although she thought the sculptor had taken such care, she thought it should include something Irish.

JOANNA: He was so proud of his Irishness. I thought how like Spike – getting involved.

NORMA: As she was leaving she looked at another photograph on my sideboard – there are so many of them – it is of Spike and Eric Sykes with their arms round each other. I told her Spike and Eric had shared the same office for fifty years.

JOANNA: Isn't that extraordinary. That doesn't happen now, it isn't required to happen, nobody wants it to happen.

NORMA: She looked quite wistful, I didn't want to end her memories on such a sad note so I asked her: did she have a favourite Spike story? It was wonderful – pure Spike and pure Joanna.

JOANNA: Oh God, I wish I had a favourite story. Oh yes, a journalist once told me Spike had been asked what would be his dying wish and he said, 'A full moon and Joanna Lumley.' [We both laughed. She thought for a while.] Oh, with a compliment like that I might get it tattooed on my heart.

ALAN J. W. BELL

Alan J. W. Bell is a BBC producer and director with more hits to his name than perhaps any of his contemporaries – *Last of the Summer Wine, The Hitchhiker's Guide to the Galaxy, There's a Lot of It About,* Ronnie Barker's film *By the Sea, The Hello Goodbye Man, Dogfood Dan and the Carmarthen Cowboy* and so it goes on. Hit after hit.

Alan directed Spike's shows on many occasions. But when Alan talks about Spike, I sometimes wonder who he is talking about. It's certainly not the Spike I know but that is how Alan perceived him. I've reflected on this many times because Alan produced and directed Spike in *There's a Lot of It About* and I remember mini-tantrums, but Alan can't recall them.

Alan was gentle, I never heard him raise his voice, and if he had to tell Spike that a part of the script wasn't working, he did it in such a way that Spike listened and they would start again. The first time I witnessed this I was amazed – no histrionics. He wasn't being sycophantic, just quietly pointing out what was best for Spike and trying to give him all that he wanted. This was such a change from Ian MacNaughton, the highly volatile, multi-talented producer/ director of the *Q* series. If you can believe this, Ian had a shorter fuse than Spike so the change to Alan was dramatic. It was like the calm following a hurricane.

————————

ALAN: I first met Spike when I was a production manager – they call it assistant producer nowadays – in a rehearsal room way out at Riverside Studios The rehearsals were so much fun because he was enjoying it. He loved to work. He was one of those people who never looked at his watch to see if it was time to go home. On the contrary, he wanted to have as much fun as he could get. We moved to the studio where we were showing a clip from a very old film with the actors singing 'Goodnight, Vienna'. Spike was supposed to accompany this on his trumpet but he found it difficult because of the playback sound. I told him not to worry, I would conduct him because I could hear the track. It wasn't easy for him. He didn't say – as some might – 'My God! Stop everything! We must get this right.' No. He wanted it to be realistic – human. That's what mattered to Spike. And to me. I never had any trouble with him. I remember watching other people deal with Spike and I thought how wrong they were. They wore the face of the BBC. Spike used to say 'The BBC is there to stop me from enjoying myself.' He called those people 'suits'. They were always doing the wrong thing. Fuss, fuss, fuss. He didn't like that.

NORMA: Later on you worked once more with Spike on the Q series.

ALAN: I think it was the last in the series. Now, my predecessors had experienced what was described as 'a bumpy ride' but I remember the wonderful Ian MacNaughton. He was one of the great producers – a legend in the BBC – but just as mad as Spike, zany but brilliant. Somehow he managed to keep Spike under control without stopping the flowering of his brilliance. Result! Success. I'd always enjoyed working with Spike so to me this was a great challenge.

I remember one evening when we were filming by the river at Thetford, not far from a hotel. It had been one of those sweltering days and the evening was very hot and sticky. When we'd finished, about midnight, Spike said, 'Let's all go for a swim.' Someone pointed out that we didn't have any costumes. Spike said, 'Don't worry about that. We don't need costumes.' He stripped off and so did everybody else and plunged into the river. We were all laughing and splashing about when I saw a blue flashing light come along the towpath. A policeman gets out of the car. People were using their hands to cover themselves. Trouble, I thought and said to him, 'It's such a hot night.'

'Swim in the river in the buff if you like,' he said, 'but don't make such a row. You're waking up the guests at the hotel. Now just move round the bend.' And with that off he went. But he'd made sure that all the fun had gone out of skinny-dipping. But the whole idea of skinny-dipping had been fun to Spike. That was typical of him. If it's fun, do it. I remember he said something to Huw Wheldon who was doing a portrait of Spike in a *Monitor* programme that I thought was profound and summed up the way he saw life. 'I think when you stop being childish,' he said to Huw, 'you stop enjoying life because a child enjoys life more than anybody else. Everything is so new and exciting.' When I spoke to him about it he didn't remember saying it but what he did say was that people accused him of being childish and he took that as praise rather than criticism. Now, to be with Spike and get a glimpse of life as he saw it could be equally exciting. Working with him was a wonderful experience for me. The only problem I had was that I went home at night with sore ribs from laughing. It wasn't only what he said to camera but behind the camera. He used to say, 'To think we get paid for doing this.' He was such a funny man.

NORMA: Well, you seemed to get his good side, most likely because he got on with you.

ALAN: I think Spike respected people who understood him and his humour, who didn't laugh because it was Spike Milligan who had said something. I believe he could tell when people were laughing to humour him. I never appeased him or laughed when I didn't think what he had said was funny but, having said that, most of the time I did laugh. However, there were some sycophants who laughed at anything he said and I felt they were driving him up the wrong path. If I didn't think something was funny I would say, 'That's very funny but I think we can find something funnier.' He would tear up the script and start all over again. I can honestly say that I never appeased him. I believe that was the best way to work with him. You do a disservice to everyone if you don't tell the truth.

NORMA: Did you know about his girlfriends?

ALAN: Not really. I knew that he had girlfriends. I saw the documentary about him which mentioned them but they never got involved in our working relationship. You see, Spike liked people and I think he would obviously like girls more than he would men, but I took the view that what went on in his private life was up to him.

NORMA: Did you ever have any problems because of his mental illness?

ALAN: I remember one day when a black mood came over him but apart from that never. Everyone gets bad days and the weight was on him. As I've told you I took over the series after it had experienced a bumpy ride. At the time I was doing *Summer Wine* and Bill Owen asked if he could come to the studio to watch Spike at work. Now what we did at that time was to rehearse a scene with Spike and then record it. Afterwards, when we had put all the scenes together, the finished article would be shown to a studio audience and their response recorded. Bill sat at the back and when we had finished he said, 'I know I shouldn't say this but you're doing it all wrong. Spike and an audience fuse together. Once you cut out the audience you've only got half of Spike Milligan.' I think he was right, as painful as it might have been. I think we lost a bit of Spike's sparkle because of the way we did it.

NORMA: How did the Q series finally come to an end?

ALAN: We had started to plan the next series of Q after the BBC bought Elstree Studios. Elstree was so spacious that we felt we would be able to do all sorts of things, then when we were geared up to go ahead we got a call from the head of comedy to say that the controller didn't want another series. Now dare I say it but this followed sketches where Spike had gay or suicidal controllers jumping off the roof of Broadcasting House. And another sketch I had directed ruffled feathers because someone decided it was racist. The thought never entered my mind when we were doing it. A very proper BBC announcer said,

'And now we're going over to the Albert Hall for a concert by Mrs Lily –' I've forgotten the surname we used – and there was Spike, looking like a Jewish lady playing dad a de dum da, the Warsaw Concerto, I believe – and as the camera pulled back you could see she was playing a cash till. I didn't think there was anything wrong because Spike had a go at everybody but there were letters saying we should never have shown it. Then the chairman of the board of governors wrote a letter of complaint to the head of department and the scene was cut out of repeats.

NORMA: Do you think Spike was racist?

ALAN: It never crossed my mind that he was. I think most people saw that Albert Hall scene for what it was – satire. I think people should be free to say what they want to say. If you look at what he did he was saying how absurd life is. He did a sketch about cashpoint machines and a policeman who is watching then takes out some money, an abuse of his position. Another thing I can't stand is what happens when a celebrity comes on to a talk shows – all that whoop whoop nonsense. They're encouraged to do it like trained chimpanzees.

NORMA: Did you ever meet any well-known people who were apprehensive about meeting Spike?

ALAN: We had Billy Connolly as a guest to do a voiceover. He was a great Spike fan but he was apprehensive of him. I think it was because of Spike's reputation, you know, that he would do wild things. He didn't have that seventh skin that we all have that stops us from saying something. Now, with Spike he knew what he wanted to say and damn it, if people didn't like it, too bad. I believe people should be free to say what they want to say.

NORMA: John Fisher [a well-known television producer and writer] said that in a hundred years' time we won't be watching Spike but people would still be reading him.

ALAN: I think that's right. He has a place in literature. And his drawings are fun. They're on greetings cards now.

NORMA: What was he like to work with?

ALAN: In my dealings with him I found he didn't want to be adult and sensible about things. I know this sounds strange but I found him to be extremely professional in an unprofessional sort of way. He would go to enormous lengths to make sure he got the most out of a scene. He knew the disciplines of television and because it's expensive he always turned up on time. One day I came a cropper when we were filming a boxing scene. David Renwick had written the script but Spike changed it out of all recognition. I apologised to David but he told me not to worry because it was now much more Spike. In the scene his opponent was a Jehovah's Witness who wouldn't fight back. I asked him to give me an outline of what he was going to do but he actually did the whole business there and then. It was hilarious and all the technicians were laughing. At the end he turned to me and asked, 'Did you get all that?' He looked whacked. Now, I knew we could be on dangerous ground but I said, 'No, Spike. I asked you to show me what you were going to do.' He gave me a long look and then without as much as a protest did the whole thing again so we could film it. What's more it was just as funny, though he was drained by the end of it. That's what I mean about being professional, though we did have problems. He would arrive on a Monday at the rehearsal room and go through the script. He always got a lot of laughs. Tuesday, the actors would do it again, still very funny. By Wednesday everybody has heard it so there were fewer laughs. By Thursday Spike was saying, 'I've got to take that out. It's not getting any laughs.' No, I would tell him. Everybody has seen and heard it in rehearsals. Then the technicians would come along for their rehearsal because they had to decide where to put the lights and the cameramen came to position themselves to get the best shots and the designers to make sure the sets were big enough. They were all familiar with the show by then but if they didn't laugh Spike thought it was doomed. I used to tell him that they were concentrating on what they had to do and weren't really listening to what he said. No, he would protest, they're not laughing and they should be. So then he would cut bits out and write new bits in. He just wanted to make people laugh. He needed the sound of laughter.

NORMA: People have said that he was a selfish actor.

ALAN: I never witnessed that. On the contrary, I found him to be generous and supportive of new actors and willing, no, determined, to work as long as necessary to get things right. I couldn't stand anyone on the set looking at their watch because it was knocking-off time.

NORMA: That's probably why you got on with him.

ALAN: I think we both believed in working until we got it right. I loved to work with him. He was so professional. That's what's lacking in the BBC now. Senior executives make the decisions. We haven't got the people with showbusiness experience. Bill Cotton had it oozing out of him and so did Michael Grade. They knew what the public wanted to see, what would entertain them. Now you find that someone who is working in a department totally alien to showbusiness becomes the head of entertainment and makes the decisions about what the public are going to see. I think that's very sad. Spike would hate the way things are today and he would hate those executives making those decisions – and he'd let them know it.

Spike's dedication and determination to get things right was very impressive. [He laughed.] Let me give you an example. He was doing a sketch where he played the part of a suppository tester and one of his lines was that it started at the bottom and stayed there. There was a pause in the recording so we could connect the water to the tap behind his back. While this was being done he said, 'I expect it'll be the ice cold water as always.' Now before we recorded again the effects guy turned up the heat, not maliciously, just trying to be helpful, but it came out of the shower steaming hot. I could see the look in Spike's eye and the effects man went 'Oh God!'

Spike didn't know whether to stop the recording or not but he knew if he did it would take half an hour to dry the costumes off so he carried on until the end. Then he screamed and all the bitterness came out – 'You bastard' . . . this and that. I said, 'If you'd kept your mouth shut you'd have had the ordinary water temperature.' He didn't say a word though I knew there could have been an explosion, but he'd brought it on himself. When we'd finished for the day I said to him, 'Are you still taking me to dinner tonight?' He looked at me – you know that expression of his – then smiled and said, 'Of course.'

On another occasion he was playing Long John Silver leaning on his crutch. In a cabinet, which was in shot, was an artificial leg. He had to point with the crutch and say, 'I used to have one of those.' In the sketch, because he was pointing with the crutch and had no support he had to fall over – on to a mattress that was out of shot. Every take we did he put out his hand to break the fall far too soon and it was in shot. I said, 'Spike, it isn't working. It'll be funny only if you fall on to the mattress without putting out your hand to break your fall. You've got to point to the cabinet with your crutch and then fall over – without putting your hand out. Right?' He said, 'There's a problem. I know what to do but this crutch is about a foot too short.' It wasn't but I didn't argue. 'Let's try it again,' I said to everyone. This time he didn't put out his hand. But this time neither did the props man put the mattress in place to break his fall. Spike bounced on the floor, right on his shoulder. He leapt up and shouted into the lens, 'You're a fucking sadist! I'm off. I'm going home,' and shot off to his dressing room. I waited a few minutes and then went in to see him. 'Look, Spike,' I said, 'these things happen. The guy didn't know we were going to shoot it and that's why the mattress wasn't in place.' There was a pause and he said, 'Oh, all right. Give me a few minutes. It's aching a bit. I won't go home. I'll just rest it and then I'll be back.' 'Great,' I said, and patted him on the shoulder – the one he'd fallen on. He screamed, 'You are a fucking sadist!' But he came back and we did the shot. That was how it was with Spike, so don't tell me he wasn't professional. I learned a lot from Ian MacNaughton. He got on very well with Spike.

NORMA: He was wonderful, just wonderful.

ALAN: They were both on the same wavelength.

NORMA: Did you know Spike's pet name for Ian?

ALAN: No. What was it?

NORMA: Rage. 'Is Rage here?' Spike used to ask. Then, 'Rage. He's always bloody late, raging around somewhere, and he loses his temper. He's unbelievable. I don't understand him.' 'Well, you should,' I said. 'There's a pair of you.' [Ian MacNaughton died after a car accident when a car going the wrong way crashed into him on the autobahn.]

ALAN: Ian was an eccentric; there's no doubt about that.

NORMA: Spike told me that John Cleese and the boys got Ian to produce and direct *Monty Python's Flying Circus* because he was sufficiently eccentric to have worked with him.

ALAN: Well, you needed someone who understood what Spike was trying to do and Ian certainly did. A director has to have simpatico with his performers and the boys no doubt thought that if he had that with Spike he was the man for them. If you don't capture what the performers want to do the instant they do it you've lost it forever.

NORMA: Do you think Spike was such an influence on Python?

ALAN: Totally. I've heard the boys say so. He had an enormous influence on them and Michael Palin has said as much. Spike went beyond the natural confines of the envelope, far beyond. He wanted people to say, 'Hey, this is not the usual television format.' Take the Goons, incidentally, before my time. I've listened to them recently and there's no doubt he broke the mould with that amazing radio series. It was revolutionary, not just the funny voices but amazing characters doing wild things never done before on radio. It was complete imagination run riot. Now people have said that the *Q* series was television's version of *The Goon Show* but I don't agree. *Q* was much more of a sketch show and the Goons were never that because they had continuous stories. I don't think Spike's ever done anything, with the possible exception of appearances in drama, where he wasn't in total control. Nobody ever said to him, 'Sit there and do what I tell you.' That would have made him dull and he had too much going for him for that. I admired him greatly for what he was. Totally an original. A complex man and a generous one. He told me once about the time he paid for Ronnie Scott [of Jazz Club fame] to go into hospital [to be dried out]. It was the Waterford treatment, whatever that was. I think it was for booze. Spike said Ronnie told him he was skint and couldn't afford it, so Spike told him not to worry, he would pay. He admired Ronnie so much, because of what he had done for jazz, and he was a regular at his Jazz Club in Frith Street. Spike told me that this treatment consisted of being put into a dark room to be floated on water until the patient reached a tranquil state. I said, 'You should go. Not him.' That didn't go down very well. And that wasn't the end of it. The man who couldn't afford the treatment went on holiday to the Bahamas or Bermuda when he came out of the nursing home. He couldn't understand that.

NORMA: You might have thought he would learn a lesson from that, but no. Some time later, because Ronnie also had a drug problem, he was admitted to a very expensive nursing home. Spike told me to pay all the bills. I said it could run into thousands. After five weeks it had and I tackled Spike about it. 'Don't tell me how much. I'm not interested. He's my friend. Just pay it.' Two weeks later more bills arrived. Again I confronted him. 'I don't mind signing the cheques but it's your money and I think you should know he's ordering booze on your account and eighty bloody Benson and Hedges a day.' He shrugged. 'What can you do?' he said. 'He smokes.'

ALAN: He was a very generous man, a compassionate man. Save the Earth and all that. And wonderful company. I didn't see so much of him when he moved from Hadley Common to Rye. I think that was perhaps the biggest mistake he ever made. I'd ask him if he fancied dinner at the Trattoo and he'd jump at the chance, get into his Mini and drive two and a half hours to London. That was how much he missed his friends and London Town. What a mistake to move down there! He made himself a prisoner.

NORMA: He was a real London man but his wife [the third one] wanted to live on the south coast to be near her family. She told him that his friends would visit but very few did. Eric [Sykes] went once and said, 'It's a bloody camel ride.'

ALAN: I went there once to see him to make a DVD of his work. We called it very simply 'Spike' and it sold very well. He'd had a few operations by then and when we were recording it I asked him if he could be a little brighter. He said, 'I've got more cuts on me than Spaghetti Junction.' I wrote a draft script and said to him that he could make alterations or re-write it if it wasn't what he wanted. He said, 'No, we'll do it the way you've written it.' Now there was a surprise. I couldn't believe it. He made one alteration. He changed the name of the butler so he could say, 'All right, Piles.' He wasn't the Spike I'd known but I suppose, living down there, he lacked stimulation from the sort of people he'd worked with. Anyway, the DVD was successful and I managed to get the BBC to repeat it. It was called *Q, the final series – There's a Lot of It About*. It was a compilation of all the funniest bits from the series – very successful and people loved it. It was a very sad day when *Q* was knocked on the head for no apparent reason. It had a huge audience but whoever was in charge at the time didn't like it. I went to John Howard Davies about it but he said, 'If the controller doesn't want it, that's it.' Spike was devastated. I knew there was a huge audience out there for Spike.

NORMA: Later I sent a script to Gareth Gwenlan (at that time head of comedy at the BBC) that Spike and Eric had done about two old comics who meet and tell lies about how successful they are, with marvellous receptions in Blackpool and other top spots. Spike said that they were actually having such a bad time that they hadn't got their arses out of their trousers, they had their arses out of somebody else's trousers. It was a very funny script, as it would be from two of the finest writers in the business – and wouldn't they have been marvellous in those roles. Gareth read it and rang me to say it was the funniest thing he had read in a long, long time and he would get right back to me. When he did his voice was down and I could tell he was upset. He said, 'I don't know what to say to you. I'm having great difficulty in convincing the BBC that anyone over forty can be funny.'

What will be your lasting memory of Spike?

ALAN: He called me one morning out of the blue, and said I've just made up a joke, do you want to hear it? It's about an Irishman who goes to a talent competition. He's got this sledgehammer and he goes up on stage, and says to the man, get someone from the audience to come up here, I want him to hit me over the head with this sledgehammer. The man said, I can't do it. Of course you can. So the man hits him over the head with the hammer. He's taken to hospital, and is unconscious for about two months. When he comes round he says: 'De dah!'

That's real Milligan. Of all the people in comedy I have worked with over the years, he is the only one I can say he was a genius. It was the highlight of my working life being with him. He had a great texture to life.

DICK DOUGLAS-BOYD

Doug Dickless-Boyd – Spike got away with murder and Dick allowed him to, and knowing Spike as I did, it was sheer devilment. It was back to the old BBC days when he named one of his *Goon Show* characters Hugh Jampton, and Peter and Harry waited with controlled laughter for 'The Suits" reaction to the script. There wasn't one. Spike got away with it and nearly twenty-odd years later he was at it again with Dick Douglas-Boyd. But there was one big difference – there was mutual affection between Spike and Dick. I don't think anyone could say that with 'The Suits' at the BBC and Spike.

Dick was marketing director at Michael Joseph and Spike's dear friend and long-term editor, Jack Hobbs, introduced them after Spike had written the first volume of his war memoirs, *Adolf Hitler: My Part in His Downfall*, and was looking for a publisher.

The year was 1970. Michael Joseph did publish the book and Dick and Spike remained friends until Spike's death. In 1987 when *The Looney* was published, Spike's dedication was:

'I wish to dedicate this book to Paul Getty Jnr for helping support some of my causes, also to Jack Hobbs for his friendship and to Dick Douglas-Boyd for letting me call him Doug Dickless-Boyd.'

———————

DICK: My first contact with Spike was over the telephone. I was in my office when the phone rang. 'Hello, I'm Spike Milligan. Have you heard of me?' I was so taken aback I just said, 'Yes.' Spike told me he had written a book about his wartime experiences and, as a publisher, was I interested to read it. Of course I was and asked Spike to send me the manuscript in a taxi and I would read it. Spike told me Jack Hobbs had recommended Michael Joseph as a good publisher and I remember Spike said, 'You're a good publisher big-time and I want to be in the big time.'

The manuscript arrived and I took it immediately to Raleigh Trevelyan who is a very, very cultured, literate editorial director. He took it home that evening and phoned me the next morning and said he hadn't slept all night. We will publish it.

The next time we met at Orme Court. And there I met the redoubtable Norma who introduced me to Spike in his office. He was very amiable, asked me about myself, particularly what I'd done in the war, and I think that made a friendship because no one in Michael Joseph, apart from Raleigh Trevelyan, had served in the war. I'd flown and he called me Pilot Boyd. I got a Christmas card he sent me saying 'Pilot Boyd', with a 650-pound bomb dropping on Gunner Milligan who is saying, 'My God, he thinks I'm the Tirpitz.' That formed a personal connection with Spike. Sometimes in publishing you have to be a bit tougher and other times you can relax, and we got it right, I think, on the whole, but sometimes it was tough.

NORMA: The next meeting was at 52 Bedford Square, Michael Joseph's offices. He was going to introduce Spike to everyone.

DICK: We went to meet Raleigh, and when Spike looked in the office he said, 'Fucking hell! There's a whole load of vandals here. Look what you've done to this beautiful old building. Look at all these wires all the way up the stairs.' He was quite right but that was Spike and he made his point. That was his first visit and it seems to me that Spike's humour was mainly for me, for overgrown schoolboys like me.

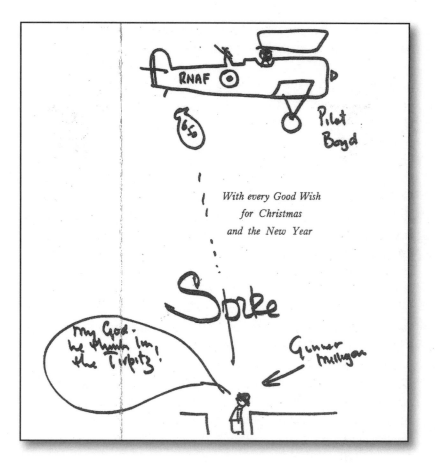

NORMA: I wondered what was the connection with preserving an old building and humour . . .

DICK: I don't think women understood Spike's humour and every time a new manuscript came into Michael Joseph a phone call would come down from the women editors saying they'd got a new manuscript from Spike and would I look at it because they didn't think it was funny. And I would ask, 'Is it the same as the last one?' It was. 'We'll publish it then because it will be funny.' Spike had already guessed what the women would think. He used to say, 'Don't let the vestal virgins read it: they are all devoid of humour.' And he wasn't wrong.

Most people at Michael Joseph were apprehensive of Spike, and they didn't like him particularly but they didn't understand him, with one or two exceptions. Alan Samson, for example, was one of them, he was a very good masculine chap.

All those signing sessions. Someone said that at other people's signing sessions you saw the queues diminishing. With Spike's, they got longer and longer as the time went on. When people saw who it was the queues got longer. I remember in Hatchards, a very distinguished bookseller's, Spike was sitting there signing all these books. Some of those waiting were men in their bowler hats (still worn in those days) and one rather prissy man came in and asked could it be signed for his Aunt Jemima. Spike said yes and was very polite to him and the man was smiling and beaming, then Spike stood up and shouted, 'Now get out.' The man didn't know how to take it, but this was his usual joke. The manager grinned, it was always pantomime with Spike whatever he was doing. He always made it fun. He always made an individual signature and chatted to everyone individually.

Then there were the launch parties. Publishers are always dubious about them because they thought they could get publicity in better ways, but authors liked them so we gave launch parties for the best authors. Spike, being one of them, would turn up and just talk to the old boys from the wartime years, but sitting in a corner there was no possibility of publicity. So the next time that a book launch was suggested, I had to fight for it. 'Spike wants a party, let him have a party, what the hell.'

The best one was my final party when Spike came along with a bottle of '22 Malmsey, which was my birth year, '22. That was Spike at his very best.

There were other difficulties in deciding on print numbers. When it came to the Q series the BBC found them politically incorrect and dropped the series, so book sales were declining and it was touch and go whether they should publish that many. Dick tried explaining to Spike who didn't really want to know and in the end wrote Dick a letter.

NORMA: But there was one party at Michael Joseph to which Spike had been invited which Dick remembers with embarrassment.

DICK: I saw Spike standing up against the wall looking at this painting. Edmund Fisher, the managing director at this time, had bought it at auction, a beautiful painting, and he'd paid a lot of money for it. Spike went up and signed his name right across the bottom in ink. Everybody was dumbfounded. It cost Edmund Fisher about two or three thousand pounds to have Spike's name wiped out, but he never complained about it. I told him in my opinion that was vandalism, and Spike should have been made to pay for it. That's one of the bad things about Spike, there was no excuse for it. Spike thought it was funny. I think it was because he didn't like Edmund Fisher.

NORMA: I disagreed with Dick about his dislike of Edmund Fisher, I just knew he was very, very fond of Raleigh Trevelyan.

DICK: I think he must have heard, probably from me, the atrocious way that Edmund Fisher got rid of Raleigh Trevelyan.

NORMA: A nightmare came for Dick when Spike was going on tour with his one-man show to South Africa. Whilst he was out there he wanted to do signing sessions in each town he visited and Dick had to make sure there were books in each of the shops.

DICK: I got from you the full itinerary – I think it was eight one-man shows. So we got the books delivered to Johannesburg and about three days before he was due to leave I got a phone call from you saying, 'You're not going to believe this. He's cancelled the tour.' I had to explain the situation to the agents who had to junk the books. But we owed Spike loyalty as he'd shown us loyalty. He hadn't moved to another publisher. A lot of people, after they'd had one big book, move to another publisher and I know you tried to keep all his books in one stable.

NORMA: He shook his head, recalling the drama and, ironically after that, praised Jack for introducing them. Dick said it was thanks to Jack Hobbs that publishing Spike all came about.

DICK: I'd met Jack as a small publisher and I liked meeting small publishers because often they have authors who are just on the way up. Jack used to take me to this place with a piano. We had some lovely evenings together, and used to meet in a bookshop called Bob Chris just off Charing Cross Road. Bob Chris was a lovely secondhand bookseller's and the place was frequented by all sorts of interesting people. And when Bob Chris died he left me £50 in his will for five of his regulars to have a meal together. I was very touched by that gesture.

I wouldn't say this to anyone else but I think my career at Michael Joseph was helped by the fact that Spike stuck with me and always wanted to talk to me. It was very useful to me.

Every Christmas the top six sellers in the list were presented with a leatherbound volume of their current book. Other authors like Dick Francis, James Herriot and Stan Barstow used to treasure them and we thought we were doing something rather nice. Spike had received two leatherbound books and then the third one came along bound in purple leather and followed by a letter from Spike:

To: Dick Douglas Boyd Esq.,
Michael Joseph Limited   *2nd December, 1977*

Dear Dick,

 Thank you so much for the leatherbound copy of Puckoon. How did you know that the colour I hate most is purple – the divine inspirational.

 If I can have a choice in future, can I have black, or brown – or red to go with my bank balance.

 As ever,

 SPIKE MILLIGAN

I conjured up a letter saying I was sorry because the binding was made from baboon bums.

Dear Spike,

My favourite leather is black shiny. I am sorry that you dont't like
purple. It cost us a hell of a lot of money because the binding is
made entirely of baboon bums and it is hard to find one large enough
to fit round anything but a paperback.

Tell you what, if we have a good year next year you'll get black. If
we're in the red you'll get red. O.K?

Yours

Spike wrote back to say thank you but 'we're all going to be in the shit, so I suggest a brown cover.' I thought it was such fun.

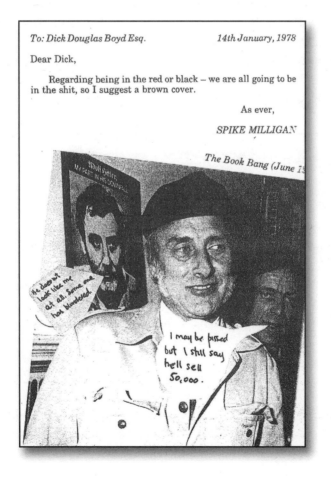

To: Dick Douglas Boyd Esq.   14th January, 1978

Dear Dick,

    Regarding being in the red or black – we are all going to be
in the shit, so I suggest a brown cover.

                        As ever,

                    SPIKE MILLIGAN

The Book Bang (June 1

NORMA: Dick told me the story of a disastrous dinner arrangement, and I wondered why he still continued to hold Spike in so much affection after that.

DICK: Spike had phoned and asked me to take him to dinner at the Berkeley Hotel, as a friend of his was playing piano there. I didn't know the restaurant, so I went along to see the maître d' to reserve the best table near the piano, ordering Spike's favourite wine, Gewürztraminer. Just as I was pouring myself a glass, starting to enjoy the atmosphere and pleased with myself that all the arrangements had fallen into place the maître d' appeared at the table. 'I'm sorry. Mr Milligan has left. Unfortunately he wanted to take some photographs in our foyer and it's strictly not allowed for anyone. We have to protect all the renowned people who come into our hotel, we have to say no to everyone whether it's Marlon Brando or whoever so he said, "I'm leaving. Would you tell Mr Douglas-Boyd he can join me at the Trattoo."' I was so embarrassed. Later Spike softened the blow by sending me a 'love letter'. That's part of the relationship really.

NORMA: Spike was a contradictory and complex man. I reminded Dick about the business with Jack Hobbs and royalties.

DICK: Yes, after about the third book we'd published, Spike suddenly said to me he thought that as his editor they ought to pay Jack Hobbs a royalty. Jack did very little. He helped trim his books and suggested movements of text. This placed me in a very difficult position – the book had been contracted. Then came Spike's usual emotional blackmail: 'Well, I think it's not very kind of you to leave Jack out of this,' and I pointed out, quite rightly, that the contract was for Spike to produce a book and for us to publish it and the terms had been agreed.

Spike remained firm, and it was down to me to persuade the directors to pay a royalty to Jack. They were very reluctant and I had a bad time. Eventually I won the day and Jack received a 2½% royalty, a lot of money. I told Spike it was for this book only and the next contract had to include Jack's royalty. Another two books later, to my utter amazement, Spike called me and said, 'What's all this. Why are you continuing to pay Jack Hobbs money from my book? I've written it, it's my book, and it's my money and you are giving my money to him.' I tried to remind him it was at his insistence that Jack got the money and a typical Spike reply, 'Well, stop it,' and so it was stopped.

NORMA: We remembered another tricky situation, this one in particular was Spike being disloyal, and Dick thought it was out of character. He was nearing the end of his time at Michael Joseph. He'd been with the company twenty-five years and was very reluctant to retire, when he heard via the grapevine Spike had written to M.J. saying he wanted to start his own publishing company, Monkenhurst Books, with his family, and he immediately phoned me to find out what the undercurrents were. I confirmed Spike's latest madcap impulsive disaster.

DICK: I couldn't believe it, because we'd had such a good relationship. We'd published everything he wanted us to do and we published them well. It would have been a big act of disloyalty, and I heard you had had a row with him about his bad behaviour and you had refused to get involved with Monkenhurst Books, so it all came to nothing. And then he wanted to come back to M.J. and you made him write a letter asking to come back. I was so surprised by the whole incident, and found it hard to believe.

NORMA: It wasn't the only time Dick witnessed Spike's bad behaviour.

DICK: June [Dick's wife] and myself had arranged a special outing to hear Johnny Dankworth who was playing at Kipling's House in Sussex. We invited a party of friends, which included Spike and his wife. June went to a lot of trouble preparing food for the picnic. When we met Spike at the venue, we could see he was in the middle of the black dog. We'd planned to go down to be as near to the band as possible, but half-way down to the spot Spike decided he didn't want to go any further, but wanted to sit under a hedge and listen to the music. The trouble was we were so far away, we couldn't hear anything. Judy, my daughter, commented that he was wearing the same sandals he once wore in a pantomime 'like wizard's boots' and he sat on the grass refusing any food or drink, looking thoroughly miserable. My family and friends were disamused.

NORMA: I asked why he thought people forgave him when he was behaving badly.

DICK: Two reasons why I forgave him. One, it was politic for me to do so because I was his publisher and secondly, because of the very many kindnesses he did. There was that other side when he couldn't have been kinder to me. Genuine kindness and thoughtfulness. He dedicated his book *The Looney* to Jack Hobbs and me for letting him call me Doug Dickless-Boyd. He wrote inside: 'To the only man who ever said yes to me.' That's because I was the one who first said 'yes' to *Adolf Hitler* and I did say yes when other publishers might have said if you can get it round to us we will consider it. And I said 'We'll do it' and we did.

And I remember the times when Spike would phone me on Fridays and say 'It's the England/Ireland rugby tomorrow. Come down and watch it with me.' And we would watch it together, drinking cold white wine plus the great rugby stories.

My lasting memory of Spike is of being in a taxi, we were going back to Orme Court, wishing I'd got a tape recorder with me, buckled up with laughter with his surreal conversation, when he was taking a simple thing and expanding it into something absolutely looney. I remember bursting with laughter at something I knew I wouldn't be able to conjure up again.

NORMA: I came away with the feeling that Dick had been delighted to share his memories with me, and for all the ups and downs and the heartaches Spike had caused him, he was grateful to have such memories.

spike milligan

9 Orme Court,
LONDON. W. 2.

17th November, 1982

Dick Douglas Boyd Esq.,
Pelham Books Limited,
44 Bedford Square,
LONDON. WC1B. 3DU.

Dear Dick,

Thank you for your letter of the 4th November.   In this
wonderful correspondence that we continue, all I am trying
to do is find out the secret of my book sales, and nobody
has ever told me whether my books have sold or whether
there are any left in the warehouse, and I want to be
business-like in future, I think it would be nice to know
the numbers printed, the numbers sold, and the numbers left
in the warehouse, and I would be able to help you with the
right amount to be printed, the type of book I write, I mean
as you said you printed the wrong number with Get in the
Q Annual, so maybe having seen the figures, I could have
dis-suaded you from over-printing (what I clever little
bugger I am).   So, I can assist you in getting a larger
grass-cutter for your lawn, and you don't have to sit
there and do the work, you can be swinging in a hammock.
You see, I can make more space in your warehouse, and less
space in your overdraft.
You realise, of course, that I love you, it is only being
of the same sex which screws it up for us.
Jack Hobbs is alive and well and living in a bathful of
tears, every half an hour I add a bottle of Beaujolais
Nouveau to ease the degree of suffering. He is gradually
coming around to my way of thinking, if only I was.

/Contd..

- 2 -

A complete translation of this letter will be available
through Her Majesty's Stationery Office next Monday.
Now, if you read between the lines you wont see any
writing at all.

Love, light and peace,

Spike

P. Spike Milligan.

P.S. This is a sworn Affidavit that I am genuinely in
love with you, it has been witnessed by a Christian
Scientist Monitor, a Red Indian Spirit Thrower, and
Mrs. IrishSquirt from Barnsley.
I know you are not a book publisher, you are the fourth
mole in MI6, and that your father is A) Pagan, or B)
Prime.
I will be sending back the ring by separate post.

31st May 77

Dear Dick,

As the phone is no longer a reliable means of communication, I write to tell what sheer delight it was to get the book, 'Country Diary of an Edwardian lady. What a delight! to have the 4 seasons locked within its covers - its a book that sings in your hand. Reading it, I feel in love with that lady of seventy years ago -

Thank you all.

Spike.

JONATHAN MILLER

Thirty-six years with Milligan should have shorn me of any nervousness about meeting famous people but I had a dose of it as the taxi took me through Regent's Park to the home of a man renowned for his blazing intellect, a famous director whose analytical ability has made famous tenors and divas realise they had never before grasped the essence of their roles, and actors challenge the traditional interpretation of the characters they are to portray. A far from easy man, I had been warned, intolerant of fools.

Sorry! Sir Jonathan Miller is a charmer. He was waiting for me on the pavement outside his house and took my arm as we mounted the steps to the front door. In the porch was one of his carvings, something he does extremely well whenever he finds a spare moment. Far from being prickly I found him considerate, rounded, obviously multi-talented and with the manners that an English gentleman is supposed to have. He took my coat and sat me in a chair in a warm kitchen with its pictures of his children and grandchildren.

'Would you like a drink?' he asked.

He brought the camomile tea in a pot and we sat round the kitchen table where I listened to an erudite analysis of Spike's work. I suppose I should have known I was about to hear some entirely original views about Spike. Certainly, Jonathan is daunting but after one has put forward the accepted interpretation of one of Spike's works to have it demolished by a withering but constructive criticism, there is no feeling of either humiliation or inferiority because his warming smile is an assurance that he is satisfied you had never before had the opportunity of hearing the one and only correct exposition.

JONATHAN: I believe I first met Spike when I became known as a comedian in *Beyond the Fringe*. It was when I appeared as a minor officer in a pastiche called *The Bridge on the River Wye* with Sellers playing the main part. Peter Cook was also in the cast. I then got to know Sellers slightly and later I directed him in my film of *Alice in Wonderland* when he played the King of Hearts. He was absolutely wonderful but as mad as a hatter and often very difficult to control. He would arrive looking rather gloomy because he had passed a black cat on the way to the location. He had already called his astrologer who warned him not to start filming until his mood had improved, so we wasted three hours out of a very short shooting schedule. It was about that time that I occasionally came across Spike in the BBC studios or on social occasions. I never knew him really well and when we met he was always slightly insultingly jocular, as if he wanted to put me down.

I could never get a straight answer out of him. It had to be an enigmatic joke of some sort, at my expense. I wasn't offended but found him very odd and very difficult to engage in normal conversation. I would have liked to talk to him about the origin of some of his *Goon Show* characters that became so famous – national characters in fact, deeply embedded in the British consciousness. And famous in America where the *Goon Shows* were broadcast. He had great fans over there. His characters became as famous as some of the most comic characters in Dickens and *Alice in Wonderland*.

Spike had the most extraordinary sort of logical imagination. I can remember a wonderful line when Eccles called out to Bluebottle, who was walking along a branch being pursued by a jaguar or something, 'Jump, lad, I'll catch you. The ground will break your fall.' Well, of course it could, but in doing so we all know it could also break his neck. That's the sort of joke I relish. And there is a wonderful moment when Eccles and Bluebottle are in a trench waiting to do something the next morning and Bluebottle asks, 'What time is it?' and Eccles says, 'Just a minute. I've got it written down on a piece of paper. A nice man wrote the time down for me this morning.' Bluebottle says, 'Let me hold that piece of paper to my ear, would you?' 'Ere. This piece of paper ain't goin'.' To me the charm of that is that something written down at some previous time would count at a later time as it did at the time it was written down.

NORMA: [He smiled, a gentle smile and asked, 'Are you warm enough? Are you sure?' This from the man I had been told could be fierce and intimidating, but one I found to be considerate and charming, original and informative, his face often illuminated with a smile. And an expert with the *Goon Show* voices!]

JONATHAN: You see that joke about the time is very close to the sort of thing that Lewis Carroll did. I think that if *The Goon Show* had been a piece of printed literature – difficult though that might be to imagine – I think it would be on a par with *Alice in Wonderland*. Quite apart from that the characters themselves are so memorable. They're such a wonderful pastiche of various social, military and political stereotypes, many of them played with great brilliance by Sellers. The character of Eccles and his relationship with Bluebottle is absolutely wonderful. I'm not surprised that someone like Prince Charles talks so much about *The Goon Show* and its characters. There are lots of us who grew up with the show for whom these characters are as familiar as Mr Micawber. They are part of our national heritage.

NORMA: Did you ever work with Spike?

JONATHAN: I think I did a radio programme with him. It was impossible. He had to dominate in some way, take control and one had simply to take a back seat.

NORMA: Do you think that was evidence of his insecurity?

JONATHAN: No. I think that would be a rather glib psychological explanation. What actually motivated his very often insufferably bad behaviour is extremely hard to say. Why should he be insecure when *The Goon Show* made him into a national figure? If he had started with some sort of insecurity the success of the show should have given him absolute confidence.

NORMA: He resented the fact that he didn't have a university education.

JONATHAN: University could have blighted his life and many of his ideas would have been formalised. It might have killed his natural talent that came spontaneously out of his imagination. He didn't have to know anything but I believe he knew everything. He wrote some things that were a wonderful pastiche of boys' romancing about being Biggles and things like that. He may not have been educated and in the Forties and early Fifties people who hadn't been to Oxford or Cambridge or didn't belong to a propertied family might have been made to feel small, but by the mid-Fifties that was breaking up. All sorts of things were beginning to favour talent for its own sake. It had started in the army when my father, as a psychiatrist, ran the War Office selection board, quite different from the First World War when you had to be classy to be an officer. Gradually merit had begun to replace birth, yet when Spike was in the army he may have encountered some of the officer class who looked down on him because he was uneducated and didn't speak nicely.

NORMA: Having been born in India probably didn't help.

JONATHAN: I think India would have had a profound influence. In India under the Raj in the Twenties and Thirties the English lagged behind what was happening in England. It may have been that someone born in pre-war India like Spike might have been affected by the snobbish condescension of the class system over there that was dying in England. I have friends who were at Cambridge with me, working-class boys who got there on scholarships and so forth, who haven't a trace of inadequacy. My brother-in-law, Karl Miller, came from a very humble Edinburgh family – his father was a signwriter and a communist but an educated man and a rather good painter. Karl hasn't a trace of inadequacy. He became a very important scholar and ended up as Professor of English at University College, London. Spike did not become professor of a college but he became one of the most famous men in England.

NORMA: He always felt that there was something else that would be better. He always wanted to move on.

JONATHAN: Yet he never made a move in any other direction. It's true that he wrote his war books, creditable works and very good accounts of war.

NORMA: He wrote over eighty books, which are still selling.

JONATHAN: But he will be remembered for *The Goon Show*. I didn't meet anyone at university, including classy figures, who were not absolutely familiar with *The Goon Show*. To this day Prince Charles does *Goon Show* voices. They populate the English imagination in much the same way as *ITMA* that preceded it. All sorts of characters in *ITMA* – what a cast – like Mrs Mopp. The scriptwriters captured with uncanny accuracy the diction and style of their characters. Mrs Mopp for instance with her 'Can I do you now, sir?' or 'I brought this for you, sir.' 'Oh! What is it?' 'It's one of the lodger's leavings, sir.' And then all those characters like the German spy, Funf. When the phone rang we got 'This is Funf speaking.' And I remember the wonderful Welshman called Sam Fairfechan who said, 'Good morning. How are you? As if I cared.' They are not dissimilar from those characters with their catchphrases in *The Goon Show* who became internationally famous. Who can forget that wonderful moment when someone makes a splashing noise and a voice says, 'He's fallen in the water!' And then when Bluebottle is teaching Eccles about gravity he says, 'Jump up!' So Eccles jumps up. 'There you are,' says Bluebottle. 'You've come down. Why do you think you've come down?' Eccles says, 'Because I live here.' That's absolutely Lewis

Carroll. In one of his stories someone says, 'Who did you see coming down the road?' 'No one.' And then the someone says, 'No. I never saw him.' Wonderful!

NORMA: I wonder whether you agree with many of his friends that Spike was totally trustworthy?

JONATHAN: I have no idea if he was trustworthy or not. I never had cause to invest trust in him. I had friends who worked with him, one in *Oblomov*, who said he was swinish from beginning to end. It wasn't that he was untrustworthy. No. Quite the reverse. One actor friend of mine said you could trust him to let you down. Not let you down by deceiving you into thinking that you were going to do one thing rather than another. He just behaved horribly because he was so vain as a performer. He wanted to dominate to the exclusion of everyone else. Actually, I'm amazed that he allowed Secombe and Sellers to make their characters as famous as his own Eccles. They became identified with those extraordinary characters he created for them but there's no sign in the performances that he tried to shut them up. Some of the characters must have emerged from his wartime experiences in the army. Major Bloodnok for example, and those endless allusions to his incontinence. Remember the fort on the North-West Frontier in the smallest and coldest room in the house when the Major is in some difficulty. Then we hear this vast explosion and the Major saying, 'I'll never eat Bombay Duck again!' Wonderful!

NORMA: You've got the voices.

JONATHAN: I can do all of them. You know, Milligan created all sorts of wonderful, imaginative Lewis Carroll-like distortions of time and space – the fact that there were months of the year which didn't exist like Octember and the fact that one could travel in time or span enormous distances in space in the course of fifteen seconds. One of the things that I think Milligan understood perhaps better than almost anyone was the extraordinary elasticity of space and time. You could do that on sound radio but not on film. I very much doubt whether any of those characters would have survived if we'd been able to see them.

NORMA: That's why he was very much against the idea of televising *The Last Goon Show of All* to celebrate fifty years of broadcasting by the BBC. Eventually, and very reluctantly, he agreed to it some time later. Moving on, did you or any of your acquaintances experience Spike's treachery?

JONATHAN: No. I heard a lot about people he had let down and those he had betrayed but I had no personal experience of it. All I had from him was a rather grudging facetiousness because he probably felt I was posh and had been to university.

Now neither Harry Secombe nor Peter Sellers had an education but they managed to live with it without any embarrassment and be who they were, but Milligan was incapable of that. He was clearly an angry, resentful person who did badly by people in order to get even with them, even with those who had done nothing against him. You repeat the belief that in Milligan there were two people. On the contrary, I believe the answer is that there was one person there and he was inconsistent. It pleased him to present himself as someone lovable, having previously proved himself as someone absolutely despicable, but there weren't two people there. It's just that he had a double aspect to his personality. After being despicable to someone he would then invite admiration for his magnanimity. I don't believe he was genuinely magnanimous. You can't switch it on and off.

To alternate between magnanimity and treachery betrays some sort of fundamental weakness of personality. Magnanimity is an all-round business. If you genuinely love people you would be aware that you couldn't make up for your treachery by being apologetic, re-morseful and then magnanimous.

NORMA: I always thought Sellers was more treacherous than Spike and didn't have a conscience.

JONATHAN: I don't think either of them had. There are a lot of people in the theatre who don't have personalities. That's why Sellers was such an astonishing creator of different personalities – he didn't have one of his own. Peter Cook had a lot of that. I never really had a conversation with him unless he adopted an accent. His inventiveness was comparable to Spike's. For instance, that character of his sitting on a park bench saying that he could have been a judge but he couldn't get through the Latin exam. 'Very rigorous, compared to the mining exams which are very unrigorous. They only ask one question, who are you and I got seventy-five per cent on that.' That's absolutely in the same line as one of Spike's jokes. Peter could do all those voices and he could turn them on at will. The number of times I succeeded in having a conversation with him when he used his own voice can be counted on the fingers of one hand.

NORMA: He used to come to the office occasionally. Spike thought he was very special.

JONATHAN: Those things he did with Dudley after their television broadcasts were absolutely wonderful.

NORMA: Do you think Spike has influenced those who have followed him?

JONATHAN: No. Some of the most interesting people have no influence. They are unique. It's true that someone like Dickens had an influence but not in the way one would think. The people most deeply influenced by Dickens were Kafka and Dostoevski. There are things about Kafka that are not unlike *The Goon Show* – the curiously surrealistic succession of events, for example. But nobody is carrying on the *Goon Show* tradition. Subsequently, some of us did comic things like *Beyond the Fringe* and after that came *Monty Python* but it would be very rash to say that *Python* was in any way a continuation of what had been established by the Goons. It was a different sort of surrealism.

[Jonathan was looking at Spike's drawings of *Goon Show* characters.] I find it rather distressing to see them. I hadn't the faintest idea what Major Bloodnok looked like, or Bluebottle or Eccles. Show me Eccles. You see, I didn't visualise any of them. It isn't that it's wrong that I have a different picture in my mind; it's wrong because those are real pictures and that is a very subtle difference. If ever I did conjure up a picture of Eccles – and I don't think I did – the voice sounded like Disney's Goofy.

[He then did a remarkably accurate imitation of Goofy's voice.] I think you'll find an amazing number of people who can do Goon Show voices and talk to each other using them. There are elderly people who come to my door and say in that unmistakeable voice, 'Well, halloo.' And I say, 'You're eighty years old and you are still doing Goon voices.' You tell me that people are still buying recordings of *Goon Shows* by the thousands, not necessarily people who listened to the original broadcasts. What is it that they like about *The Goon Show* because they are too young to have met any of the types that are represented? What are they laughing at?

Like other people of my age do I like the *Goon Shows* because I get a sense of a world of rationing, of few cars on the road, the difficulties of public transport and so forth. They have a nostalgic fragrance, a smell of that period that can mean nothing to younger generations. In thirty years' time I suspect nobody will be buying a recording of them.

I saw very little of Spike. My own life in showbusiness was a reluctant one. I felt I had made a mistake by being in it at all. I'm a doctor and I think I fell out of medicine in a way that I shouldn't have done. Spike would have thought I was some sort of 'fucking intellectual' but I am an old-fashioned intellectual and I actually never talk to anyone in the theatre. I regret having gone into it. [He pointed to an anatomical chart on the wall.] It's not an accident that it's there. For me, how we work is the reason I went into medicine.

I wasn't interested in helping people. I didn't go into it to do good. Not that I wanted to do any harm but I wasn't in the least interested in doing good. I was curious about how we worked. My interest in the theatre is consistent with my interest in how we work. I have such contempt for ninety per cent of what goes on the stage and on the screen. It doesn't reflect what human beings are actually like. People ask me what directing consists of and I tell them it is very simple. It's nothing else than reminding my performers of what they knew all along but have forgotten and getting them to forget what they ought never to have known in the first place. The result is that I never spend any time with the people I'm seen with on television or those I join for a discussion on radio. I directed Peter Sellers and put up with his bad behaviour because I had to tolerate his moods but I never saw him at any other time. We had absolutely nothing in common, absolutely nothing at all, and I don't think I would have had anything in common with Spike because he was in showbusiness, ENSA and the world of entertainment. I don't think we would have got down to things that interest me, such as why do we laugh at things. But maybe if the two of us could have sat down in this kitchen with nobody else present we could have talked about why laughter happens. On the other hand, he could have suddenly reverted to nastiness because he felt I was pulling his leg. You believe he would have been enthralled and that pleases me. He was so inventive and I would have loved to have got into the deep origins and the roots of where that came from. When he says his humour came from thinking sideways he's not quite right. It's a very good metaphor but he didn't know enough about the structure of thinking to say anything else.

NORMA: Robert Graves said Spike was the most educated uneducated man he had met.

JONATHAN: That's brilliant!

NORMA: Spike said 'What the fuck does that mean?'

JONATHAN: That was his sense of resentment. As I said earlier the worst thing that could have happened to Spike would have been if he had gone to university. If he had, I doubt we would have had such gems as 'Jump! The ground will break your fall.' It's a wonderful joke. You see, we are at home on earth and therefore the idea of falling back down to earth could be said to be coming home. If I had spoken to

Spike in those terms he would have been exasperated. He would have thought it was pedantic hair-splitting. His jokes came so spontaneously from his imagination that he would have felt it inappropriate and boring that someone who can't make jokes was insistent on trying to analyse how they work. The best jokes occur when people are reminded of what they knew all along but have forgotten.

NORMA: [He waved goodbye as my taxi drove away. I left warmed by his charm, stimulated by his intellect but saddened by what seemed to be his lack of Spike's limitless capacity to share with his friends an enduring love of life.]

MICHAEL PALIN

'There's something unusual about him. He's a good human being' –
Spike's description of Michael Palin. How many times did I hear him
say, 'Oh, how I hate the human race, oh, how I hate its ugly face.'
Obviously, Michael Palin didn't come into that category but most
people, at one time or other, were to fit that description, depending
upon Spike's mood/whim/black dog days. As he wrote in 1971:

> Pull the blinds
>   on your emotions.
> Switch off your face
> Put your love into neutral
> This way to the human race.

or in a black mood also written in 1971:

> God made night
> But
> Man made darkness.

Hardly the words of a lover of his fellow man, but he was definitely
a lover of animals and his beloved planet:

This evening in the twilight's gloom
A butterfly flew in my room
Oh what beauty oh what grace
Who needs visitors from out of space.

Written in 1984 and to prove his love of butterflies. Also, written in 1989:

Butterfly Butterfly
Making colours in the sky
Red white and blue upon your wings
You are the loveliest of things.

This contradictory man warmed to Michael Palin and I told Spike it was either because Michael was a true Yorkshireman, or the fact he had been educated at Shrewsbury public school. What is it about this school? Other pupils included Richard Ingrams, Willie Rushton and Christopher Booker, all with the same sense of fun, wit and humour. When I informed Spike of this connection with the school he thought it was incredible, but a typical Milligan dismissive shrug, 'Maybe it was something they put in the water.'

Whatever! Spike became a fan of Michael's after watching *Ripping Yarns*, and discovering that he had co-written it with Terry Jones. 'They've got it right.' So, on my way to meet Michael, whom I hadn't seen for some years, I was so looking forward to the laughter which I knew we would share and enjoy together.

MICHAEL: I first met Spike around the time of *Monty Python*, but I already felt I knew him because I had been so immersed in his works since I discovered *The Goon Shows* in 1954. I listened to them with my friends when I was ten or twelve years old and I was always interested in who wrote the shows. I realised, even at that age, that Spike was brilliant and was creating a new kind of comedy. Instead of someone opening a door and letting someone in, there's a knock on the door and someone comes all the way down the stairs and says, 'What do you want?' 'I want to come in.' 'Oh, I'll go and get the key,' and they go up again. After listening to Richard Dimbleby commentating on royal occasions, this was so liberating. I'd also been brought up with radio sitcoms like *Take It From Here*, and stand-up comedians like Tommy Trinder who were funny but conventional, and Spike was completely unconventional.

I finally got to meet him through Ian MacNaughton who directed *Q5* which the Python team admired so much. It was probably 1970/71 in the Trattoo, and Spike was having dinner with Ian MacNaughton. I was in awe of the man and I was a bit wary. There were a lot of other people around and we shook hands and I think he said something like, 'You bastards nicked my fucking show,' and I thought, 'Hang on here. This is not your normal sort of showbiz figure. Tread carefully. Is he really serious or is he just having a joke at my expense?' So there was an edgy quality to Spike.

NORMA: Over the years you got to know each other and Spike was always very warm towards you when you approached him to appear for you in *Comic Roots*.

MICHAEL: Spike had to sit in a mock-up of his house with his actual radio playing *The Goon Show*, the two of us chatting. I was telling him what it was like to meet the Goons and said, 'I passed Peter Sellers once in the passageway in the studios,' to which Spike replied, 'Oh, very painful,' and we didn't get much further than that. It was after the first series of *Ripping Yarns* that we became closer. I received a card from him which just said: 'Love the *Ripping Yarns*. More please. Spike.' It was written in that lovely, loopy handwriting he had and this was the first time I really believed that he did like what I was doing. From that time on, whenever we met, I felt a little more confident, but neither of us were gushy people. We didn't like showbiz euphoria. We would sit and chat, it was comedy we understood. I didn't have to tell him how much I liked the Goons. He'd heard that from everybody.

NORMA: When Monty Python's *The Life of Brian* was being filmed in Tunisia, Spike happened to be on holiday in the same place, Monastir. Pythonesque or what. It was inevitable you would all have dinner together in a strange restaurant.

MICHAEL: I think it was called The Frank Arab or something like that. Spike spent the whole evening talking about *Ripping Yarns*, describing the show, sometimes verbatim and sometimes nothing like the original, but in a way he had added lots of Spikisms. I was left in no doubt how much Spike appreciated my work.

NORMA: Do you remember that awards dinner? It hadn't started off well. Spike had arrived in not what you would call a sociable mood. Apparently I had asked you to sit next to Spike to try and calm him down, and you were deeply flattered to think he might have some effect. It was short-lived.

MICHAEL: Yes, some comedian was doing his bit, but had gone on far too long and Spike said in a loud whisper, 'When is this going to end?' and 'Get on with it,' and started heckling. I would have said privately, 'Why did we need this?' but not Spike.

There were some days when he was a bit dangerous. He couldn't stop himself and that's why he was so different from any other comedian. You could feel it all buzzing in his head like electricity. It's almost like Tourette's. It had to come out. We had to stop it all buzzing in his head.

After the outburst we sat and talked for the rest of the evening. Among other things we discussed *The Goon Show* and I thought Spike would say, as usual, 'It drove me mad.' Instead he said, 'You know, it was like one very good summer.' I never forgot that. It was a beautiful description. It wasn't literally what he meant, but it's the feeling you remember about a golden time. Of course, it wasn't because we all make a fine summer, and there was never really a fine summer. There were good days and bad days, but the fact that he remembered it was 'one very good summer', I thought, yeah, I feel a bit like that about *Python*. Everything came together and it's a bit nostalgic, but you know probably there won't be anything quite like that again. But it's a past you can go back into and say, 'Yeah, that was good,' and I thought that was a nice thing for him to say.

NORMA: What were your memories of *The Other Spike*? [A documentary made in 1972 in which Spike re-enacted his mental breakdown, in the mental home he had been in at the time. This was quite a brave thing to do.]

MICHAEL: Spike was supposed to have peace and quiet and was under sedation. When he screamed, 'Four o'clock in the morning and down below they're emptying bloody dustbins, clanking and shouting,' I thought that was a very good observation about hospitals. I applauded the fact that Spike had the courage to appear in *The Other Spike* and because of his mental fragility he was more aware of life's problems – whereas most people go through life with an even temperament, nothing happens either up or down – and that was why so many things meant so much to Spike, whether it was trees or animals, he did get very upset about things and couldn't really hide it. It was a very sharp awareness of life and all that was around him. I always felt with Spike there was a raw edge.

Sometimes when you were with him he would be very comfortable and easy, and he would be in a nice reflective mood, but only one thing had to happen – a waiter putting something on the table at the wrong moment [he laughed at the thought] – then he would crackle with this raw energy. And at other times he was just so miserable. He could be down on himself when he was writing. 'I didn't think I could be this fucking unfunny.' I heard him say that.

NORMA: Spike regretted not having gone to university. If Spike had done so, would it have had an effect on his writing?

MICHAEL: No, I don't think so because he had such an original mind, and such an original approach to things. It's all hypothetical, but if he'd had a university education all that would have happened is, maybe the edges would have been knocked off and maybe we would have got a

Spike who was more gentle, possibly even-tempered. But you wouldn't have got down to the depths of what came out when he was writing. A lot of the best comedy is a reaction against something – you can't laugh at this, you mustn't do that. In his war memoirs – which was wonderful stuff – while others were writing about the heroics of war, Spike could see through all that and I'm sure that must have been very much his early inspiration. Being in danger, knowing you could be killed the next morning. That concentrates the mind, either on fear or laughter, which is so close to fear, making someone laugh. It's the same sort of uncertainty – which way are you going to go?

University education might have reduced his level of anger and resentment, but that would have been a disaster because it was such a key element in his writing, and in all his work. Maybe university would have reduced his originality, you just don't know, because education is very much about references and increasing the technical stuff you have available to you but Spike had a natural ability to write and there was such an edge to everything he wrote, even his wonderful children's stories. I absolutely adore *Badjelly the Witch* – it's one of my children's favourite books. I read it to them with such evident joy that they laughed and said, 'Please let us have that bit again where his trousers fall down!' That was the sort of kind, nice, ingenuous Spike – it wasn't an educated Spike.

NORMA: Spike wrote a *Goon Show* every week. It took discipline and energy to control the characters and maintain the standard.

MICHAEL: Writing the *Goon Shows*, delivering one show a week, was a difficult time for Spike, and those were the years when I became even more interested in him. I felt that this is probably where good comedy comes from, not from people looking out of a window saying, 'What are we going to make a joke about today?' It's often from seeing what a rotten mess we've made of the world.

Of course, there were good and bad *Goon Shows*, as with *Monty Python*, but there was so little repetition. It was all so fresh each time, and Spike was very hard on himself. I have wondered if Spike wanted to be a more serious writer, but I don't think he could have been anything other than what he was – a totally original comedy writer. Spike's voice was very much his own voice. I've heard people say they have caught a certain style, echoes of Evelyn Waugh or whoever. But they can't deal with something that is absolutely incomparable, and Spike was incomparable. We all try to emulate him, believe me. Frank Muir and Denis Norden, Ray Galton and Alan Simpson were among the most important comedy writers of this country. Ray and Alan had an ability to create characters that moved you and were very funny. But Spike occupies a different sort of plinth, as it were, in the pantheon of great British comedy writers, because he really did take things in quite a different direction and you can't really see where he came from. But nobody produced a body of work like Spike.

NORMA: What did you think about the nasty and cruel Spike Milligan.

MICHAEL: I didn't witness it personally, or perhaps I've blotted it out. I saw Spike being very hard on Ian MacNaughton and witnessed his dark side. I couldn't understand it because they were close and good friends. Spike's pet name for Ian was 'Rage'. Ian went into terrible rages, which always amused Spike and that in turn infuriated Ian. But Ian was one of the very few people who understood Spike and his work, and he always wanted to give Spike what he needed in his work. There was definitely a love/hate relationship between them.

There were days when Spike was diffident and miserable. We'd meet and I would say, 'Hello, Spike. Lovely to see you,' and he'd say, 'Not so lovely. Fuck off!' I never took it personally and preferred that greeting to someone avoiding me with an icy smile. Spike's 'Fuck off. What are you being so cheerful about?' was preferable. Some days he just didn't want to talk to anyone. I saw him at several book launches where he would sit in a corner on his own and would be very terse when people went to speak to him. Other times he would be very gracious to everybody. He didn't do bullshit. He didn't know how to pretend to be nice, as we all do just to get through the day. With people we don't like we're even nicer, but Spike could see through that, and what's the point. He got round it by being rude to everybody, even the people he really liked. That was his way – anti-nice.

NORMA: Why did people forgive Spike's rudeness?

MICHAEL: Because he wasn't a grump who sat around, here was someone who provided wonderful comedy shows, books for children
and for grown-ups – such a body of work. And the wonderful lines –
'Nelson fell here. I'm not surprised, I nearly tripped over it myself'–
clips you can recount with great joy and affection.

NORMA: What will be your lasting memory of Spike?

MICHAEL: That time in Tunisia when Spike regaled me about how
much he loved *Ripping Yarns*. At the time I was getting quite embarrassed. He was just making up this tale, roughly approximating to
what I'd done. It was lovely – such an affectionate thing for him to
do. I'd inspired Spike to be more Spikish, and that was great because
he'd inspired me so much. And of course there was that time you put
me next to Spike to keep him quiet, and he was having a go at the
situation which quite honestly was hysterical. Awards are incredibly
tedious. I felt sorry for the guy who was told to get up there and do
twenty minutes and there's Spike in the front row! This poor guy, and
Spike's not enjoying it.

I think the only other person who comes close to that sort of
behaviour is Maggie Smith. I worked with her on *The Missionary* and
A Private Function. She is adorable, but doesn't suffer fools at all and
tells it how it is. When I talked to her about her brilliant acting she
said, 'Oh, how I hate it, darling. Rehearsals are great but the rest is a
bore.' It was a similar kind of thing with Spike. People who are so
good and so uncompromising with themselves don't have to prove
themselves to others. They are what they are. Spike spent half his life
campaigning about something or other, but whatever the cause he
believed in it passionately and fiercely. There was no compromise in
the way he approached things. He would fight to the end.

NORMA: What do you think Spike's legacy will be? [He didn't hesitate
with his reply.]

MICHAEL: Undoubtedly it will be the way he created a new form of comedy with the *Goon Shows*, which people say led to *Python*, and in that there was definitely a connection. *Python* did on television what Spike had done on radio and television. He was in the back of our minds. He was someone who really carried a burden on his shoulders, who took British comedy in a whole new direction, who wrote with humour and honesty. His memoirs are the work of a unique and original writer.

STEPHEN FRY

Stephen Fry for Prime Minister. Spike would have been amused by that.

I had gone down to Rye to see Spike and over dinner, completely unrelated to the conversation, Spike asked me, did I know Stephen Fry? When I answered No, he proceeded to give me a detailed analysis of Stephen's character. When I asked him, What's brought all this on? he told me he had been speaking to him. He thought Stephen was a 'sensitive soul and what you see is *not* what you get. There's something much deeper, and I think he has more demons than I have.' He went on to tell me that we all need to be loved but Stephen more so than most, and that 'air of pomposity' he has hides insecurity. He thought he had great intellect and 'uses it like a crutch to hide the insecurity'. And he had an amazing amount to offer his friends: 'He's like me – he likes loyalty. But also like me he knows he's alone, and that's the cross we have to bear – that's the illness.'

I never did find out what it was all about. I know Spike, something had triggered Stephen in his mind because he ended, 'Yes, I'll take him to dinner and we can talk.' It never happened, the moment had gone.

Stephen Fry walked into my office, even before I greeted him – and on reflection I may have been a little curt – I said, My God, I'd forgotten how tall you are. He is at 6 feet 5 inches. He then proudly told me he had lost six stone; he looked like a whippy overgrown sapling attempting to defy the wind. His overwhelming politeness is matched by his charm and deprecating smile. As he uncoiled in the armchair I was waiting for him to joke about the cassette machine I use. Not a bit of it. 'You aren't using an iPod. A good old-fashioned cassette, I love it.' I loved his enthusiasm which shone throughout our time together. Not for nothing was he voted the most popular choice for Prime Minister.

———————

STEPHEN: My first memory of Spike is when I was about 16 or 17, at the time I was studying for a scholarship to Cambridge University, which I later won. After being expelled from two public schools and spending three months in Pucklechurch prison on remand for stealing a credit card from a family friend – not an auspicious start – but I did graduate from Cambridge with a degree in literature.

I had gone as a dippy fan to see the show he did at the Theatre Royal in Norwich with Jeremy Taylor, the guitarist and singer. Spike was absolutely extraordinary. I went to the theatre bar after the show, not expecting to see Spike, but he was there, though I didn't see him, he must have come in afterwards. There was I, at the bar, this rather pathetic 16-year-old, when a hand batted the cigarette out of my lips, and a voice said, 'There! I've saved your life.' I turned around and it was *the* Spike Milligan. He literally stood next to me. He'd seen a young man smoking and just pushed the cigarette out of his mouth. That was the mood he was in and of course it was the greatest compliment one can ever be paid, and I said, 'Oh, sorry, sorry,' and he said, 'No, I should be the one who is sorry, but then I'm not,' and he turned and joined some people.

Many years later I did mention the occasion to Spike, who didn't remember a thing about it. Yet it was a memory that had burrowed its way into my mind, never to leave. I thought it was a great introduction, and not untypical. It demonstrated a lot of Spike's obsessions, not caring about normal manners, his hatred of smoking, and that fabulous eccentricity which one hoped one would experience. I don't suppose from that meeting onwards I ever grew less scared of him than I was the first time.

NORMA: Were you aware of Spike's feeling of inferiority because of his lack of a good education, his regret at not going to university, and do you think it would have diminished his originality if he had gone?

STEPHEN: He could be chippy about it, and for that reason I was never completely at ease with him. You mentioned to me about Jonathan Miller never being able to get on with him; both Jonathan Miller and I are very typical Cambridge students, he more so than me. A true deep-dyed intellectual of a particular kind whose ranges of reference are enormous. We both have compendious memories and have read a great deal, Jonathan infinitely more than me, but nonetheless we both give off, whether we like it or not, an air that somebody who has not had our education would probably find forbidding. And they would imagine in us all kinds of arrogances that I hope are not there, but one must be realistic enough to recognise that they give that impression, especially to someone like Spike, who on the one hand could not be called a Marxist and a class warrior, but on the other hand no one could call him a toadying snob or an upwardly mobile aspirant to middle-class comfort and respectability. He inhabited a space between.

He was proud, and yes, the Irish Anglo-Indian sort of ordinary squaddie if you like. And yet he also had a great fascination and love of the eccentricities of the English upper classes, particularly the stupid majors rather than the more refined figures. Yeah, I'm sure he resented not going to university because he knew his worth. He knew that his mind was an extraordinary, original one and one of immense imaginative power and remarkable skill in writing. His poetry shows above all that he was not just a scattergun surrealist, that he had the discipline to focus on small things with immense delicacy, and it would be wrong to think he was the man that made jokes about porridge and custard and so on. So I think because he knew his worth he realised there was another Spike who never got a chance to be born, who maybe would have been a more settled and happy figure. I don't think that's necessarily true but I can see why he might have thought it.

And then the other side of your question is, yes, I absolutely agree. I think he would have been a weaker and a less original talent had he gone through a conventional education. It sounds terribly patronising. It's like Ben Jonson's lines about Shakespeare's 'small Latin and less Greek and his native wood notes wild'. I mean, who would have tempered Shakespeare's natural exuberance and extraordinary power and imagination and so on by sending him through Cambridge like Marlowe and all his contemporaries? There is that sense of an unfettered imaginative energy that was all the more remarkable because of its complete originality. A trained tree has got straight branches with pears against a gable end, but a wild tree is a much more beautiful thing, and Spike was wild.

NORMA: Did you admire Spike as a person, his free spirit?

STEPHEN: I admired his originality. I admired the fact he was afraid of no one. I admired the fact that he didn't toady to anyone. He didn't demand to be liked. That's so exactly the opposite of myself that I can't but admire it because I have this appalling habit of trying to be whatever I think people want me to be. It makes me easy company, generally speaking, but even my best friends sometimes get frustrated by the level of my politeness and my chameleonlike qualities to be similar to people I'm with, and to be liked all the time. Spike had none of that and that is an admirable thing. It genuinely is. It also creates all kinds of difficulties. For instance he was a rude man. There is no question of that. He didn't consider other people's feelings and the beginning and end of good manners is to consider other people. He couldn't do that. Because of his prodigious talent and the general knowledge that he was not a happy person people forgave him because they knew it was not an affectation but a characteristic, a trait that did not necessarily give him any pleasure. I used to see him at the *Oldie* lunches. He liked Richard Ingrams very much, they are both prickly figures. I think he always made an effort to be there for Richard's sake. He could be jolly.

He was never directly rude to me. In fact, I remember one occasion we were filming in Rye – *Cold Comfort Farm* – doing the scene in the tea shop with Kate Beckinsale and Ian McKellen. They were lighting it and I was wandering down a very pretty lane. A car was going past and

I stepped aside. It stopped and the window wound down. It was Spike and he said, 'And what brings you to my manor?' And I said, 'Oh, we're filming.' 'What are you filming?' I said, '*Cold Comfort Farm*.' And he said, '*Cold Comfort Farm, Cold Comfort Farm*. I read that book. I remember Alastair Sim in it.' We talked about Alastair Sim for about ten minutes and we agreed that he was a genius and one of the best character actors Britain had ever produced. It was a really nice conversation. He was in a calm mood. He was neither slumped in his melancholia nor was he, you know, madly throwing apples at people or whatever. Another car came behind me and I had to move on. It was a very touching moment. It's a lovely memory. It was very sweet.

NORMA: If he didn't like you, yet knew you were going through some trauma, he'd still ring you up. I think that's total compassion. If somebody had been rude to him or he'd been rude to somebody or whatever and I said, 'You know, they're having a very bad time,' he'd ring up and say, 'Norma said you're having a shitty time.'

STEPHEN: As an example, I remember he made one of the most powerful poetic and insightful remarks I've ever heard about another person's unhappiness. We were talking about Peter Sellers for an interview years ago and he mentioned a row and the way Peter had grown way beyond the Goons, obviously, and become an international star. Poets travel the shortest distance to the truth without the need for education or intellect and he said, 'I think the trouble was he was a man without a fireplace in his life,' which is an extraordinarily profound remark. I'm not sure that he knew this, but hearth and heart are from the same root and also the Latin for hearth is 'focus'. Since the beginning, the definition of a family is sitting around the fire, having that sense of hearth and home. Peter lived in hotels in the South of France, in rented villas, rented accommodation and rented woman, almost. It was a miserable existence and however miserable people think Spike might have been, he always had a hearth. People put up with him and you were close enough to him to give him that sense of a focus of a hearth around which his family and friends gathered. He looked at the extraordinarily talented Peter Sellers and saw the misery of a man without a fireplace, and I thought it was just so beautifully put. I don't know that he even knew how brilliant it was as an observation.

NORMA: Spike once said to me, 'My mate's so unhappy. You know, he doesn't have a fireplace in his life.' Obviously that was a symbol in his head, focus on hearth and home. The difference between Spike and Peter was compassion. Peter could be mean, genuinely mean in a way that was just cruel. There's one difference. Milligan has heart.

Do you think Spike had changed the face of comedy after he had written *The Goon Show*? Quite a few people have said that, for them, Spike changed comedy in the twentieth century.

STEPHEN: I think it's absolutely incontrovertible. I mean you've only got to see the comedians who came after and the absolutely unforced and honest way in which they confessed their debt to him. I was of a generation just too young really to have experienced the Goons when they were broadcast. My great heroes in the early Seventies were the Pythons, but of course John Cleese and the others have expressed their debt and how much they owe to him. My own father was an enormous fan of *The Goon Show*. He used to run through the sketches but I didn't quite understand them. Then at some point in the early Seventies they began repeating them on the radio and you could get cassettes and records of them so I began to listen to them. I bought the scripts, watched *The Last Goon Show of All* on television and started to do the voices like everybody else.

I remember – and this is going to sound ridiculously pretentious but I wouldn't be the first to be this pretentious – I remember I was reading Samuel Beckett at the time, you know, *Waiting for Godot*, and I thought, My God! These two are very different, both Irish as it happens, and both with this extraordinary way of looking at reality and subverting it, and making it funny. In the case of Beckett, obviously much bleaker with much less of the kind of entertainment that Spike managed to achieve, but there are some jokes, like Eccles keeping the time written for him on a piece of paper, that are as good as any great humorist has managed to come up with – ever. I mean, they are just simply miraculous. One can talk of the standard *Goon Show* but what was brilliant was he could write for all the characters. The Eccles humour people remember particularly, because it is so him and so utterly upside down, yet unpredictable. And obviously the Bluebottle humour, because it was so adorable. Peter Sellers was absolutely best as Bluebottle but then the way Spike wrote for Minnie Bannister and for Moriarty and all these characters, and for Seagoon, who was really a straight man, though that's a bit unfair on Harry Secombe, but in a sense he held it together, usually narrating whatever story there was. The other thing was the class business, I mean, it's so enormous. Without Spike, I think the two streams of comedy at that time would have carried on separately. There was what you might call your ENSA working-class sort of thing. That was fed from the music halls and that became Variety. Then the working men's clubs and the panto tradition, plus the new thing that had come up at the same time as the Goons, which was the university tradition – Jonathan Miller, Alan Bennett and Dudley, obviously. And then came Cleese, Eric Idle and Graham Chapman and so on. And then all the way up to people like me. What he did was unite all those sides. No one could call him a university graduate humorist, but he was something more and richer than the end-of-the-pier sort of thing, that standard ENSA fare that you would expect. Therefore he could influence both, and particularly he influenced the graduate humour. He was an original and his energy awoke the whole nature of comedy. In a sense, I suppose you could argue (and I think he might quite like this himself) that he was the first one to use the principles of jazz in comedy, because he loved jazz of course and knew a huge amount about it. In his lifetime he grew up with the absolute classic greatness of Louis Armstrong, right through to the bebop revolution, and he was the kind of bebop of comedy. Not necessarily because he improvised but because he was able to take elements of it to twist and find the blue note in a joke, as it were, to flatten that fourth, to do those extraordinary things to meaning and to language, and just delight in texture and stupidity.

NORMA: Some people have said to me that you have taken on Spike Milligan's mantle regarding depression.

STEPHEN: Yes. Well, in as much as I started life in comedy and I've come out, as you might say, about my own condition, I suppose it's natural that people would make that connection. I'm terribly honoured to think people might make that link. We were both in showbiz, in a position where it's easier for people to be open about all kinds of things, about their life, whether it's their sexuality or mental condition, because we're surrounded by much kinder, more loving, forgiving people. Nobody is going to sack us because of things like that, whereas obviously many other people have had a much tougher time. I think whatever the nature of the differences between Spike's condition and mine, we would probably both agree that stigma was the major problem. That people should be ashamed of what happens in their mind is the biggest shame of all. It's bad enough having to deal with it. It would be bad enough to deal with diabetes as Harry [Secombe] did. It's a chronic condition but you don't have to hide away. You just say, 'It's a bit of a bore. I've got diabetes.' 'Oh, that's a shame,' whereas you have to have immense courage to admit that your mind is letting you down. If your body lets you down everyone seems easy about it. And I'm glad to say my manic depression is more under control at the moment. The thing is, for some reason, it's been worse for me because of my absolute obsession with not upsetting other people, which I think comes from my mother, who is a very divine and lovely person. I tend to bottle things up much more and hide it, and people were always astonished when they discovered that I had a three-month period of a living hell or whatever, because I'd either go away and they don't see me, or when they do see me I'm just perhaps a little quieter than usual. I'm terrified of showing it to people.

I can remember the last time I saw Spike was when he was in *Gormenghast*. There was one particular day when he was in a foul mood, being pushed around in this wheelchair, and it was just the way his body was slumped, his eyes, everything about him just told you that he was in a horrible depression. When I was in my depression if there was anyone else in the room I would stare and my eyes would be a bit unfocused. I think his is probably a healthier way of facing up to it, to be honest. I mean, it doesn't make you any happier to be like that.

NORMA: With Spike I could tell when he was going into a depression. He'd start shouting at things. The picture on the wall not being straight, 'This phone is fucking filthy.' Then he'd have a go at everybody. Johnny Speight once said to me, 'Don't ever get upset. He's just shouting at the world.'

STEPHEN: Yeah. It's true, and of course he would never have meant you to be the one who is hurt. That's it. You have to be on your own.

NORMA: Sometimes, when it was bad, I had to slip a note under his door saying 'I'm here, I'm going home. I'm on the other end of a phone.' Then for three days, four days, nothing, and then suddenly I'd come in and he'd say, 'Fuck off and leave me alone.' I thought, Oh, he's getting better.

STEPHEN: That's moving up. Yes, the changes. The mood dies.

NORMA: Do you get like that?

STEPHEN: Absolutely. The thing is until about four and half years ago I did what is known in the trade as self-medicating, which I know Johnny Speight did. Self-medication is often a euphemism for alcoholism and drug addiction of the non-prescriptive kind. I used to take cocaine for ten years and drank a lot. If you take cocaine it lifts your spirits for as long as you're taking it and then eventually you have to stop and crash down, and if you are completely manic drink drops you down a bit. It's taken me a long time, mostly for me exercise, walking. I walk four or five miles every morning.

NORMA: With Spike, it was squash, three times a week.

STEPHEN: Yes, fascinating. So now, obviously, I've given up smoking, not all drink. I still drink, but I've given up drinking to excess, and

I've certainly given up cocaine. It took a long time for that to work its way out of my system. My body expected any mood to be suppressed and now I let the mood happen, but I find that they are less severe. My cycles have always been much slower to emerge.

NORMA: With Spike it was up and down. We talked about the programme *The Other Spike*. He was fifty-two when he filmed that and I begged him not to do it, I begged him with all my heart because I knew the effect it would have on him but he said, 'I have to help those people who think they are the only ones.'

STEPHEN: It's unbelievable the effect these things have, isn't it? I've never done anything that's had more effect than the programme I did called *The Secret Life of a Manic Depressive*.

NORMA: Spike never took what he described as schizophrenic drugs. They lift you up and then suddenly, boom, you're back where you where when you bloody started.

STEPHEN: Well, that's very smart of him because most of us are too dumb. We just like the lifts.

NORMA: In the late Seventies Spike was taking rohypnol as a sleeping pill long before it was known as the date rape drug. His biggest problem was insomnia.

   You were appearing in the West End in Simon Gray's *Cell Mates* when you dramatically left the show after three performances and fled to Belgium.

STEPHEN: Yes, I did. I mean, I knew I had this problem. I knew that my mood swings were greater than other people's so I knew I could get so black as to have suicidal thoughts, which is always the thing doctors are most obviously worried about and rightly so. But I didn't have active suicidal thoughts. The thing about depression is it robs you of all sense of a future so you cannot see the point of anything. You lose energy because you can't make plans, because you think, well

– it's like the poet Arthur Hugh Clough – the Ten Commandments – 'Thou shalt not kill, but needst not strive officiously to keep alive'. I get this feeling, Oh God! If only I was run over or something. I'd so hate to upset my parents by taking my own life. I couldn't bear that. Then when the mood switches all you can think about is the future. You have this amazing ability and you're rich with plans and sometimes they're absurd, grandiose plans that can never come to fruition, but at best and at a medium level it allows one a force of creativity that you believe is essential. As W. H. Auden said, 'Don't take life's demons away because you rob me of my angels too.' It's something I asked in the programme I made. Here's a button and it would take away your life hurts or your manic depression and you would be on an even scale all the time, neither manic nor depressed. Would you press the button? Out of about twenty-two people I'd interviewed only one of them pressed the button. That's the extra-ordinary thing and some of them are people who have tried to kill themselves many times, have miserable lives, gone through alco-holism and divorce and lost their children, but they still found that the elevated mood gave them the feeling of supremacy and joy and contact with the infinite. So what one would like, of course, is for a doctor to say, 'Okay, you can just have the mania.' But if you talk to their families they would say the hardest thing to deal with is when these people are manic. If they're depressed you feel sorry for them, and generally speaking they just want to be alone and sit in a darkened room. But if they're manic you just don't know what they're going to do next. You know they're going to go absolutely loopy. They're going to embarrass you. And I found out from a lot of wives and husbands of partners with manic depression that they preferred it when they were depressed.

NORMA: Spike explained it so vividly. 'Physical pain cannot come close to the raging pain in your head. The burning sensation that starts, it's as if the inside of your head is on fire, then the blackness that envelops you, it overtakes everything else in your life.'

He captured that pain in a poem he wrote called *Manic Depression*:

The pain is too much
A thousand grim winters
grow in my head.
In my ears
the sound of the
coming dead.
All seasons, all same
all living
all pain
No opiate to lock still
my senses
Only left, the body locked tenser.

STEPHEN: When Spike was manic he could be so rude. You must have experienced that, Norma?

NORMA: Oh, many, many times I'd say to him that wasn't very nice, and he'd ask, 'What, what are you talking about?'

STEPHEN: That's what one means by disinhibited. All inhibitions disappear. Inhibitions may seem, oh, a middle-class bourgeois thing, but actually they are there to make one's life easier. A loss of inhibition leads you to make an exhibition of yourself.

NORMA: A lot of people didn't like him for it.

STEPHEN: No, they didn't. I mean, I'm sure you'll be honest about this. For all the admiration, for all the love of his work and who he was in our cultural history, he was a hard man to like.

NORMA: Yes, he was.

STEPHEN: Because he got so little out of the people who knew him. I don't know many who would say that he exhibited a curiosity about them. And one of the greatest compliments someone can pay you is if they want to know more about you, and especially if it's a great man.

And he was a great man, so if he's not interested in you it's a bit wearing. Nor does he want compliments. It's not as if he wants you to talk about his work either, so what the hell do you talk about?

NORMA: That lane near Winchelsea where you talked, that was a lovely moment for you.

STEPHEN: That was really great.

NORMA: That's when he was okay. I used to say 'You can be nice.' Were you ever the butt of Spike's treachery?

STEPHEN: No, not really but there was something I chose to regard as genuine confusion. On the second day of filming *Gormenghast* I said, 'Hello, Spike,' and he just said, 'Who are you?' and I thought, fair enough, but he said it in such a way, so direct, a Spike-like way of being rude.
   I bought a wonderful photograph of Spike – I should have bought two – it was by a very fine photographer called John Swannell. Black and white, it was really beautiful. Spike was standing in front of a wall. John signed it as well and I gave it away as a wedding present. John Swannell told me when Spike arrived for the shoot he was in a really bad mood. He came into the studio and said, 'How long is this going to take?' John said he would just do a test photograph and then a second one, which he did, and was about to say 'Let's start' and Spike said, 'Okay, that's good' and off he went. John was heartbroken and thought, 'Oh God, I only took two test photographs,' but it turned out they were absolutely perfect, and he said if they had taken all day they wouldn't have been any better.

NORMA: Did your attitude towards Spike's mental illness change after you had suffered from bipolar disorder?

STEPHEN: Yes, it did. It reminded me of the fragility of one's ability to concentrate and continue as a writer. I also thought that the sheer effect of writing all those *Goon Shows* so early on and having so much to do all on his own must have exhausted and depleted his spirit enough to somehow make him more vulnerable. I don't ever want to be in such a position that I'd overdo it like that, but also I think that the negative side of his response to it and the negative side of his professional life, if I can call it that, was somewhere between an artist and a professional, if you know what I mean.

You know, the Q series and things like that had some absolutely wonderful moments but also he lost quite a lot of self-judgement. It saddened me when I saw, for example, something that wasn't really the best joke he'd ever written or the best sequence he'd ever done when he would try and get it through by laughing it in, as comedians say. By going [here he laughs to demonstrate] and I wondered 'Why are you laughing, Spike? If you had a good joke you'd do it deadpan and it would be brilliant.' And he had all those wonderful people like John Bluthal that helped him out. The one thing that's easiest in the world is to become bitter and resentful when young people come up and you're being passed over. Now, to some extent I think he probably was being passed over for all kinds of reasons. In the end organisations like the BBC and Hollywood are pretty simple. They just want contact, as they call it nowadays. They want material and they want it good and if Spike, for all his moods and Spike-iness, had produced top-quality stuff that they could rely on when they needed it and in the way they needed it, they'd put up with anything. But in the end I think he wasn't really being at his best and his heart wasn't in it and you could sense it. But, on the other hand, he may have rightly felt that perhaps he wasn't given the respect he was due. He watched other generations come up and make so much more money, not that he was a greedy man, but they did. I remember doing a Terry Jones film, a version of *The Wind in the Willows*. We were at Shepperton and in those days I was still a smoker and having a cigarette outside the set. John Cleese came up. There was a Ferrari parked there and John asked, 'Whose Ferrari is that?' I said, 'I think it's Steve Coogan's.' He said, 'How old is Steve Coogan?' I said, 'I think he's twenty-eight,' and I could see John's mind thinking back to when he was twenty-eight. And he said, 'Fucking hell,' and walked off. It was so funny. I'm sure Spike thought that when he first saw John Cleese in a Rolls-Royce or something.

I sensed in Spike a resentment, a slight bitterness, to be honest, and that's a terribly sad thing.

I love the business of comedy. I always have. My brother and his contemporaries had rock 'n' roll and I had comedy, and I literally would play records of Golden Music Hall Hours. I listened to the early days of radio comedy after the war as well and so I knew about *Take It From Here* and I knew about Frank Muir's period as a BBC executive and how influential he'd been and how much he'd helped other comedians, including the Pythons and so on. I knew, therefore, that he was more than just a jovial soul in a bow tie, and that he'd made a real contribution to the comic history of Britain. I think Frank Muir felt that the current generation of BBC executives had no idea who he was, and they didn't, and that really was offensive to him and rightly so. Do you know that story of Fred Zinnemann, you know, the great director who made *High Noon* and *A Man For All Seasons* and all those things, and the story of him going into a meeting with a twenty-five-year-old, one of those executives who was chief of production at Twentieth-Century Fox. This executive said, 'Okay, Mr Zinnemann, Mr Zinnemann, okay. So can you just run by me what exactly are your credits?' And Zinnemann said, 'You first.' Isn't that great? And there's a really sad story of Rod Steiger who was a genius, a brilliant actor. He had a meeting in the studios, in the late 1990s. He also suffered from manic depression, and was a very unhappy man. I believe Elizabeth Taylor, who has this extraordinary genius for friendship and is an unbelievably kind woman to people she has known, befriended him, and I do think she helped him enormously. Well, anyway, back at the studio this young executive said, 'So Mr Steiger, very nice to meet you. Tell me, do you think it would be a problem for you to do a southern accent?' to which Steiger replied, 'It's been a pleasure talking to you,' and walked out. He had won an Oscar for *In the Heat of the Night*, for fuck's sake. This kid couldn't even be bothered to check that. That's so insulting.

NORMA: A similar thing happened with Eric Sykes and Jimmy Edwards when they were touring Australia with *Big Bad Mouse*.

STEPHEN: I saw that production three times at the Theatre Royal in Norwich, and it was different every night.

NORMA: This was the same production. Eric and Jimmy were being interviewed on television to promote the show. I think it was in Melbourne, the interviewer was late and Eric and Jimmy had been waiting when he rushed in and said, 'Hi, now which one of you two is Sykes?' Eric stood up and said, 'The one that's just leaving,' and walked out.

STEPHEN: I wish I had known Jimmy better, he used to shoot with my grandfather in Norfolk. I've got a photograph of the pair of them in tweeds, both looking like Edwardian country gentlemen. It's hilarious. He was a very naughty boy, Jimmy. He came to Cambridge when I was there, and the president of the union, a rather pretty boy, went to meet him at the station. I was there when the cab arrived and the boy shot out, pink-cheeked. Jimmy stepped out and proclaimed, 'Well,' he said. 'You couldn't make an old man happy, could you.' Shameless but he was very, very funny.

NORMA: What's your lasting memory of Spike and what do you think his legacy will be?

STEPHEN: I suppose my lasting memory of him is a little kaleidoscope of my heart beating faster whenever I went into a room or a party where he was. It was beating faster out of hero worship and out of fear, because I just didn't know what he was likely to say if I tried to speak to him. He could sort of brush me off as an imposition or just be polite, but there are certain figures in one's life one is glad to have shared the planet with, not for long, but to have been alive when they were.

I think of myself at school reading Puckoon and I think of myself with his poems, learning them and reciting them with friends. And I think of those hours spent over Goon Show records, trying to perfect the voice of Eccles and Bluebottle and all the Cruns, and yeah, his place in our comic university is absolutely assured. He is there in my lifetime.

Two of the greatest influences on me, unquestionably, are people I have met. Maybe I would say three, although one of them is less well known, and they are Spike, Peter Cook and Vivian Stanshall.

They made me who I am and they all had in common that absolutely glorious way of looking at things differently, and yet understand language so extraordinarily. A great man.

EDDIE IZZARD

'Eddie Izzard is the one that will stay the course. Out of all the new breed, he's the one' – Spike's assessment of Eddie. That's why when Spike died and we had a memorial service for him, I asked Eddie would he read at the memorial. I was so pleased he agreed and, being very selfish, I asked him to read 'Have a Nice Day'. It's my favourite from Spike's poetry collection. It's one of the longest poems he wrote – 28 lines, unusual for Spike. It's such a complicated poem. Very funny, very Spike. The reason I mention this, it was some years later and I was having lunch with Eddie when casually he told me that he was dyslexic. But had I known I never would have asked him to undertake such a gigantic task. It says a lot about Eddie: he never told me at the time.

Absolutely nothing to do with anything, but at the memorial Eddie asked Eric (Sykes), 'Can I read at your memorial?' And Eric's quick-witted reply, 'Only if you let me read at yours.'

In certain aspects Spike and Eddie share the same qualities, one of them being mind over matter. Eddie's marathon runs – 43 marathons in 51 days; Spike in his fifties decided to take up the game of squash, late in life for such a hectic sport, particularly when he was playing four times a week, the same obsessive nature. Both staunch Labour supporters, with the attitude that you can achieve anything if you put your mind to it, 'And I'll do it to prove to myself I can.' Both complex people. Then, of course, they go in different directions. With Spike you got what you saw. He led his life like an open book, anything came out, you never knew what he was going to say because *he* didn't know what he was going to say. Eddie, on the other hand, is quite secretive, and doesn't readily share his thoughts.

———————

EDDIE: I was born in the Yemen where my father was working for BP, and I was only 12 years old when I first heard a recording of *The Goon Show*. My father, who was a huge fan, said to me, 'You'll want to listen to this: it's the Goons.' It had come from Radio Dubai and it was introduced by an Arab woman who was speaking good enough English but with an Arab accent and I seemed to put those crazy sons of fun in my head. I think the first *Goon Show* I ever heard was 'Shifting Sands'. I was with my father in Abu Dhabi for about four weeks, so I heard four episodes and by the time I returned to England and was at school in Eastbourne I was a fan. Not only of the Goons but of Spike Milligan. My father then recorded them every week from Radio Dubai and they would come all the way from Arabic lands, back to me at school.

I read *Adolf Hitler: My Part in His Downfall*, and a large chunk of it was set in Bexhill-on-Sea and I thought no one from Bexhill ever went off and did anything except Spike. In my teenage years I wanted to concentrate on comedy, and I thought this was my big link to comedy. Bexhill is flat, apart from Galley Hill, and Spike was stationed on top of it manning the guns. Probably it would have been 1940, after the fall of France, so in 1976 I was stationed at the bottom of Galley Hill in a kiosk selling ice creams, totally different, but geographically that linked me to Spike, so my idea was if he could make it out of Bexhill-on-Sea, maybe I could. There was a *Goon Show* called 'The Dreaded Batter Pudding Hurler of Bexhill-on-Sea' and I had read in *Adolf Hitler* that Spike played the trumpet in the De la Warr Pavilion. There were other places mentioned in that book, so with a map I got on my bike and went around trying to find these links to see if there was any of Spike's essence lying around.

NORMA: Eddie thought Spike was the 'Godfather of Alternative Comedy', just as Lenny Bruce started alternative stand-up comedy, followed by Billy Connolly.

EDDIE: But Spike was the engine of ideas and without him there would be just mainstream stuff and there wouldn't be *Monty Python*.

I think when he won the Lifetime Achievement Award it should have been an occasion all on his own, just a one-off thing. He made that fantastic speech and I remember roaring with laughter. I was watching it on a television monitor (I wasn't in the room but I was in the building) when I heard that wonderful reference to Prince Charles, 'the grovelling little bastard', and the whole room erupted. That night was when I first met him, but at a 'do' like that you can't sit and chat. I remember saying to him, 'I first heard your stuff on Radio Dubai' – he must have thought I was completely nuts. We talked rubbish together which I knew was the right way to talk to him. We said inane or crazy things and for me it was wonderful and I thought, 'It's such a long way from Galley Hill.'

NORMA: I wondered whether he thought Spike's mental illness had had anything to do with his rudeness.

EDDIE: I recall that Harry Hill, who is a huge fan, had said to Spike at some bash, 'Hi, Spike, how nice to see you.' Spike told him to fuck off and leave him alone. I'd heard that Stephen Fry got the same treatment.

I don't think it did and this myth that comedians need to be angry is rubbish. I assume that Spike's illness was revealed in his comedy and it figured in his whole life and how he went about things, but with or without it he would have been funny.

NORMA: I asked Eddie what he thought about Spike's womanising. He was quite philosophical about it, and gave a remark you would expect from Spike.

EDDIE: In this industry, and in politics or in fact anywhere, the affairs of the heart and relationships don't matter as long as people are happy.

NORMA: I pointed out that they shared a similarity – they both adored their mothers. Spike dedicated *Small Dreams of a Scorpion* to his mother: 'This book is dedicated to my mother, who spent a lifetime dedicated to me.'

EDDIE: I wasn't that fortunate. My mother died at the age of 41 from bowel cancer when I was just six years old. I was then sent away to school, and I remember crying for almost five years.

NORMA: Spike was in his seventies when his mother died but the pain was no less. The day after she died he telephoned her home in Woy Woy. When I asked why, he said, 'Just to be near her.' For both Spike and Eddie, the death of their mothers left them emotionally vulnerable.

I asked Eddie when he first discussed his own work with Spike.

EDDIE: When I met Spike at one of these celebration dinners, he was talking to Terry Wogan. His facial expressions lit up the conversation. We met later in the evening and he said, 'I like your stuff' – he actually said those words! I didn't believe it! It was such a strange, magical moment, and I wanted to know had anyone else heard it, because I wasn't sure I was hearing it. I thought, 'Wow! If there is a short straw and a long straw, I've just got a bloody long plank of wood.'

Years later we met at a photo shoot for *The Times* newspaper. We were being featured as 'the early generation and the later generation' and I considered it a great honour. It was a magical afternoon and Spike sent me a lovely letter after the meeting, and I thought of doing a gig outside his house. I tried to get my father to find out if there were any venues near to Spike's house so I could do a gig that would make it easy for Spike to attend. I decided against it: in the Nineties, when I was breaking through on the comedy scene, I reckoned Spike could see the video anyway.

Times were changing in the industry, and in the end I think it must have affected Spike in some way. Once you get to a place where you are doing good stuff you are wanted, and if you have struggled to get there you want your level in the country, or the world, to stay there or move up. It's like a balloon that needs pumping up, and as you get older the young people become commissioning editors, and they say we are not interested in this any more. So you need to keep the stand-ups going. Rely only on yourself. Spike worked this out long before other people. He was doing solo shows sporadically, but I don't think he was very happy with what he was doing and I felt for him. The BBC didn't treat him with the respect I felt he was due. They were probably only interested in numbers, and younger generations.

I was talking to Paul Merton about the same thing. He is widening his cause, as Spike did. He's in about the eighteenth series of *Have I Got News For You*, and he works like crazy but I think he's mindful of what can happen, so I don't think of Paul as having that vulnerable thing, unlike Spike, he had such a vulnerability about him. Lots of people in the entertainment industry wonder how long they can keep it all going before it might all drop off, and you know, some people have ended up in places which are not very pleasant.

There was one thing I regretted in the late Eighties and early Nineties when Spike toured the world with his two-hour one-man show and that was that I never saw a performance. I've tried to find a recording of it but failed. It taught me a lesson though. I was talking to Ross Noble and he told me that he videos every performance he gives. I'm now doing the same because every now and then you get a golden one, and what a tragedy Spike didn't do that. I suppose in those days nobody thought about it. I certainly didn't until I spoke with Ross.

NORMA: I asked Eddie what he thought Spike's legacy would be.

EDDIE: Spike was the godfather of alternative comedy and alternative comedy has now become mainstream. Alternative comedy is self-written comedy, you become a comic philosopher, and he was our first comic philosopher. Within that kind of comedy writing there is your own point of view, your attitude to life and the stuff in the Goons was all coming from his life and his experience and attitudes, so he created the modern comedy and it won't go away now and he won't go away. You can go around and do the racist/sexist tour, the old mother-in-law stuff, which still happens. But hopefully at some point with Barack Obama as president of the United States of America, you feel we are moving forward, and some old racist comedy hopefully will drop off the bike. Maybe it will, maybe it won't. Way back then it wasn't thought of as racist or sexist. It was silly emotional, it was puncturing balloons and its a great legacy. He would have actually been the godfather of all alternative comedy in the world. Of course, there were Americans coming through like Ernie Kovacs who was doing interesting stuff in the Fifties so Americans were influenced by that. The *Saturday Live* shows in the Eighties were influenced by *Python* who were influenced by Spike and the Goons, so it all flows through.

I heard Spike had written over eighty books. I loved his poetry, but I'm a bad reader of books because of my dyslexia. It takes me hours to get through books people knock off in a night, but I loved his poems and if I was writing poetry I know it would be in the same area. [He smiles and recites:]

> The new rose
> trembles with early beauty.
> The babe sees the beckoning carmine
> the tiny hand
> clutches the cruel stem.
> The babe screams
> The rose is silent –
> Life is already telling lies.

I don't think I'm really a positive person, and I have my doubts about Spike's positivity too. I think it must be given out with your genetic cards at the beginning.

NORMA: I pointed out to Eddie that he shared something else with Spike – a passion for military history. Spike was the fifth generation of a military family and all the history that goes with it. His seven volumes of war memoirs were applauded by the army's hierarchy, the consensus being that it was the definitive history of WW2 from the point of view of the ordinary soldier. Eddie's interest in military history was a strong bond between them. Spike never witnessed Eddie's pilgrimage to France to scatter the ashes of a D-Day veteran, and he personally donated £100,000 for a group of war veterans to travel to Normandy to mark the 65th anniversary of D-Day. There would have been a Milligan missive of appreciation winging its way to Eddie with 'Let's have dinner and talk.'

The more we talked the similarities grew. Spike was driven every day of his life and I could see the same drive in Eddie. The striving to do better. Spike pushed the envelope out, he extended the boundaries of what was funny. Eddie is now doing the same thing.

Finally, and for me the most important of all, Eddie has the same childlike quality, the enthusiasm, the eagerness to make you laugh and the joy both get when they see you laugh. But there the similarity ends and they become as far apart as Marmite and caviar. Eddie and his two-million-pound show travels with an entourage of forty-five people, plus seven lorries to transport his technical paraphernalia. Spike had a company manager, David, who was in charge of one skip, which housed several false noses, one bald wig, several different hats, a Margaret Thatcher lifesize dummy and an assortment of bits and pieces, together with a 3 x 3 Comedy and Tragedy gobo. His beloved trumpet travelled with him. He didn't trust anybody with that, and that 'included God'.

As we left my office Eddie looked at the bookshelves, some housing many of Spike's books.

EDDIE: I had no idea he was so prolific. What an original we had in our Godfather.

... ON SPIKE

JOHN BLUTHAL (actor): I was liberated working with Spike. He's a bit of an anarchist in a way, and so am I. It was surreal and I cottoned on straight away and I loved it.

He was very sensitive and his perception of an audience reaction was very, very acute, within a hundredth of a second he could sense what the audience wanted and then he would go along with it.

JOHN HEGLEY (poet): He shows the hurt. He lets you see the emotion. You don't have to dive for it. He really enjoyed the freedom he fought for. The freedom of speech, freedom of association, and once someone has broadened the gamut out you move from that and you move further, but he broadened it out. Freedom of comedy.

NEIL SHAND (TV scriptwriter): He challenged us with where he was going with jokes. They didn't always make me laugh, I have to say. I'd think, hang on, this is probably very funny but it's not making me laugh. It didn't matter to Spike, it made him laugh, and he would push it through relentlessly.

He was a manic depressive in the clinical sense which resulted in a circular behaviour. Working with Spike there would be a forty-day period coming up to a wonderful peak and that period when he reached the peak always seemed to be the excitingly creative time. By the time you got to the peak it was all too fast. The ideas woud be spinning around the room and bouncing off the walls and you couldn't really catch them, and then you start going down the other side which meant the door was locked and he sat there and he was just on his own, feeling – God knows what he was feeling. None of us in this game can be funny all the time but he had a higher scoring rate than most.

ROBIN WILLIAMS (actor): *The Goon Show* is pure madness. What we have in common is the desire to be bizarre. Spike had a lot of levels. Please help get Spike Milligan appreciated in America.

HUMPHREY LYTTELTON (musician and composer): You can never say Spike was influenced by anybody. You can't think of anybody who was a forerunner of Spike. The great thing he had was his irreverence for everything, especially the conventions of comedy and the conventions of broadcasting. Anybody that ever met him or heard him talk will know he's a frustrated musician.

TERRY WOGAN (radio and TV presenter): When he was on top form there was nobody like him in the whole world but equally, he could change just like that. He wasn't called Spike for nothing because Spike he certainly was.

LARRY GELBART (American TV and film writer): You can't think of Spike without thinking of the word 'unique'. He was flying blind, working without a net. He was very bold, he just walked to the edge of the cliff and did something funny all the way down. He wasn't daunted by the fact that he was expected to come out with something funny – he just came out with something funny.

I remember Spike came down to the footlights and sang an awful rendition of 'God Save the Queen' and the audience of course got to their feet and he said, 'If you'll stand for that you'll stand for anything.'

JOHNNY SPEIGHT (scriptwriter): Spike was truthful and funny. He didn't mind kicking people up the arse. He has had a tremendous influence on British comedy. Monty Python and the Cambridge

Footlights copied him. Everything is derived from something of his –
it's almost idolatory.

He had integrity, honesty and talent. He was irreverent and could
be offensive, in fact he did it a lot, but he was a breath of fresh air, a
great innovator.

I discovered he didn't have a word processor and went to his office
to persuade him to buy one, pointing out to him all the advantages:
'Spike, you really should have a word processor.' Without a pause
came a vintage Spike response, 'But I am a word processor.'

TERRY NATION (**creator of *Dr Who***): Spike Milligan actually gave
me my very first break in the business. I had been failing miserably at
everything I had been trying to do. I had failed as a stand-up comic,
and got an introduction to meet Spike, and as far as I was concerned,
he was a big star. *The Goon Show* was on and every young person in
the country was a *Goon Show* fan. I went to meet him, and he chatted
for a minute, and then he took a longer look at me and said, 'When
did you last eat?' I said, 'Well, Thursday,' and this was Wednesday, I
suppose. My hair was long, and I was starving to death. He instantly
wrote a cheque for ten pounds, and that was a lot of money in those
days. Milligan was a very generous, warm man, and I would have quit
had it not been for his coming up with that opportunity. When people
ask me how I got started, I got started because of Spike Milligan.

JOHN FISHER (**author and TV director**): Spike was more than
an innovative and exciting comedian. More than any of his contemporaries, he represented a major cultural figure, whose legacy will
one day correspond with names as various as Lewis Carroll and
Mervyn Peake, John Betjeman and Roald Dahl, as much as with
Groucho Marx and Max Miller.

The multi-faceted nature of his achievement – performer, poet,
novelist, soldier, musician, conservationist – was matched by the para-
dox of his personality. Was there anyone who could be so horridly
mean one moment and so overwhelmingly generous the next? Was
there a performer who created such a cocoon of peace, calm and
serenity around himself one day and then on the morrow exuded such

turbulent disagreeability and suspicion that you shirked from contact with him unless it was absolutely necessary? I had the good fortune to conduct the last interview with him before he died. When asked to nominate his ideal chat show guests, he expressed the wish to have interviewed Hitler and Churchill together. Jesus Christ would have been around too. In Spike, all human life was there. But in hindsight I know that for all his faults and venalities he was intrinsically a good man and a great one and I deeply miss him to this day.

JANET BROWN (impressionist): I can think of Spike on one particular occasion when he took a great dislike to the audience, a very strong dislike, and so after the first performance when he came off he went up to his dressing room. He had a very good voice and he could sing and play the trumpet jolly well. He was singing 'Laura' and he played a wonderful solo on the trumpet. Well, come the second house, he just didn't want to have anything more to do with the audience, can you believe it. We all have to get on there, but he didn't. That was Spike.

DES O'CONNOR (singer and entertainer): When you got Spike on a good day, you got gold, there was nobody to touch him, you always knew when he had that twinkle in his eye. He had the odd day when he wasn't happy with the world and he would arrive looking down at his feet and you knew you had to be careful.

I remember we were doing a Christmas Special for Thames Television. In the sketch I was a carol singer visiting people's homes, and wherever I went singing the lights went out, or people locked their doors. In the afternoon I asked the director what Spike was going to do. The director had spoken to him and Spike said, 'Don't worry, I'll think of something, so I didn't know what he was going to do. On the show when I knocked on Spike's door I started to sing 'Good King Wenceslas', he opened it and facing me was this bloody cannon, a real cannon, and he lit it and I ducked. He was such a joy because he was so different from everybody else.

We won't see his like again.

... ON THE GOONS

SPIKE: It was a loose assembly of very hungry young comics. Eventually by sheer hunger we were forced to do something and somebody said, How about doing a non-hungry show and get paid? So we went to Pat Dixon. Pat was revolutionary: he had the Confederate flag behind his desk. He looked at the script and said, Yes, yes, I'll do it, and that was the right answer for us.

PETER SELLERS: I think that Sunday get-together used to put a charge into Spike, and the thing used to get off the ground. We really had a marvellous time. Looking back it was probably the most happy time professionally I've ever spent.

HARRY SECOMBE: It was like children being let out of school, it's the only way I can describe it, and you could always hear me, Peter or Spike giggling in the background. Little private jokes we dare not repeat. But for Spike, having to keep up the standard all the time, it was very difficult and it resulted in a breakdown of his health and I don't think it helped his first marriage. It was strange – four fellows on a Sunday afternoon, getting slightly sozzled on brandy in between shows, made such an impact on the world of comedy.

ERIC SYKES: Spike was in a complete world of his own. Some people said it was just anarchy. It wasn't anarchy. Some of the jokes that Spike wrote, in particular 'Eccles and the Law of Gravity', were spot on and very different. It was such a hectic show for him to do every week. He wasn't feeling very well and he asked me to help for a time and what I remember is the laughter we had in the writing of it. It was a great part of my life.

The first time I heard a *Goon Show* on the radio, it was like walking through clear air after being stranded in a fog.

JOHN BROWELL (the last producer of *The Goon Show*): Pat Dixon, the BBC producer, was enthusiastic about getting *The Goon Show* on air but he didn't particularly want the hassle of producing it himself so he arranged for other people to produce the show. When you are a producer working with Spike Milligan, he is a mixture of resenting the fact that you are BBC and also wishing to get on with you in order to get the programme done. So you always had this ambivalence between Spike and yourself and it could raise problems of temperament at times.

TERRY PRATCHETT: One of the key things about the Goons was the delight in language, the delight in language for its own sake. I hope I do that in the Discworld books. But I think what I owe most to them is the fact they went there and they opened up new territory. It was up to me and lots of other people who came along afterwards to build cabins and cities and carve little farms out of the wilderness, but they were the guys that went out first and actually said, There's a whole new continent out there, guys, and the rest of us were just colonists.

JIMMY GRAFTON (christened K.O.G.V.O.S. Keeper of the Goons and Voice of Sanity, licensee of Grafton's and radio scriptwriter): I always told him Eccles is the true Milligan and the rest is just for cover. His ID or alter ego. A simple happy soul, content for the world to regard him as an idiot, provided that it does not make too many demands on him. He was the most complex member of the Goons but the ultimate mainspring. When Spike was told what I had said about Eccles he replied, 'He's right, yes, that's it, I don't want to know about all that stuff, all that thing about earning money – I just want to be an idiot.'

DENIS NORDEN: It needed the courage that a good musician has to know about how long to go on and when to change key. Nobody else in radio made that use of repetition, the pure sound of letting things go on. Any normal person would say, that's enough, they would get fed up with it, but Spike went two miles beyond that. That still has never been equalled. I think one of most perfect pieces of radio writing is the piece where Eccles writes the time down on a piece of paper. It is comedy they should teach in schools as an example, that's a jazz riff.

DICK LESTER: He was on the edge of a cliff and he was determined to jump off to see whether there was a better way of doing something. My experience with Spike was that he would sometimes sacrifice the easy in order to try to explore. It's a passionate surrealism and that's maybe a contradiction in terms. Spike was a very passionate man. It's a thin-skin surrealism and that's very rare. He had the ability to care about something and turn it into nonsense in order to prove a point. He remains the finest comedy mind that I have ever met in terms of explosions of extraordinary originality and ability to turn a thing on its head, and I have worked with some great people like Buster Keaton, but Spike remains unique.

JOHN CLEESE: The Goons were my childhood heroes. I became almost obsessed with them. I am glad that I did. Many years later I was able to understand the audience response to *Monty Python* in a way that I would never have done if I hadn't been such a fan of the show. Once you'd heard Grytpype-Thynne or Eccles you could never forget them. They weren't characters that would drift away. He created them incredibly vividly and he knew how to play them off against each other, so he had this extraordinary little group of characters and each one had a different relationship with everyone else. It was a world of his own and the greatest comedy writers do exactly that, they create a world of their own.

JONATHAN MILLER: I have come across strange, marooned, landlocked Goon enthusiasts in upstate New York. People who come to you from Ithaca who say, 'I am the president of the Ithaca chapter of the Goon Show Fan Club. All hail. How interesting to find you in this neck of the woods.' *The Goon Show* has never been rated as an important contribution to British popular culture but I think it is of the same importance as *Alice in Wonderland* and *The Pickwick Papers*. It is a major monument in British cultural life and I believe Milligan should be seen not only as a comic entertainer but – and this may seem to be rather pretentious – as a major imaginative artist of the twentieth century.

MICHAEL PALIN: The great thing about listening to the Goons was a series of anticipations as to when your character was going to come in. It was rather like hearing Elvis Presley doing 'Heartbreak Hotel' for the first time – you knew this was very, very different and it wasn't just that my father looked askance at the radio when he heard it. It was that there was something in the form of it that was different. Spike never lost a sense of the absurd and that's why I feel most close to him.

EDDIE IZZARD: It was just very loose, you could flip off anywhere. It fuels your imagination if you listen to it, it gives you the possibilities of where you can go which is anywhere. It was the birth of alternative comedy. That was it right there, and people don't know how to analyse it or define alternative comedy any more. It is the other thing, it isn't mainstream. You have to buy into it.

RORY BREMNER: It was a picture in Spike's mind, it was a picture in their minds. It was just the enjoyment of language as well – the enjoyment comes searing through. You look at the Goons and you see a line that runs straight through. You can hear the Goodies, Monty Python, and you can hear Vic Reeves and Bob Mortimer. You can hear all these things that are subsequent, it's almost like Captain Scott and Amundsen. The Goons got there first, they pitched their tent and everything since has been looking back to the originality and the creativity or the madness, in fact, of Spike and the Goons. I sent him a letter when I read in a newspaper that he had had a heart by-pass. I wrote: 'After all these years of campaigning, they put a by-pass through you.' He loved that.

SPIKE ON SPIKE

Irish doctors have carried out the world's
first haemorrhoid transplant.

All I ask is the chance to prove that money
can't make me happy.

Contraceptives should be used on every
conceivable occasion.

Are you going to come quietly, or do I have to
use earplugs?

And God said, 'Let there be light' but the Electricity
Board said he would have to wait until Thursday to
be connected.

A sure cure for seasickness is to sit under a tree.

How long was I in the army? Five foot eleven.

I'm not afraid of dying. I just don't want to
be there when it happens.

A baby rabbit with eyes full of pus is the work
of scientific us.

For ten years Caesar ruled with an iron hand. Then
with a wooden foot, and finally with a piece of string.

And God said, 'Let the earth bring forth grass'
and the Rastafarians smoked it.

I can speak Esperanto like a native.

Is there anything worn under the kilt?
No, it's all in perfect working order.

It was a perfect marriage.
She didn't want to and he couldn't.

I have the body of an 18-year-old. I keep it in the fridge.

I thought I'd begin by reading a poem by Shakespeare,
but then I thought, Why should I? He never reads
anything of mine.

It's all in the mind, you know.

I shook hands with a friendly Arab. I still have my right
arm to prove it.

I spent years laughing at Harry Secombe's singing
until somebody told me that it wasn't a joke.

God made night, but Man made darkness.

Some calming words for you – Valium Librium Mogadon.

Money can't buy you happiness but it does bring
you a more pleasant form of misery.

I'm a hero with coward's legs.

Money can't buy you friends but you get a better
class of enemy.

My father had a profound influence on me,
he was a lunatic.

Listen, somebody is screaming in agony –
fortunately I speak it fluently.

Chopsticks are one of the reasons the Chinese
never invented custard.

Copulation equals population equals pollution.
Answer – birth control.

If I die in war you remember me.
If I live in peace you don't.

I thought I saw Jesus on a tram. I said, Are you Jesus?
and he said, Yes, I am.

It's like swimming in porridge.

Don't worry. It only happens all the time.

On my tombstone I want 'I told you I was ill.'

He left an indelible blank on my mind.

LIST OF ILLUSTRATIONS

Letters have been kindly provided by the interviewees. All efforts have been made to seek permission for use of the photographs reproduced. Unless stated below photographs are from the private collections of Norma Farnes and Desmond Milligan. The publishers would like to apologise if there are any omissions and will be pleased to incorporate missing acknowledgments in any future editions.

Plate One
 5 (Bottom) Courtesy of Liz Cowley
 6 (Top) Courtesy of BFI Stills
    (Bottom) Courtesy of Marcel Stellman
 7 (Middle and bottom) Courtesy of George Martin
 8 (Top and bottom) Courtesy of George Martin
10 (Top left and right) Courtesy of Alan Matthews
    (Bottom) Courtesy of Barry Humphries
11 (Top) Courtesy of Richard Lester
    (Middle and bottom) Courtesy of Richard Ingrams
12 (Top) Courtesy of Jimmy Verner
    (Middle and bottom) © BBC
13 (Top and middle) Courtesy of Peter Medak
    (Bottom) Courtesy of Alan J. W. Bell
14 (Bottom) Courtesy of Dick Douglas-Boyd
15 (Top) Starstock/ Photoshot
    (Bottom) Python (Monty) Pictures Ltd
16 (Top left and right) Joss Barratt/ © BBC
    (Bottom) Courtesy of Eddie Izzard